Andrzej Glass

Lublin R-XIII

Army cooperation plane

KAGERO

Lublin R-XIII Army cooperation plane • Andrzej Glass • First edition • LUBLIN 2020

• **ISBN 978-83-66148-31-4**

Translation: **Liudmyla Butenko** • Cover: **Arkadiusz Wróbel** • Color profiles: **Arkadiusz Wróbel** • Drawings: **Andrzej Glass i Witold Szewczyk (Technical drawings: Maciej Noszczak)** • Perspective drawing: **Robert Pietracha** • 3D visualizations: **Marek Trojanowicz (www.polskie-samoloty.pl)** • Photos are taken from the collections of: **Jerzy Cynk, Andrzej Glass, Mariusz Konarski, Tomasz Kopański, Volker Koos, Tadeusz Królikiewicz, Fr Robert Kulczyński, Andrzej Morgała, Lechosław Musiałkowski, Jerzy Rozwadowski, C. Smit, Witold Szewczyk, August Zdaniewski, Archives of Mechanical Documentation, Polish Aviation Museum and from the Internet.** • Design: **KAGERO STUDIO – Łukasz Maj** • Printed in Poland

KAGERO Publishing
Akacjowa 100, Turka, os. Borek, 20-258 Lublin 62, Poland, phone/fax: (+48) 81 501 21 05
www.kagero.pl • e-mail: kagero@kagero.pl, marketing@kagero.pl
w w w . k a g e r o . p l
Distribution: **KAGERO Publishing**

Mechanical Works E. Plage & T. Laśkiewicz (ZMPL)

In 1897, Emil Plage founded the Factory for Building Machines and Boilers in Bronowice, Lublin. In 1899, he formed an alliance with Teofil Laśkiewicz and the factory was renamed into Mechanical Works E. Plage & T. Laśkiewicz (Polish: Zakłady Mechaniczne E. Plage i T. Laśkiewicz, ZMPL); that was a mechanical workshop and steam boiler manufacturer. The Russian Army retreating in 1915 set their premises on fire yet those were restored.

On the initiative of the Polish Air Force, Mechanical Works E. Plage & T. Laśkiewicz in Lublin began to produce aircraft in 1920. The firm owners were engineers Kazimierz Arkuszewski and Roman Laśkiewicz. It was located in the south-western district of Lublin, at Fabryczna st., 26, near the aerodrome. Teofil Laśkiewicz was managing director, Engr. Witold Rumbowicz worked as technical director, Engr. Stanisław Cywiński headed the technical office and the production preparation office was headed by Engr. Kazimierz Kazimierczak.

The Works occupied the area of 14 ha. That territory comprised: a building housing the company's management and construction offices, a joinery, a fitting shop, a tin shop, a tool shop, mechanical workshops, an upholstery shop and a paint shop, a propeller shop, a final assembly department, hangars, warehouses, a laboratory and a dope shop. Next to those were buildings of non-aviation departments producing boilers and, later, car bodies. In 1921, the factory employed 500 people.

On February 17, 1920, the Polish Air Force concluded an agreement with the Works for the provision of 300 aircraft: fighters Ansaldo Balilla and combat biplanes Ansaldo A.300 that would be constructed under the Italian licence within 1,5 years. In August 1920, Ludomił Rayski delivered a sample copy of Ansaldo A.300 from Italy (Turin) to Lublin by air. On June 15, 1921, the first Ansaldo A.300 built in Lublin performed a test flight and on July 21, pilot Adam Haber-Włyński running the test flight of the first Ansaldo Balilla plane died because of his too daring pilotage.

During two years since receiving the order, they only produced 100 planes. A.300 aircraft manufactured in Lublin were called 'flying coffins' because there were several cases when wings were torn off as they were heavier and weaker than examples built in Italy. The reasons were thicker plywood of the poorer quality used in their construction and improper execution. At the beginning of 1924, Gen. Armand Leveque suspended the production. In total, 75 Ansaldo A.300 planes and 57 Ansaldo Balilla planes had been built by then.

Irrespectively of the licensed production, the Works had to develop their own designs. In August 1921, Stanisław Cywiński created the project of a two-seater reconnaissance aircraft Arla-1 (shortened Arkuszewski and Laśkiewicz) which was later sent to the military authorities for approval. That was a monoplane with braced mid wings and 300hp engine Fiat A.12bis. The project was not realised. However, in 1923, S. Cywiński built two gliders at the factory – the Lublin I and Lublin II that participated in the First Polish Glider Contest in Białka near Nowy Targ.

In April 1924, the factory received an order from the Aviation Department of the Ministry of Military Affairs for licensed production of French combat planes Potez XV; to assist in starting the production, French engineers were brought. In September 1924, a flight of the first Potez XV led by Col. Serednicki came to Poland from France; a few among them were to be used as sample copies by aerospace manufacturers. In the middle of 1925, the first Potez XV planes of the Lublin production were ready.

Meanwhile, the firm's board was being changed. Starnawski was managing director for a short time, Tadeusz Piasecki was his successor and, eventually, Engr. Zygmunt Zakrzewski

Mechanical Works Plage & Laśkiewicz in Lublin.

Mechanical Works Plage & Laśkiewicz and the aerodrome from a bird's eye view.

took that position. A French engineer Rastoul became technical director and Engr. Władysław Świątecki succeeded him. Engr. Jan Dębowski acted as administrative and commercial director, Engr. Jerzy Rudlicki headed the construction office and Jan Luboiński headed the production preparation department.

In 1927, the factory started to build licensed reconnaissance bombers Potez XXV; 100 were constructed in 1928-1929 and 50 more in 1932. They produced 20 three-engine bombers Fokker F.VIIb/3m under the Dutch licence in 1929 and 11 Fokker F.VIIb/3m airliners (10 for LOT Polish Airlines and 1 for export to Belgium) in 1930. Working on Potez planes enabled them to build fuselages welded from steel pipes, while production of Fokkers allowed to construct cantilever wooden wings skinned with plywood. In addition to manufacturing, the factory also provided repairs of Potez XVs and XXVs.

Since 1927, they started working on their own prototypes. Those were designed by J. Rudlicki and his team of more than a dozen people including engineers Marian Bartolewski, Jerzy Dąbrowski, Antoni Uszacki, Janusz Lange, Jerzy Teisseyre, Witold Grabowski, Jaworski and others.

The factory's first own product was a reconnaissance bomber Lublin R-VIII built in 1928. Its airliner variant, the R-IX, was constructed in a short while. In 1930, they produced a pilot series of 5 Lublin R-VIIIs, 3 of which were converted to seaplanes in 1932. At the beginning of 1929, they performed a test flight of a liaison aircraft prototype designated R-X; a pilot series composed of 5 examples was built in 1931. Prototypes of the Lublin R-IX airliner (1929) and Lublin R-XI airliner (1930) as well as its improved variant, the R-XVI, failed to meet the requirements of LOT Polish Airlines so the production was not started. However, 5 examples of an air ambulance variant R-XVI were built in 1933-1934. In 1931, they created the R-XII sport aircraft that was not put to use.

In 1930, they created the R-XIV trainer aircraft, a development of R-X. A reconnaissance variant, the R-XIII (1931), became the factory's biggest success. In 1932-1936, 273 R-XIIIs in-

1921-1922 1923-1930 1931-1935

Plage & Laśkiewicz's logomarks in 1921–1935.

cluding 19 examples of a seaplane variant on floats were produced. The last design introduced by the factory was a prototype of a two-engine torpedo bomber aircraft R-XX (1935).

Engr. Rudlicki was also running his experiments. He had the idea of a tail configuration called Rudlicki's V-tail or a butterfly tail. They tested it in 1931 on the Hanriot H-28 and in 1933 on the R-XIX, a development of the R-XIII. Some Rudlicki's projects were not realised. Those were an army cooperation plane R-XV (1931), a reconnaissance bomber R-XXI (1932) meant to be a development of the Potez XXV with landing gear retractable in wings and better fuselage skinning; there were also projects of a two-engine bomber biplane R-XVIII (1933) with Rudlicki's V-tail sent to the contest and competing with planes *Żubr* (*Bison*) and *Łoś* (*Moose*), an observation aircraft R-XXI (1934) and a torpedo seaplane R-XXII (1934) – an improved R-VIII variant.

It is worth noting that the concept of the R-VIII was similar to the Potez XXV. Likewise, the arrangement of wings on R-XI and R-XVI high-wing airliners and on the R-XX torpedo seaplane was undoubtedly based on Fokkers' wing configuration.

In 1935, the factory employed up to 1100 people; 800 of those worked at the aviation department. Since 1934, Col. Józef Zajączkowski

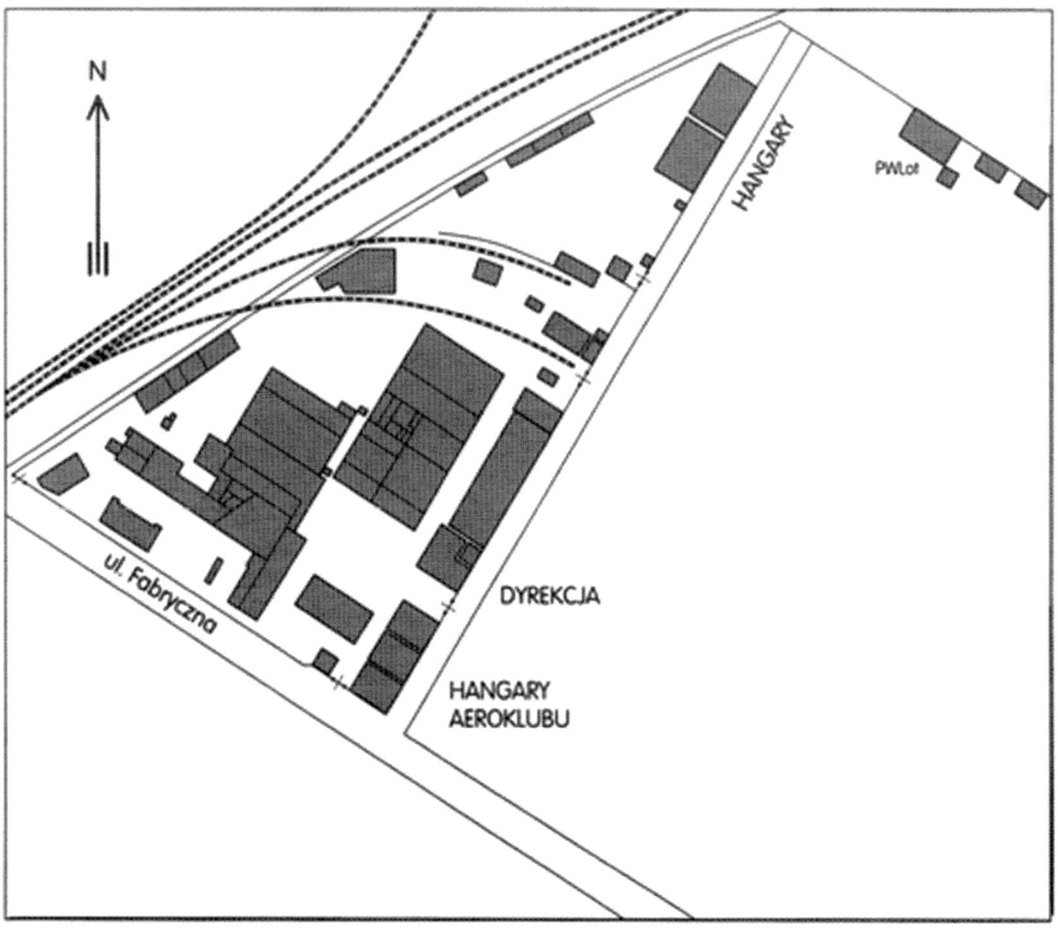

The plan of the Plage & Laśkiewicz premises and the aerodrome.

Lublin Aircraft Works' logomark.

was managing director. Adam Haber-Włyński, Stanisław Pawluć, Antoni Mroczkowski and Władysław Szulczewski worked as test pilots.

At the end of 1935, Air Command willing to nationalise the factory cancelled the order for 50 R-XIIIFs, some of which were near completion. The aircraft were estimated as scrap and the factory declared bankruptcy on December 7, 1935. Then it was nationalised and the renewed order for the R-XIIIF enabled them to operate without debts and losses, now with a new name – Lublin Aircraft Factory.

Lublin Aircraft Factory

Upon their nationalisation on February 1, 1936, Mechanical Works E. Plage & T. Laśkiewicz in Lublin received the name Lublin Aircraft Works (Polish: Lubelska Wytwórnia Samolotów, LWS). Formally, it was a private limited company 98% of which belonged to the Podlasie Aircraft Factory (Polish: Podlaska Wytwórnia Samolotów, PWS) and 2% to Maj. Aleksandr Sipowicz so it was actually owned by State Aviation Works (Polish: Państwowe Zakłady Lotnicze, PZL). They leased the premises from Plage &

Plage & Laśkiewicz hangars.

The fighter aircraft Ansaldo A-1 Balilla.

The general-purpose aircraft Ansaldo A-300.

The general-purpose aircraft Potez 25.

The airliner and bomber Fokker F.VIIb/3m.

The reconnaissance bomber Lublin R-VIII (1928).

The seaplane R-VIIIa (1932).

The airliner R-IX (1929).

Laśkiewicz, a debtor. In 1936, the factory employed 600 people and in 1938-1939 that number was 1100-1400. Maj. Aleksandr Sipowicz was managing director, Engr. Zbysław Ciołkosz was technical director replaced by Engr. Ryszard Bartel in autumn 1937; Zbysław Ciołkosz headed the study department (the construction office). Since autumn 1937, that position was taken by Engr. Jerzy Teisseyre; Władysław Szulczewski was experimental pilot.

During a short time, LWS continued testing a prototype of a seaplane R-XX; the project of a serial variant received the designation LWS-1. In 1936, the factory completed 50 R-XIIIFs building of which had been started before the nationalisation. In the same year, PZL passed to LWS the documentation on the bomber PZL.30 *Żubr* (designed by Ciołkosz), the first prototype of which crashed in November 1936. The plane was designated LWS-6 *Żubr*. Its floatplane variant, the LWS-5 for the Naval Air Squadron in Puck, was not built. They constructed another prototype, LWS-6 *Żubr*, and produced 15 LWS-6A in 1938-1939. In 1937, they drafted a project of a light fighter aircraft designated LWS-4 (PZL.39). In the same year, the factory completed rebuilding 47 Potez XXVs, on which they installed Jupiter radial engines instead of Lorraine-Dietrich engines. In 1937, the factory finished a prototype of the LWS-2 ambulance plane designed by Z. Ciołkosz and J. Teisseyre.

In 1938, LWS started the licensed production of the RWD-14 *Czapla* (*Heron*); 65 examples were built in 1938-1939. In 1938, they introduced a reconnaissance plane prototype LWS-3 *Mewa* (*Seagull*) designed by J. Teisseyre and Engr. Władysław Fiszdon according to the project draft by Z. Ciołkosz. In 1939, the factory started the serial production of 200 planes of that type; 30 planes was proudly announced in the middle of the year. By the end of August, some *Mewas* were near completion and two were ready. The factory's last project, the LWS-7 *Mewa II*, was at the final stage of development when the war broke out.

In spring 1939, the expansion of the factory was started.

The airliner R-XI (1930).

The sport plane R-XII (1930).

The airliner Lublin R-XVI (1932).

The army cooperation plane

As the term 'army cooperation plane' was non-typical, critical remarks about the Lublin R-XIII could be made: such a kind of an aircraft did not exist in the other countries' air forces. Meanwhile, during WWII, they all used liaison-observation aircraft classified similarly to the R-XIII: the Fieseler Fi 156 Storch in Germany, an armed variant of the Polikarpow U-2 (Po-2) in the USSR, the Piper Cub in the United

The air ambulance aircraft Lublin R-XVIb (1933).

The torpedo floatplane aircraft R-XX (1935).

States Air Force and Auster Taylorcraft in the Royal Air Force. The R-XIII had already been in service in Poland in 1932, whereas the other countries only implemented their aircraft in the course of the war.

Being used by the side that had advantages in the air, observation-liaison aircraft were able to fulfill tasks yet they were defenceless against fighter planes of an adversary. That is why the R-XIII did not play a big part in September 1939, not because they were obsolete. When an adversary had more power in the air, reconnaissance operations had to be carried out by quick reconnaissance aircraft. Nowadays, the role of observation-liaison aircraft is performed by helicopters, drones and satellites.

The air ambulance aircraft LWS-2 (1937).

The reconnaissance aircraft LWS-3 *Mewa* (1938).

The bomber aircraft LWS-6 *Żubr* (1937).

The reconnaissance aircraft RWD-14 *Czapla* (1938).

The aircraft concept

The concept of an infantry cooperation aircraft was developed on Marshal Józef Piłsudski's request, when troops were in use during the May coup in 1926. In the guidelines by the General Inspectorate of the Armed Forces on organisation and use of aviation dated October 13, 1926, they outlined the importance of adjusting the aviation to 'to the changing conditions of the civil war'. That was also stated that 'in the course of the war, working to ensure intelligence and communication must be the first priority of the aviation'. On October 14, 1926, it was stated in the report of the Polish General Staff about the guidelines fulfillment:

1. 'At present, infantry and cavalry divisions lack aviation. A battle squadron is unsuitable for the inherent aviation of these divisions. That is typical army aviation.'

2. 'Therefore, besides the mighty Air Force and Commander-in-Chief, it is necessary to implement light aviation, cheaper and more manoeuvrable, that would not require ideal aerodromes and hangars and involve less trained personnel. The tasks for this aviation are: cooperation with the divisional artillery and accompanying the infantry. An inherent unit for an infantry or cavalry division would be a platoon of 4 planes.'

A military aircraft of this type also had to solve the problem of limited funds for aviation within the military budget.

In *Memoriał w sprawie lotnictwa* (*Memorandum on aviation*) of March 12, 1928 prepared for the General Staff, the chief of the Aviation Department colonel Ludomił Rayski demanded to create the army cooperation aviation, the first three squadrons of which had to be formed in 1929.

Col. Marian Romeyko, who described the genesis of army cooperation aviation on the pages of *Przegląd Lotniczy (Aviation Revue)* in 1930, says that they wanted 'an aircraft that would be able to land almost on any airfield, would be easy to maintain, easy to transport, would not require a tent hangar, would be cheap to construct and use and simultaneously have appropriate speed, lifting capacity and service ceiling'. He specifies that it had to be a two-seater metal high-wing plane with folding wings and very broad and durable landing gear, unable to turn over and capable of taking off and landing shortly. Also, it had to have a place for a radio station.

The contest

In 1927, the Aviation Department of the Ministry of Military Affairs announced a contest for an aircraft of that kind and specified requirements for it. In the technical requirements, it was stated that a plane had to be powered by a 162kW (220hp) engine Wright J. 5, armed with an observer's machine gun and have the maximum speed of 170 km/h, be capable of a short takeoff and short landing at an unprepared airfield, have folding wings and be pullable by an automobile moving its own chassis. At the end of 1927, two factories became interested in the competition: the Podlasie Aircraft Factory located in Biała Podlaska and Mechanical Works E. Plage & T. Laśkiewicz in Lublin. State Aviation Works in Warsaw was also supposed to enter it in December 1927. On March 28, 1928, Podlasie Aircraft Factory received an order for 2 prototypes and 5 aircraft of pilot production, whereas Mechanical Works E. Plage & T. Laśkiewicz started designing the aircraft at their own risk.

Three aircraft were introduced for the contest: the PWS-5, the PZL Ł.2 and Lublin R-X.

PWS-5

At Podlasie Aircraft Factory in Biała Podlaska, Engr. Aleksander Grzędzielski and technician Augustyn Bobek (who later changed his second name to Zdaniewski) designed a wooden biplane PWS-7 that soon received a new designation, PWS-5. The first prototype of PWS-5 flew for the first time on December 28, 1928, whereas the second one, a little improved PWS-5a, was flown in February 1929. In spring 1929, the planes were sent to the Institute of Aviation Technical Research (Polish: Instytut Badań Technicznych Lotnictwa, IBTL) in Warsaw for testing. Simultaneously, they started pilot production of five PWS-5t2 planes modified according to conclusions about their prototypes testing. In autumn 1929, the factory delivered five PWS-5t2 planes to the Air Force. PWS-5 aircraft had military numbers type 51 as well as serial numbers from 51-1 to 51-7. At IBTL, the PWS-5 aircraft received negative evaluation as its takeoff distance was long, it had a low rate of climb and its landing was long so it could not be used on unprepared airfields.

Using the experience of testing his trainer biplane PWS-12, the designer of PWS-5 quickly created the improved project, PWS-6, at the beginning of 1930. The prototype equipped with slats was built in 1930 but it could not compete with other aircraft because of the worse handling qualities.

PZL Ł.2

State Aviation Works in Warsaw had privileges. In the second half of 1928, Jerzy Dąbrowski who had already gained the experience of designing the R-X in Lublin joined the factory's construction office. Being consulted by Władysław Zalewski, he and Franciszek Kott were commissioned by PZL to design the PZL.2 liaison aircraft (later designated PZL Ł.2) intended for entering the contest in 1927. As a state manufacturer, the factory had big chances of receiving orders on a priority basis. The PZL Ł.2 had the all-metal construction: its fuselage was welded from steel pipes, its wings and empennage had a duralumin skeleton and were covered with canvas. A PZL Ł.2 prototype with the military number 55-1 (that later received a registration SP-ADN) rose into the air at the end of 1929, after both competitive aircrafts had been tested at IBTL. That enabled

The PWS-5 (1928) participating in the contest, seven examples were built.

The winning aircraft – a liaison plane PZL Ł.2 (1929), 36 examples were built.

fixing some drawbacks of the PZL Ł.2 found in the aircraft mentioned by making changes in the course of construction. The aircraft passed tests at IBTL at the beginning of 1930. The comparison of the aircraft revealed that the PZL Ł.2 had considerably better performance indicators. The PZL Ł.2 took first place in the contest, the R-X came in second and the PWS-5 was disqualified. The factory received an order for 35 PZL Ł.2. In 1930, they completed 10 aircraft, among which the example no 55-10 was made as a civil sport variant and received a registration SP-AFA. Flying Captain Stanisław Skarżyński and eng. Andrzej Markiewicz flew it around Africa (February 1-May 31, 1931), a total distance of 25,000 km. In 1931, another 25 PZL Ł.2a were completed. Yet the exploitation showed that the aircraft could move well at low speed but it also entered a spin, which led to two accidents. As the factory was commissioned the PZL P.7 fighter aircraft, the manufacturing of the PZL Ł.2 stopped soon and they were written off fairly quickly.

RWD-3

On account of good results demonstrated in 1929 by a sport aircraft RWD-2 designed by Stanisław Rogalski, Stanisław Wigura and Jerzy Drzewiecki, the Polish Air Force requested its liaison variant with folding wings, which received the designation RWD-3. Its prototype performed the first flight in April 1930. However, this construction turned out to be heavier than expected. Using the engine of the power of 59 kW (80 hp), its payload was too small. The aircraft was not qualified for comparison tests.

Lublin R-X

In December 1927, at the Lublin factory, Jerzy Rudlicki started designing the Lublin R-X two-seater liaison aircraft that would eventually be able to function as a mail plane. In 1928, an airframe example for static tests as well as a prototype were made. Only upon their introduction, the Aviation Department of the Ministry of Military Affairs commissioned the plane. The static tests took place in December 1928

The RWD-3 (1930) – was not qualified for comparison testing.

Execution of the competition for a liaison-observation aircraft.

Realizacja konkursu na samolot obserwacyjno-łącznikowy

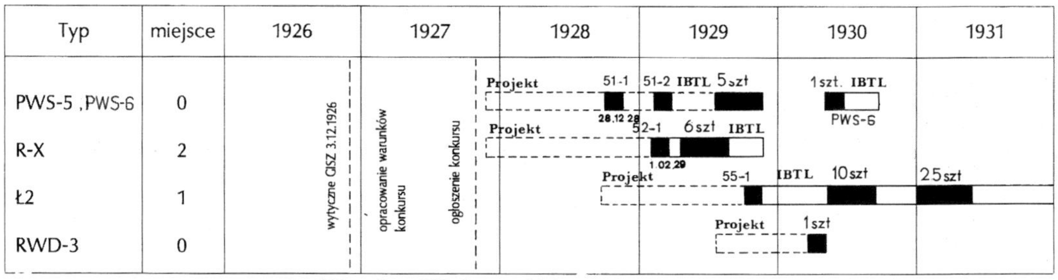

Uwagi: 51-1, 52-1, 55-1 – numery prototypów; ITBL – próby w ITBL; 5.szt – produkcja

The Lublin R-X prototype first flown on February 1, 1929. seven examples were built.

The Lublin R-X with folded wings.

An unsuccessful landing of the Lublin R-X.

and January 1929. The prototype number 52-1 was flown (with a wheeled chassis and skis) on February 1, 1929 at the Lublin aerodrome. The aircraft had military markings.

On both sides of the fuselage, the prototype had exhaust pipes with silencers reducing the engine noise very effectively. In spring 1929, the aircraft passed the tests which proved its ability to manoeuvre. Its performance and weight were distinctly worse than designated: the empty weight constituted 900 kg instead of 650 kg expected, its maximum speed was 160 km/h instead of 180 km/h and its service ceiling was 3400 m instead of 6000 m.

In spring and summer 1929, the Plage & Laśkiewicz factory completed a pilot series of five R-Xa ordered by the Air Force; those received numbers from 52-2 to 52-6.

Those aircraft had a rotary machine gun in the rear cockpit. Initially equipped with wooden propellers and, later, with a Townend ring protecting its engine and a metal propeller, the R-X was being tested at IBTL from summer 1929 until November 14, 1929.

In June 1929, one R-X was introduced at the Universal National Exhibition in Poznań. In spring 1929, the last R-Xa with the serial number 52-7 was built, that was a sport variant which received a registration SP-ABW; it was

W. Makowski's flight route in 1929 on the R-Xa SP-ABW to ▸ Barcelona.

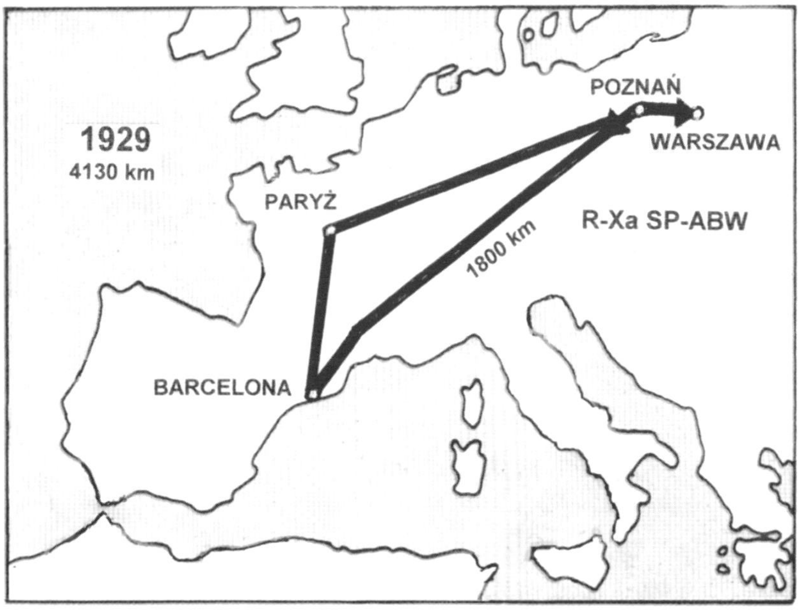

The Lublin R-Xa SP-ABW (military no 52-7) which W. Makowski flew from Warsaw to Barcelona and back in 1929, a total length was 1,800 km. The show posters are on the fuselage. ▾

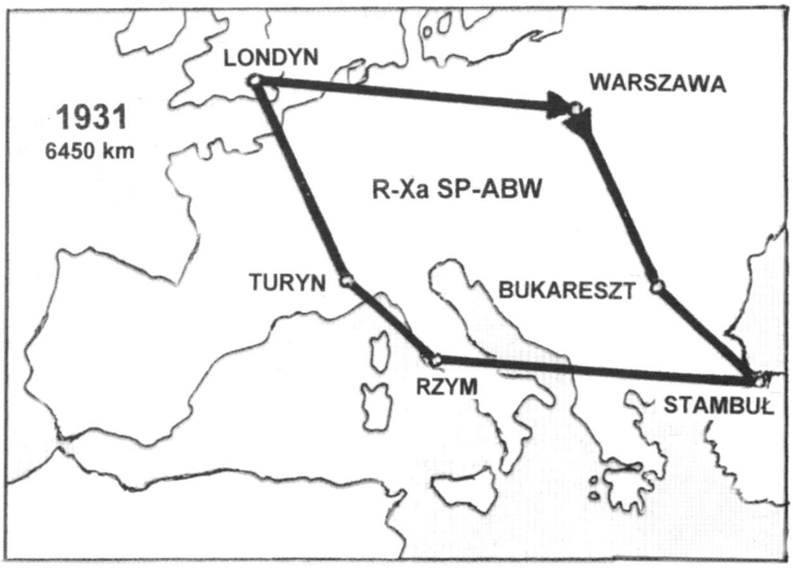

The Lublin R-Xa SP-ABW with a white-red stripe on its fuselage. The plane was flown by S. Karpiński around Europe in 1931, a total length of 6,450 km.

S. Karpiński's flight route in 1931 on the R-Xa SP-ABW around Europe.

equipped with a fuel tank for 15 hours of flying. Its distinctive feature were individual exhaust pipes for each cylinder. On September 25, 1929, an engineer and pilot W. Makovski along with a flight engineer B. Wieman flew that plane non-stop from Poznań to Barcelona (1800 km) via Czechoslovakia, Switzerland and France carrying greetings from the Universal National Exhibition to the Iberian-American Exhibition in Barcelona. The return trip with landings in Paris and Poznań ended on September 3, 1929, in Warsaw.

In September 1929, lieutenant S. Massalski piloting an R-X military variant took tenth in Kraków in the Tour of Southwestern Poland (Polish: Lot Południowo-Zachodniej Polski). Upon completion of the flight tests in the Air Regiments nos 2, 4 and 6, R-Xa were used in units, among other things, in the 2nd Air Regiment in Kraków and at the Aviation Training Centre in Dęblin in 1930-1932.

At the end of 1929, after completing comparison testing between the R-X, PZL Ł.2 and PWS-5 and concluding that the R-X had demonstrated the best short takeoff and landing, very good stability and controllability at low speeds and satisfactory performance, the Polish Air Force chose the latter.

However, the R-Xa did not go into series production as the designer created a refined model designated R-XIV; production of a better-performing development of it, the R-XIII, was approved.

In 1931, they rebuilt rear cockpits, removed rotary machine guns and installed comfortable seats on three R-Xa. Those functioned as staff planes, or liaison aircraft for commanders.

In the same year, flying captain S. Karpiński, who was planning a trip to Australia, chose the R-X for training races. On July 3, 1931, he flew 1,650 km around Poland; the plane had a registration SP-ABW. On September 23 – October 7, 1931, S. Karpiński and Engr. J. Suchodolski made a journey around Europe on the route Warsaw – Bucharest – Constantinople – Rome – Turin – London – Warsaw, a total length of 6,450 km.

In 1932, the aircraft was modified at the factory by adding a Townend ring, a metal propeller and spatted wheels. It received fuel tanks for 18 hours of flying. That model was designated R-Xa bis. On October 2-24, 1932, the crew comprising S. Karpiński and W. Rogalski took a trip on it to Africa and Asia on the route Warsaw – Sliven – Istanbul – Aleppo – Baghdad – Tehran – Herat – Kabul – Tehran – Baghdad – Cairo – Jerusalem – Aleppo – Istanbul – Lublin – Warsaw, a total length of 14,390 km and duration of 108 h 50 min.

Then the plane was sent to the 34th Combat Escadrille in Poznań as the business aircraft of S. Karpiński. It crashed on October 26, 1934 and was written off. Seven R-Xs were built.

The wingspan of the R-X was 13,5 m. Its length was 8,33 m, its height was 2,98 m and

The modified R-Xa bis SP-ABW *Srebrny Ptak (Silver Bird)* which S. Karpiński flew to Baghdad and back in 1932, a total length was 14,390 km.

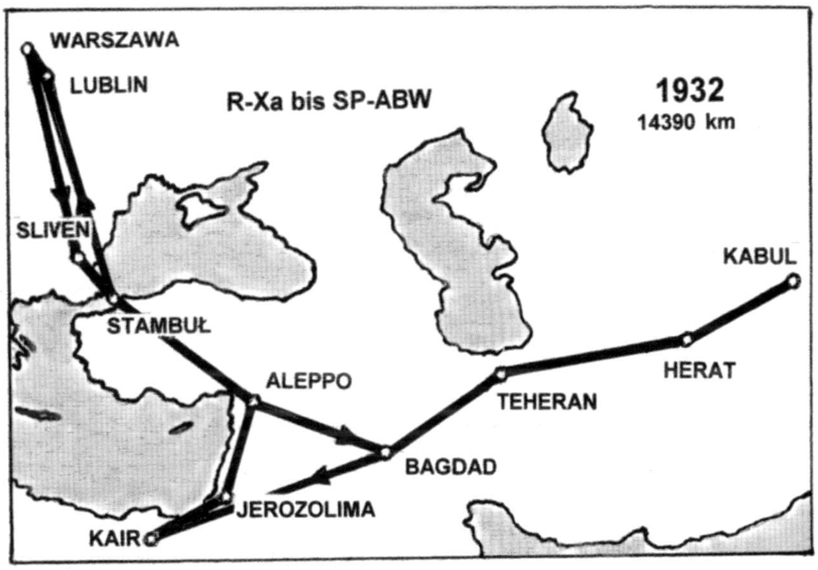

S. Karpiński's flight route in 1932 on the R-Xa SP-ABW to Afghanistan.

its bearing surface was 25,96 m². Its empty weight constituted 900 kg, the operating weight was 466 kg and gross weight was 1,366 kg. The plane's maximum speed was 161 km/h, the cruising speed was 140 km/h and minimum speed was 65 km/h. Its rate of climb was 2,4 m/s, its service ceiling was 3,400 m, its range was 670 km. It required the 40m takeoff distance and the 80m ground run. A sport variant had the operating weight of 700 kg and gross weight of 1,750 kg; its maximum speed was 176 km/h and its range was 2,500 km.

Lublin R-XIV

Good indicators of a short takeoff and landing as well as satisfactory performance proved by the Lublin R-X prototype encouraged the Polish Air Force and the designer, Rudlicki, to continue developing such an aircraft. On November 19, 1929, IBTL introduced their requirements for the R-X's successor to the factory; in December 1929, the Aviation Department of the Ministry of Military Affairs, considering the results of comparison testing between the liaison-observation aircraft PZL Ł.2, PWS-5 and R-X, chose Rudlicki's model for the Polish Air Force and provided recommendations on its further development. The Polish Air Force requested 35 PZL Ł.2 but those were insufficient. The R-X was meant to be developed in the future, whereas State Aviation Works received the order for the PZL P.7 fighter aircraft.

At that time, Jerzy Rudlicki had two project drafts finished: the R-XIV aerobatic trainer aircraft and R-XV liaison-observation aircraft, which was distinct from the first one as it had weapons, a radio station, a Standard Steel metal propeller and wheels with Bendix brakes. Both models were developments of the R-X. The Polish Navy was offered a seaplane variant of R-XV yet that was not of any interest to them. Those projects were created after the R-XI and R-XII had been designed. The ill-fated number XIII was omitted by the constructor.

At the end of 1929, the factory expected the order for 15 R-XIVs and 15 R-XIVs. However, by the contract of February 15, 1930, the Aviation Department only requested 15 R-XIVs that received military and serial numbers from 54-1 to 54-15 (where 54 was a military number for aircraft of that type). On account of big similarity of

The Lublin R-XIV prototype (no 54-1) with a big rudder, first flown in 1930.

The R-XIV prototype from the 3/4 front view.

the R-XIV to the R-X, a prototype was not built. The first R-XIV (no 54-1) was flown by Władysław Szulczewski on June 5, 1930 in Lublin.

In June and July 1930, that example passed tests at IBTL in Warsaw. Those were conducted with and without a Townend ring around the engine as well as with a wooden Hamilton propeller and a metal Standard Steel propeller. In the course of testing the first R-XIV with oleo struts at IBTL, they noticed that the plane

The Lublin R-XIV with its rudder changed.

The R-XIV no 3 in the Central Training Escadrille in Warsaw in 1933.

The R-XIV SP-ADF (nr 54-11) with a modified tail and on skis, which was used by Aero Club of the Polish Republic; participated in the Estonian race in 1931.

The R-XIV no 54-15 (89-Z) with a turret and long aileron, which became a prototype of the R-XIIIB at the tests in the Central Training Escadrille.

An R-XIIIA (56-1) prototype no 1 with short ailerons in the Central Training Escadrille.

The side view of the R-XIIIA (56-1) prototype with position lights and without a MG mount.

landed very hard. They checked the calculations and found that two times more powerful shock absorbers had been used. A person in charge of reckoning assumed that if a shock absorber was impacted by power P from below being counteracted by equal power P from above, then it would be compressed by both powers, 2P. After changing the shock absorbers, they conducted a 200-hour flight test of the aircraft (most flights lasted 2-3-minutes to test the landing gear). The tests at IBTL were run by flying lieutenant Józef Orłowski, pilot Kazimierz Kazimierczuk and flight engineer Jerzy Rzewnicki. The first five R-XIV were accepted by the Polish Air Force on August 8-11, 1930. The aircraft had wooden Szomański propellers type Hamilton, the same as the R-X and Fokker F.VIIb/3m. The last R-XIV was provided to the Air Force on July 1, 1931. Flying sergent Józef Żuromski conducted the aircraft trials.

The first example had large vertical stabilizer and rudder, the following planes had smaller rudders and the latest ones also had smaller stabilizers.

R-XIVs were used for training at the Aviation Training Centre in Dęblin and in training squadrons of air regiments. Two planes with registrations SP-AFD (no 54-11) and SP-AFG came into use in sport aviation. On March 4-16, 1931, W. Szulczewski flew SP-AFD painted olive green, with the landing gear equipped with skis in the race to Estonia organised by Aero Club of Warsaw (Polish: Aeroklub Warszawski).

Lublin R-XIII

The Air Force was willing to support the existence of all aerospace manufacturers by giving them appropriate orders. Therefore, in spring 1931, the Aviation Department commissioned an army cooperation aircraft prototype, a modification of the R-XIV, to Plage & Laśkiewicz. That aircraft was intended for communications, close reconnaissance and correction of the artillery fire. The Air Force ordered the prototype to be produced within the R-XIV series. The plane had to be equipped with a machine gun (14 kg) on a turret (8,5 kg) with 4 chargers each for 97 cartridges (8 kg), a radio station (30 kg) and a device for picking reports up, in other words, it had to meet the requirements set for the R-XV. The equipment increased the aircraft's empty weight in approximately 60 kg.

A prototype of an army cooperation plane was built as a development of the R-XIV and had neither individual markings nor a military identification number at the beginning. That was a slightly modified variant of the R-XIV. It had the same wings with short ailerons yet equipped

An R-XIIIA (56-3) with a metal propeller, MG mount and short ailerons.

with Flettner tabs. They installed a half-turnable turret (a bow-shaped handle mounted to the sides of the fuselage) with an observer's machine gun and the top of the rear fuselage behind it was flat. It had position lights. Its tail was the same as the latest R-XIV had. That prototype was flown in Lublin by W. Szulczewski in June 1931 and, in the same month, they sent it to the Institute of Aviation Technical Research for testing.

In the course of tests at IBTL in Warsaw, flying colonel Jerzy Kossowski had quite an adventure on that plane. Because of intense manoeuvring that required sudden movements of the control stick, the gudgeon pin fixing it smashed and the stick fell out of its mount. The pilot who lost control jumped with a parachute. Meanwhile, the unmanned plane continued sliding and then landed normally on a field and stopped in a ditch. After that incident, the designer realised that numbers XIV and XV were unlucky too and decided to use the omitted number XIII. So he designated an R-XIII prototype and the Air Force gave it the identification number 56-1.

In June and July 1931, the R-XIII prototype passed performance and handling qualities testing at IBTL and then was sent to the Central Training Escadrille (Polish: Centralna Eskadra Treningowa) of the 1st Air Regiment in Warsaw for flight tests. Built in accordance with the Air Force guidelines, that plane was approved as a sample copy for series production. IBTL confirmed that it provided a good field of vision for a crew and good defense conditions; it was easy for a crew to operate, maintain and store the aircraft and its engine. On the other hand, the plane's inability of being transported on the road and weak engine mount base were classified as flaws. The aircraft was equipped with an R-1 half-turnable turret.

On July 1, 1931, the R-XIV no 54-15, which became another prototype of the R-XIII army cooperation plane, performed its first flight. It was either to realise the designer's new ideas and execute the Air Force recommendations and demands resulting from testing the plane no 56-1. Its wings were distinct from what serial R-XIVs had: they

A 220hp Wright Whirlwind J-5Ab engine on the Lublin R-XIIIA and R-XIIIB.

A lifted up and folded R-1 mount on the R-XIIIA.

used ailerons of bigger span, which improved the aircraft's lateral control and manoeuvrability. To drive ailerons, they used tappets connecting the control wheel and wings instead of cables. The plane had a TO.7 rotating turret for a Vickers F machine gun (similar to what the Potez XXV had)

A serial R-XIIIB with a generator above the wing.

The experimental R-XIIIB with an individual extension arm of the winglet above its aileron.

An R-XIIIB in the 4th Air Regiment in Toruń.

An R-XIIIB no 3 from the 59th Observation Escadrille of the 5th Air Regiment in Lida.

and the top of its rear fuselage behind the turret was convex. To steering cables of the rudder were led to the outer sides of the fuselage, not to the inside as it was done on the R-XIV and R-XIIIA. Under the fuselage, the installed an anchor for picking reports. IBTL finished testing the R-XIV no 54-15 on July 15, 1931. It also passed the comparison tests together with the PZL Ł.2. The example with the serial number 54-15 became a prototype of serial R-XIIIB aircraft.

Series production of the R-XIIIA, R-XIIIB and R-XIIIS

On July 21, 1931, the Aviation Department ordered a series of 50 R-XIII that cost 46,037 zł per each example without an engine. The factory started the production in September 1931 and the first example was ready on June 7, 1932. The first five serial planes designated R-XIIIA with serial numbers from 56-2 to 56-6 were identical to the prototype no 56-1 and were later modified in accordance to the example no 54-15. The following 25 planes with TO-7 turrets received the designation R-XIIIB and serial numbers from 56-7 to 56-32; next 20 aircraft were also designated R-XIIIB, they had Rudlicki's R-2 turrets and serial numbers from 56-33 to 56-52. The last plane from that series was given to the Air Force on March 11, 1933. On October 15, 1931, the Aviation Department requested to use two-point fastening of pilot belts, enlarge the surface of the rudder bar,

A staff R-XIIIB/S without a MG mount and with a control wheel in the rear cockpit.

An engine of the R-XIIB and R-XIII bis with magnetos covering.

extend the windscreen surface and change the fuel tank mount. In 1932, another requirements were introduced: installing steps on the landing gear leg that would enable access to the fuel fill as well as adding a safety belt for an observer and a box for storing weights attached to reports. In 1932-1933, serial military R-XIIIA and R-XIIIB came into use in reconnaissance squadrons of the Polish Aviation and served there until 1935. On the request from the Air Force, R-XIIIB no 56-51 was constructed as a liaison and passenger plane and got rebuilt into a sport, or long range, variant.

The R-XIIIB examples nos 56-12, 56-13, 56-20, 56-48 and 56-51 received no turrets but passenger cabins. They were designated R-XIIIS i.e. staff planes. Those were in the aerial reserve of the Aviation Department. The plane no 56-12 SP-AFD equipped with a Standard Steel metal propeller was colonel Ludomił Rayski's aircraft. For some while, it was used with painted triangular 'birds' between the marks SP and AFD. It received fairings on fittings of

The R-XIIIB SP-AFD.

The staff silver-red R-XIIIB/S SP-AFD of L. Rayski (in the rear cockpit) with Rayski's triangle symbol.

A civil R-XIIIB/S SP-AFG with an exhaust manifold.

A civil R-XIIIB/S SP-AKK (56-48) in military spotted camouflage.

A civil R-XIIIB/S SP-AKK painted in spots, the side view.

The civil R-XIIIB/S SP-AKM. W. Makowski is in the forward cockpit and the Viceminister of Communications A. Bobkowski is in the rear one.

The forward cockpit of the R-XIIIB with flight instruments.

The R-XIIIB fuselage construction with a KZA mount. A report-picking device is under the fuselage.

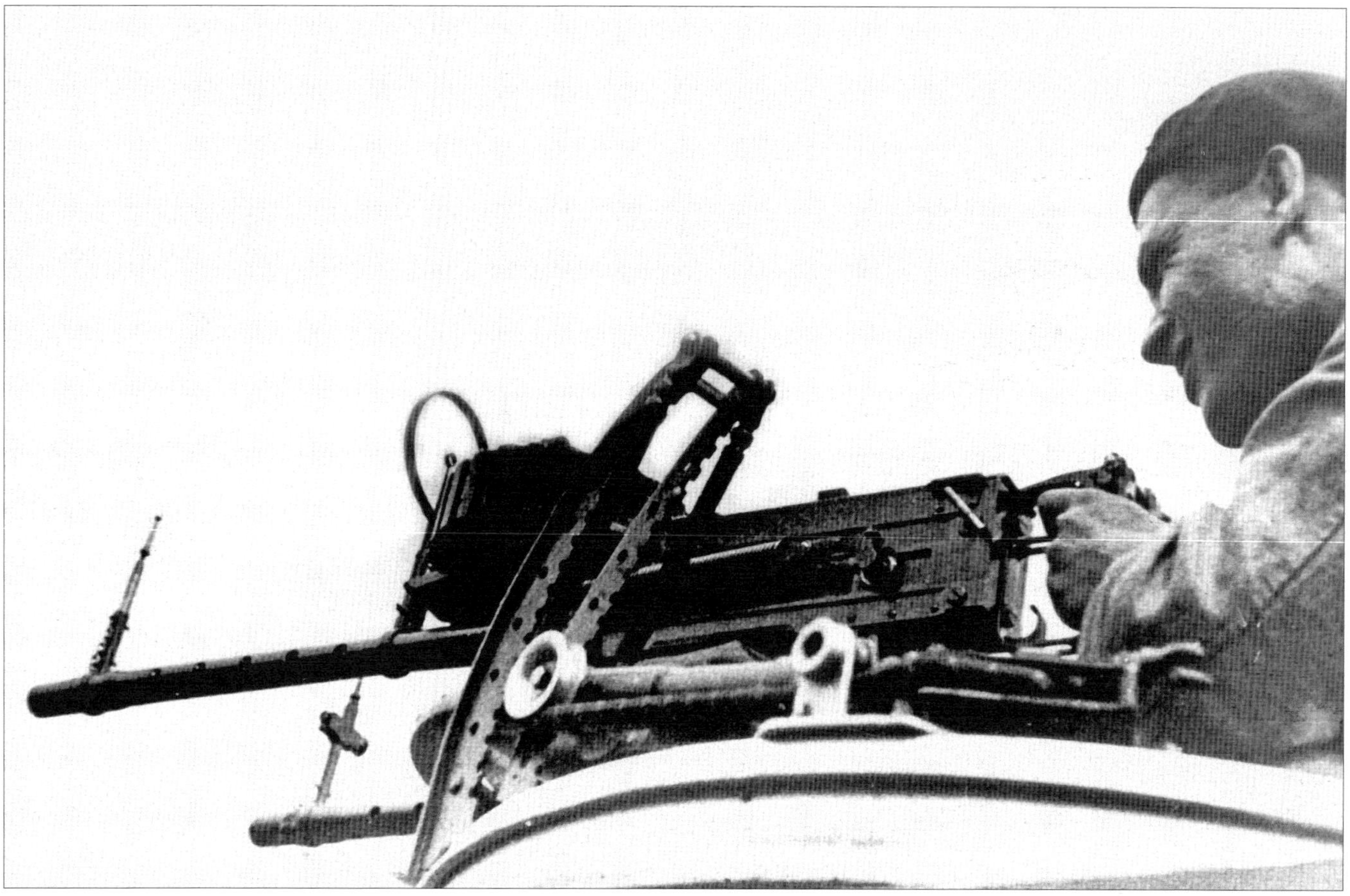

A French TO-7 MG mount with a 7,9mm dual Vickers F machine gun.

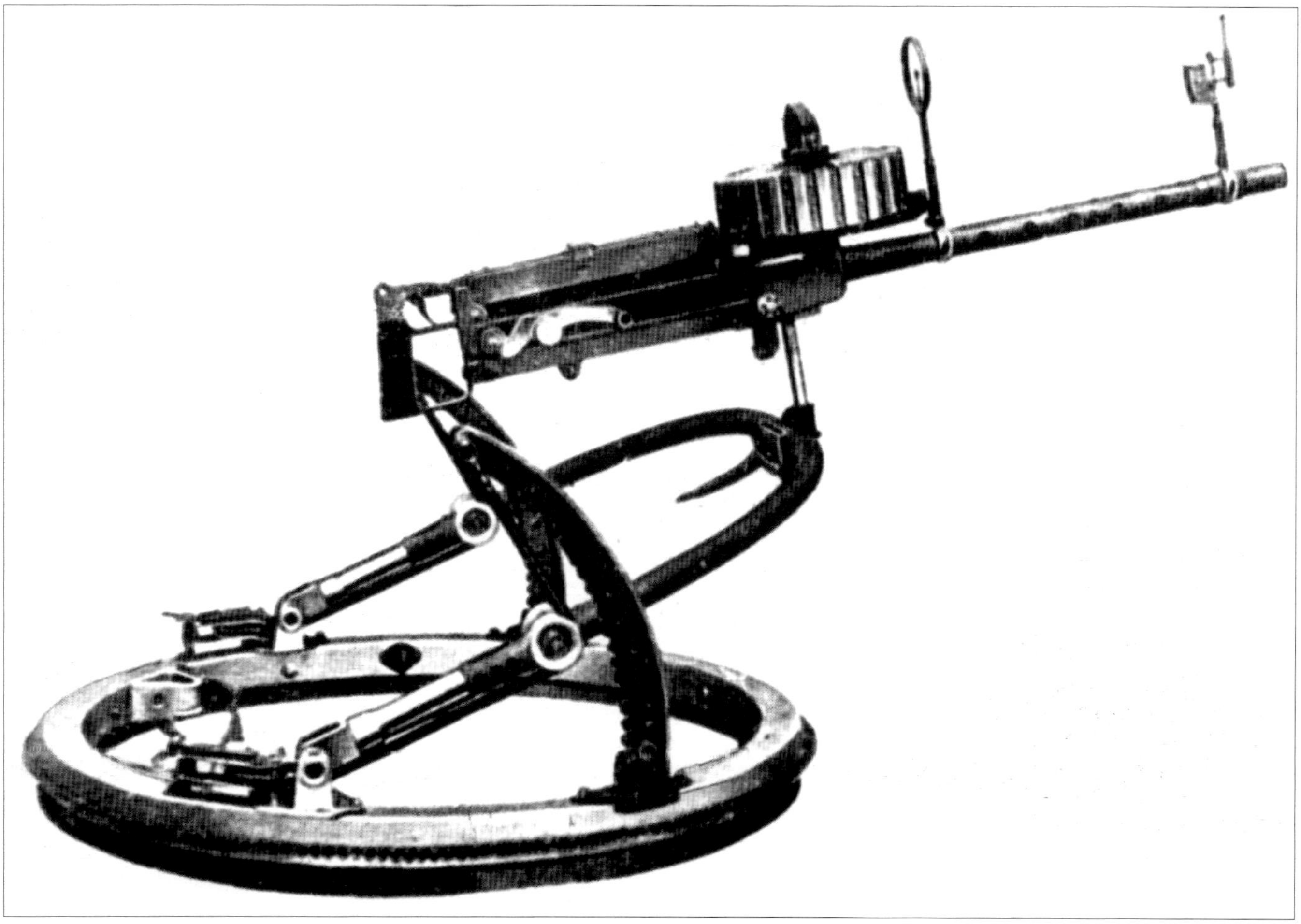

A TO-7 MG mount used on the R-XIIIB and C.

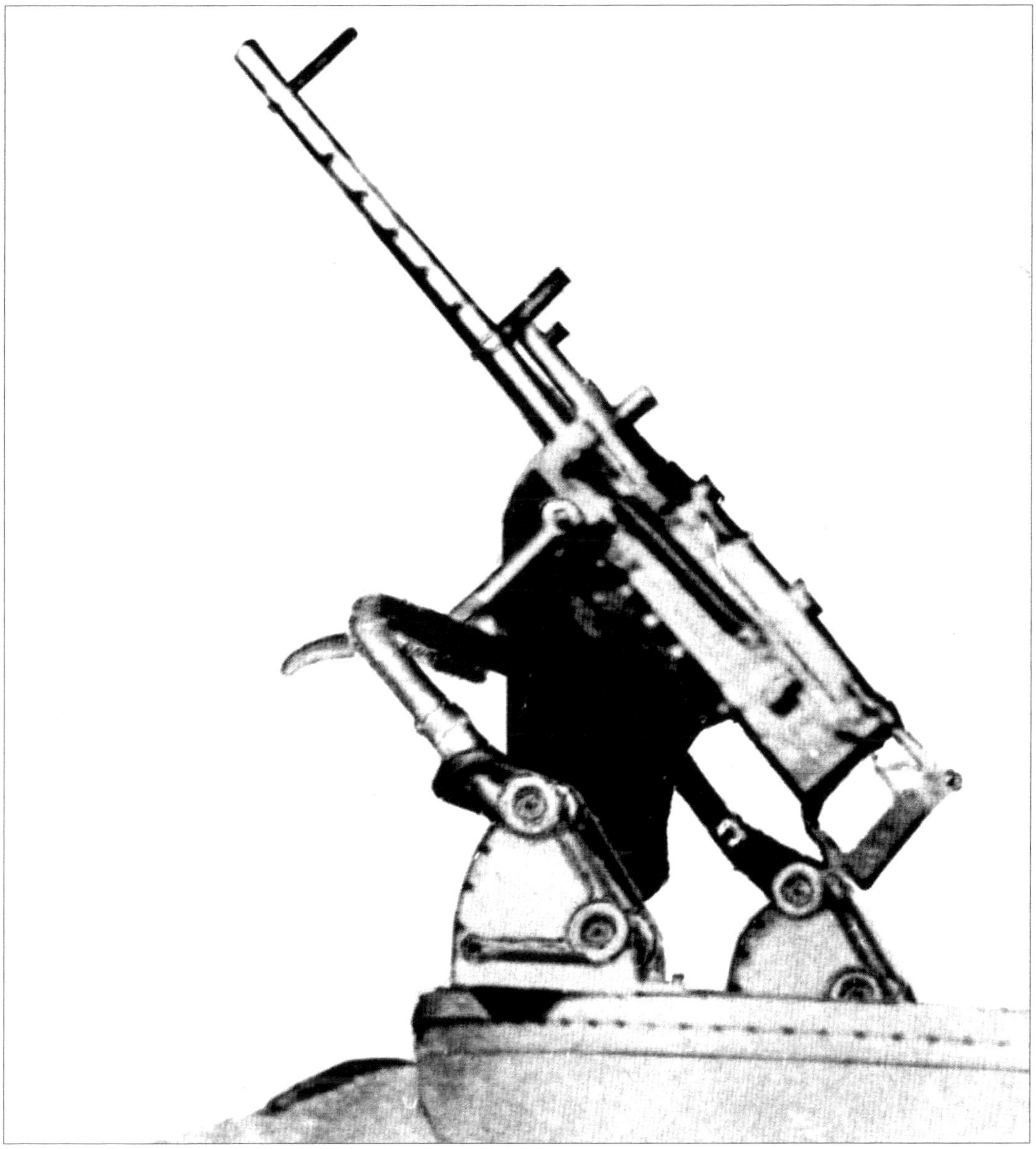

A KZA mount without a machine gun.

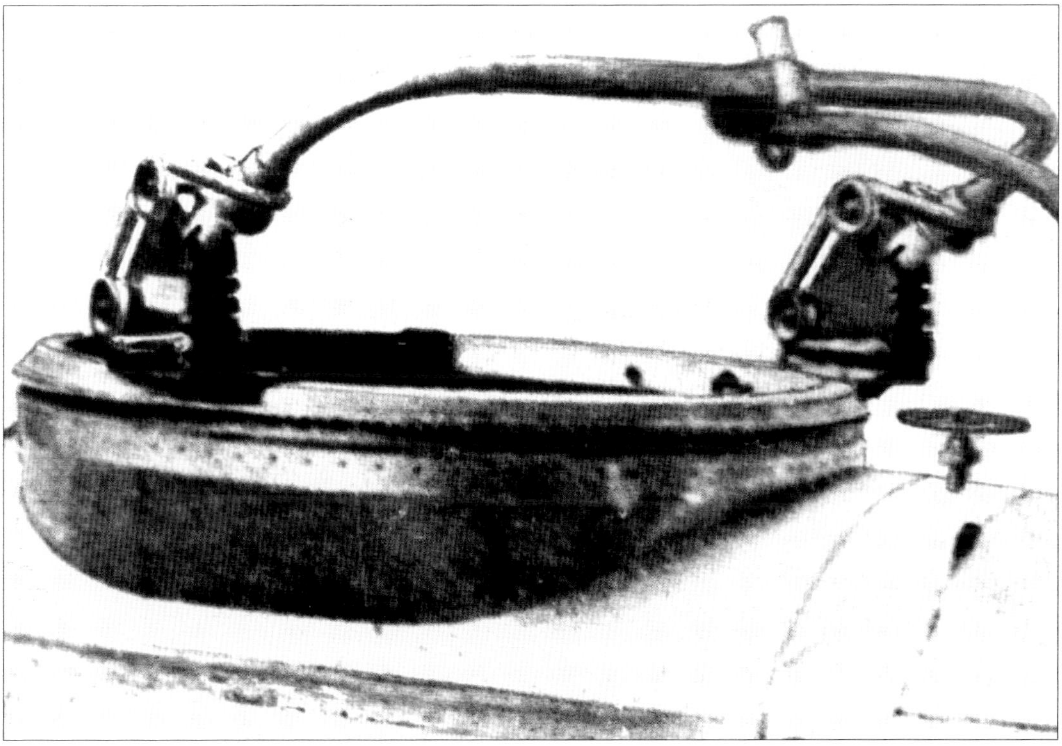

A 7,9mm Vickers F machine gun on a KZA (Kierownictwo Zaopatrzenia Aeronautyki – Aeronautics Supply Management) R-13 mount of Polish origin that was used on the R-XIIIB, C, D and seaplanes R-XIII bis and ter.

The Lublin R-XIIIC no 5.

The R-XIIIC no I from the 53th Escadrille of the 5th Air Regiment in Lida.

An R-XIIIC from the 43th Escadrille of the 4th Air Regiment in Toruń with a generator.

An R-XIIIC from the 56th Escadrille of the 5th Air Regiment in Lida on skis.

An R-XIIIC from the 63th Escadrille of the 6th Air Regiment in Lviv with a generator.

the struts as well as an exhaust manifold instead of individual exhaust pipes on the engine cylinders. The aircraft's maximum and cruising speed could exceed the R-XIIIB's in more than a dozen km/h. It had the tanks for 240 dm^3 (174 kg) of fuel, unlike the rest of the planes with tanks of 180 dm3 (130 kg) volume, which extended its range from 600 to 850 km. Initially, R-XIV no 54-11 had a registration SP-AFD. In 1933, the Polish Air Force passed four R-XIII to Aero Club of the Polish Republic (Polish: Aeroklub Rzeczypospolitej Polskiej, ARP). Their registrations were SP-AFD (no 56-12), SP-AND (no 56-13), SP-ANF (no 56-20) and SP-AKK (no 56-48). The first two were silver with red or navy blue accents, whereas SP-AKK had spotted camouflage.

On April 12-28, 1933, two civil R-XIIIS (SP-AFD and SP-AKK) piloted by Wacław Makowski and Józef Lewoniewski took part in the Balkan race on the route Warsaw – Lviv – Chernivtsi – Jassy – Bucharest – Sofia – Belgrade – Zagreb – Vienna – Bratislava – Prague – Brno – Warsaw. On April 17, in Sofia, the planes demonstrated such aerobatic manoeuvres as loops, barrel rolls and spins.

R-XIIIC

On September 19, 1932, the factory received an order from the Aviation Department for 120 R-XIII planes: 50 in an R-XIIIC variant and 70 in a modified R-XIIID variant. The R-XIIIC was slightly different from the R-XIIIB; a Townend ring was installed on its engine. Its equipment was also a little bit changed and it had a better report-picking device.

The production of R-XIIICs started on February 6, 1933 and the first examples were delivered on May 18, 1933. By adding a clause to the contract on November 5, 1934, they changed the number of aircraft from 120 to 170 including 48 R-XIIICs, two prototypes – the R-XIIIE and

A Wright Whirlwind engine with a Townend ring on the R-XIIIC.

R-XIIIF with 300hp engines, 95 R-XIIIDs and 25 planes with G-1620 engines. The last serial R-XIIIC was delivered to the Air Force on January 10, 1934. 48 serial R-XIIIC aircraft had numbers from 56-52 to 56-99. Four R-XIIICs with numbers 56-56, 56-57, 56-58 and 56-59 were adapted to training without ground visibility. Their empty weight grew from 890 kg to 929 kg. In rear cockpits on the examples nos 56-56 and 56-59, they installed a speedometer, an altimeter, an inclinometer, a heading indicator and tachometer. Several examples in a liaison (staff) R-XIIIC variant, e.g. no 56-90, with a windscreen in front of the turret rotator and without weapons, served in the 5th Staff Escadrille of the 1st Air Regiment (in the aerial reserve of Air Command), in the Central Training Escadrille on the Mokotów Field aerodrome in Warsaw and in the 6th Air Regiment in Lviv.

Flight instruments in the forward cockpit of the R-XIIIC 56-63.

A tow-plane R-XIIIC from the Central Training Escadrille without a Townend ring around its engine.

R-XIII tow-plane

Military R-XIIIs were also used for towing gliders after they had mounted special frames made of steel pipes on their fuselages and pipes with towing hitches above those. At the II International Air Meeting (Polish: II Międzynarodowy Mityng Lotniczy) in May 1933, an aerotow of 3 gliders – the *Komar* (*Mosquito*), SG-21 and SG-28 – by the R-XIIIB piloted by Jerzy Rzewnicki was demonstrated three times at the Mokotów aerodrome in Warsaw.

Within the Air Meeting in Warsaw (on September 14-15, 1935) on the occasion of the Gordon-Bennett Cup, they presented the RWD-

The tow-plane R-XIIIC no 56-89, no 3, from the Central Training Escadrille on the Mokotów aerodrome in Warsaw.

A triple aerotow of gliders by the R-XIIIC above the Mokotów aerodrome in May 1933, during the II International Air Meeting in Warsaw.

The Lublin R-XIIID prototype no 56-102 with a measuring probe under its wing (1933).

8 without a propeller (piloted by S. Grzeszczyk) being towed by the R-XIIIC no 56-89 navigated by Jerzy Rzewnicki.

R-XIIID

The R-XIIID variant designed in 1932 was considerably modified in compare to the earlier R-XIII variants. The front of the engine was protected with a convex casing with an adjustable shield. The oil cooler was covered and the propeller received a small cap. They mounted a KZA turret; the landing gear legs received joint skinning made of canvas. The length of the plane grew in 0,25 m. The first R-XIIID (no 56-102) was sent to IBTL for tests on February 28, 1933. Its weight was 915 kg.

Then, in summer 1933, another 5 aircraft from that series were built simultaneously with the production of the R-XIIIC. The planes' empty weight was decreased to 904 kg. Carefully completed and equipped with wheel fairings, those aircraft were prepared to fly as a squadron of five R-XIIID led by L. Rayski to the USSR in order to take part in the celebration of the 16th anniversary of the October Revolution. In early-November 1933, the squadron set off from Warsaw yet because of the bad weather, they only reached Minsk, Belarus and the delegation went to Moscow by train. It was a return visit of the Polish Aviation as Soviet aviators had travelled to Poland in spring 1933.

Serial R-XIIIDs were being delivered to the Air Force from March 12, 1943 to March 2, 1935.

One of 5 R-XIIID with landing gear fairings and silver-coloured engine casings commissioned to fly to Moscow in 1933.

A series of R-XIIIDs in spotted camouflage.

The R-XIIID 56-159 no 8 from the 36th Escadrille of the 3rd Air Regiment on the Warszawa-Okęcie aerodrome.

The R-XIIID no 6 (the underwing no 14 F) from the 36th Escadrille of the 3rd Air Regiment in Poznań.

The R-XIIID no 8 from the 53th Escadrille of the 5 Air Regiment in Lida without winglets above the ailerons.

R-XIIID no 2 from the 26th Escadrille of the 2 Air Regiment w Kraków. We can see Venturi tube in the case on the strut.

The aircraft had numbers from 56-102 to 56-196. Beginning from the example 56-116, their empty weight was decreased to 890 kg, however, in the middle of the production (approximately beginning from no 56-150) it grew to 956 kg because of the changes in the equipment: among other things, SS-32 bis turrets were implemented, PZL wheels with tin shields were used and so on). The latest 25 R-XIIIDs, from no 56-172 to no 56-196, had exhaust manifolds with Townend rings fitted to them and removable coverings of landing gear legs. Their empty weight was 962 kg. In 1934, the price of an airframe was 46,000 zł, of an engine – 40,400 zł; an aircraft cost 86,400 zł in total. Three R-XIIIDs with removed turrets in their rear cockpits were given to Aero Club of the Polish Republic in 1934. Those planes received registrations SP-ANE (no 56-145), SP-ANG (no 56-

An R-XIIID with the letter E, from the 2nd Air Regiment w Kraków.

The R-XIIID no 6 from the 29th Escadrille 2nd Air Regiment w Kraków.

An R-XIIID with a mosquito symbol from the 63th Escadrille of the 6th Air Regiment.

The R-XIIID N-27 (no 56-179) from the 13th Escadrille of the 1st Air Regiment picking a report with an anchor, on the Mokotów aerodrome on May 3, 1938. The plane has an exhaust manifold.

The R-XIIID no 11 picking up a report from the gate.

An R-XIIID with removable coverings of the landing gear legs.

An R-XIIID from the 66th Escadrille of the 6th Air Regiment with an SS-32 bis MG mount.

R-XIIIDs at the manoeuvres, covered.

An R-XIIID from the 63th Escadrille of the 6th Air Regiment standing on its nose after having been damaged during a landing.

A flight of R-XIIIDs from the 43th Escadrille of the 4th Air Regiment from Toruń.

Two D-XIIID from the 4th Air Regiment without winglets above its ailerons.

A flight of R-XIIIDs from the 4th Air Regiment from Toruń.

A flight of R-XIIIDs.

A cockpit of the R-XIID.

An engine of the R-XIIID with its shield and an exhaust manifold.

An SS-32 bis MG mount with a twin 7,9mm Vickers F machine gun.

148) and SP-AMG (no 56-127). The last one was equipped with wheel fairings and the type of its vertical stabilizer was changed. SP-ANG had tanks for 275 l of fuel so its range was extended to 1,000 km, whereas SP-AMG had tanks for 190 l and its range was 650 km. Those aircraft were used for technical service on the competition route Challenge 1934. In September 1934, general L. Rayski flew the SP-AMG plane on his visit to Bulgaria and Yugoslavia along with a squadron of PZL P.7a fighters. On May 19-26, 1936, one R-XIII together with three PZL P.11c. accompanied Gen. L. Rayski on his visit to Stockholm. Within repairs, the R-XIII in A, B and C variants

SS-32 bis mounts made by Stefan Stelmaszczyk.

A civil R-XIIID SP-AMG (56-127) with a rear passenger cabin.

Silver-red R-XIIID SP-AMG with long exhaust pipes and landing gear fairings. Venturi tube is on the strut.

L. Rayski visiting Belgrade on SP-AMG on September 10-14, 1934.

The civil R-XIIID SP-ANG (56-148) before the removal of its machine gun mount.

The front view of the R-XIIID SP-ANG (56-148).

were modified similarly to the R-XIIID (among other things, their turrets were changed to SS-32 bis turrets and their wheels were substituted with PZL wheels). The markings of those planes was changed (for instance, the R-XIIID no 56-27). Some aircraft only received Townend rings, no casings with shields, and their chassis legs were not covered with canvas. Some R-XIIIs received ailerons of different construction – without winglets above them.

Three R-XIII, which in 1934 were in the reserve of Aero Club of the Polish Republic – nos 56-127,-145,-148 in a liaison (staff) variant, carefully skinned and unarmed, served in the 5th Staff Escadrille of the 1st Air Regiment on the Mokotów aerodrome in Warsaw.

The R-XIII t 'deer fly' no 7 from the Air Force Officer Cadet School in Dęblin with a step-shaped flight deck. The instructor's seat is upwards.

The R-XIIIt 'deer fly' no 70-T from the Training Escadrille of the 4th Air Regiment in Toruń.

In 1938, one R-XIIID was used to test parachute ejection of 20kg pods suspended to bomb racks and 10kg pods thrown out of the gunner's cockpit at the Technical Institute of Aviation (formerly the Institute of Aviation Technical Research) in Warsaw and in the 6th Air Regiment in Lviv.

R-XIIIt 'a deer fly'

In the curse of preparations to Challenge 1934, six R-XIIIBs were adapted to training in pilotage without ground visibility (also called blind pilotage then); they had numbers 56-34, 56-35, 56-37, 56-41, 56-44 and 56-47. Those planes were designated R-XIIIt. They had forward cockpits closed with semi-transparent

R-XIIIt from the 4th Air Regiment with a semi-transparent windscreen of the forward cockpit.

The windscreen of a forward cockpit moved away on the R-XIIIt 'deer fly'.

The 'deer fly' R-XIIIt 8-U from the Fighter Pilot School (Polish: Szkoła Pilotażu Myśliwskiego) in Ułęż.

A foldable box made of canvas on the forward cockpit on the R-XIIIB in the 1st Air Regiment.

shields and raised-up rear cockpit. On account of placing an additional fuel tank atop the fuselage, the casing of its front was raised upwards too as well as the fairings behind the rear cockpit. The capacity of fuel tanks grew to 360 l and the range of the planes exceeded 1,300 km. During June-July 1934, those aircraft were used at Challenge by the Polish team that was training in Warsaw. In particular, they flew them non-stop on the route Warsaw – Paris and Paris – Warsaw. Then the aircraft were returned to the Polish Air Force. In autumn 1934, another two R-XIIIBs were converted to the R-XIIIt.

English training Spitfire Mk VIII (1946) with a step-shaped cockpit.

The Soviet trainer aircraft MiG-25U with a step-shaped cockpit.

The American attack helicopter Bell AH-1 HueyCobra (1965, 1,800 built).

Raising the rear (instructor's) cockpit upwards was Rudlicki's innovative idea that was only used abroad by the end of WWII, for instance, on the British aircraft Spitfire. Then it started being implemented all over the world on trainer aircraft and was used on combat helicopters.

At the Aviation Training Centre in Dęblin, three or four R-XIIIDs were adapted to pilotage without ground visibility – instead of turret mounts, they installed hemispherical shields consisting of milky celluloid segments that could be folded forward and back. A few liaison (staff) R-XIIIs, carefully skinned and unarmed, served in the 5th Staff Escadrille of the 1st Air Regiment (that was in the aerial reserve of the Air Command) at the Mokotów aerodrome in Warsaw.

Sport R-XIIIDr

At the end of April 1933, W. Szulczewski flew an R-XIII sport variant (serial number 56-51) that was initially designated R-XXIII and later R-XIIIDr. It was a modification of the R-XIIIB with a passenger cabin. On capt. S. Karpiński's initiative and with the help of the Maritime and Colonial League, the aircraft was made ready for a journey to Australia. Like the R-XIIIE prototype, it received a metal propeller, a wider engine casing, a Sperry artificial horizon and a Rudolf FK-3 heading indicator and wheel fairings; the bottom of its vertical stabilizer was rounded, which

The sport R-XIIIDr SP-AJT (56-127) *Niebieski Ptak* (*Blue Bird*) with a metal propeller, a broad ring covering its engine and wheel fairings.

The R-XIIIDr SP-AJT painted blue 'in the sunlight' on an aerodrome in Amsterdam.

The R-XIIIDr SP-AJT at the start of a record-breaking flight.

The R-XIIIDr SP-AJT with a swallow and the word POLAND on the fuselage.

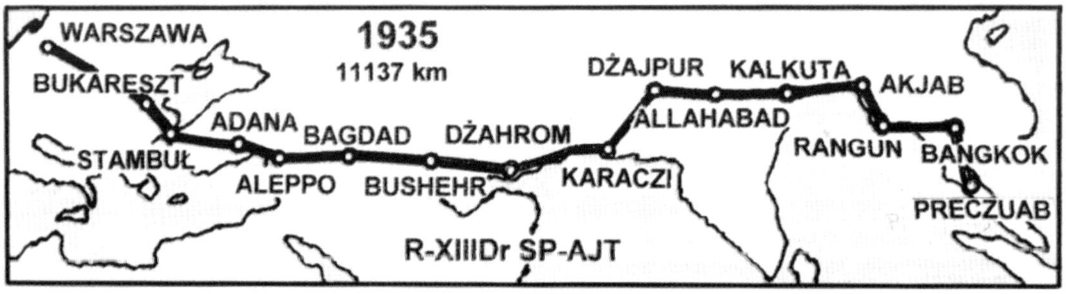

S. Karpiński's flight route in 1935 on the R-XIIIDr SP-AJT to Sinai.

changed the silhouette of its tail a little bit; it also got bigger fuel tanks – for 900 l – inside the fuselage (which allowed flying for 20 hours and could function as floats in case of water landing) and the fuselage became a little taller because of it. The plane's range constituted 2,500 km. By May 10, 1933, it passed tests at IBTL. In August 1933, landing on a clearing in the forest, it was seriously damaged and then repaired and put back in use. In June 1934, it received a reg-

Prototype of the R-XIII bis hydro floatplane no 701 (1932).

The first R-XIIIbis hydro in Puck.

istration SP-AJT. In 1935, the aircraft was repaired again in the course of being prepared for a race. They named it *Błękitny Ptak* (the *Blue Bird)* and inscribed 'POLSKA' (POLAND) on the right side of its fuselage. On October 21 – November 10, 1935, flying captain Stanisław Karpiński and flight mechanic Wojciech Rogalski flew the R-XIIIDr *Błękitny Ptak* for 11,138 km on the route Warsaw – Bucharest – Istanbul – Adana – Aleppo – Baghdad – Bushehr – Dżahrom – Karachi – Jaipur – Allahabad – Calcutta – Akjab – Ranun – Bangkok – Preczubab (Kohlak). That was meant to be a flight to Australia and back again, a total length of 42,000 km, but the aircraft crashed on November 10, 1935, within the takeoff from the sticky aerodrome in Kohlak, Siam. With its propeller twisted, its engine broken, its forward fuselage staved in and its left wing damaged, the plane was returned to Poland by sea. In 1936, it was written off.

Seaplane R-XIIIbis/hydro

The Naval Air Squadron in Puck commissioned the Plage & Laśkiewicz factory to produce an R-XIII seaplane variant. They reworked the R-XIV no 54-15 by equipping it with Short metal floats and designated it R-XIII hydro. In 1931, it passed tests in Puck that revealed that supports of the floats, so-called undercarriage, were weak and broke after landing on water.

On January 9, 1932, the Naval Air Squadron ordered 3 R-XIIIbis/hydro on flat wooden floats and with yokes. Wooden floats were manufactured by Antoni Kocjan Glider Workshops in Warsaw. The planes were completed in 1932 and sent to the Riverine Air Escadrille in Pińsk stationed on the river Pina in October-November. Those three seaplanes received numbers 701, 702 and 703. Under their fuselages, they had racks for six 12,5kg bombs, one machine gun and a gun camera, an Eagle III camera retractable in a vertical pipe under the bottom of the fuselage as well as spare landing gear and skis that could replace the undercarriage. In summer 1932, they installed a Townend ring around one plane's engine, which improved its performance. In 1933, the aircraft no 702 was adapted to training in pilotage without ground visibility by installing a foldable box made of canvas on the forward cockpit. The R-XIII no 701 sank

The R-XIII bis 702 in the Riverine Air Escadrille in Pińsk.

The R-XIII bis no 703 on wheels, with an F-28 gun camera on a strut and a telescopic sight in front of the cockpit. A generator with a single-blade propeller.

Prototype of the R-XIII ter floatplane on wheels, after being flown in Lublin.

The R-XIII ter floatplane no 704 in Puck. The number 7 is covered.

The R-XIII ter no 706.

The R-XIII ter no 707 on a transport trolley. A generator is above its wing.

The R-XIII ter no 707 on a trolley, the rear view.

The R-XIII ter no 710 anchored in Puck.

The R-XIII ter no 711 on a trolley.

on October 23, 1934. When the squadron was dissolved in 1937, the planes were brought to Puck and written off. The price of one R-XIIIbis/hydro airframe was 77,313 zł and one engine cost 35,000 zł.

The factory offered R-XIIIbis planes to Estonian aviation authorities yet the deal was not concluded.

R-XIIIter/hydro and R-XIIIG/hydro

On May 5, 1933, the Naval Air Squadron ordered 10 R-XIIIter/hydro. Those were an R-XIIID seaplane variant. They received KZA turrets. Their numbers were from 704 to 713. In their forward cockpits, the aircraft received yokes in place of control sticks. Each plane had a spare set of a wheeled chassis and skis as well as

The R-XIII ter no 712 with a KZA turret.

The R-XIII ter no 713 at close range.

The R-XIII ter no 713, the front view.

A flight of R-XIII G no 714.

Four R-XIII hydro flying.

The R-XIIIG in the rear view. The Hel Peninsula is on the horizon.

The R-XIII hydro flying. A small number on the fuselage was used in 1939.

The R-XIIIG no 718 standing on its nose in Puck. The edge of the camera is visible.

a yoke and Short metal floats; its undercarriage between the floats was braced with pipes, not tie rods as on the R-XIIIbis/hydro. Metal floats for the R-XIII based on Short floats were later produced by State Aviation Works. The floats were interchangeable with wooden floats from the R-XIIIbis. What made R-XIIIter distinct from the R-XIIIbis were steps and handles added to facilitate the engine maintenance when the plane was on the water. On one example, they tried using a Standard-Steel adjustable metal propeller. Above their wings, the planes received lifting bails for being moved from the water to the land by a crane. The aircraft's fabric covering was laced behind to facilitate the control of fuselage corrosion. The trunk behind

The R-XIIIG no 719 with a wheeled chassis, after it turned over in Puck.

The R-XIIIG no 719 after it turned over.

The R-XIII ter 711 pulled out of the water.

the engine was accessible from the both sides of the fuselage. The aircraft had position lights on edges of their wings, in the middle section of the wing and on their rudders. R-XIIIter/hydro were delivered to the base of the Naval Air Squadron in Puck in spring and summer 1934. A few planes were later equipped with racks for three 12,5kg concrete bombs for training. They used them in bombardment training with rafts on the Bay of Puck.

On May 23, 1934, the factory received an order for 6 R-XIIIGs from the Naval Air Squad-

The R-XIII ter fuselage with a yoke and KZA turret.

The tail of the R-XIII ter no 712 with a tailskid. There are no weights written on its rudder yet: Cw – empty weight, Cu – operating weight, Cp – fuel weight, Cc – gross weight.

Cockpit steps on the R-XIII ter. The plane has a wheeled chassis.

The R-XIII ter tail.

ron. Besides, they constructed one R-XIII landplane for the Naval Air Squadron instead of the fourth R-VIIIbis the rebuilding of which was not completed (it was dismantled for spare parts). R-XIIIGs received numbers from 714 to 720. The plane number 720 represented a landplane variant. The R-XIIIG was just a little bit different from the R-XIIIter and R-XIIID. The planes had landing gear interchangeable with Short metal floats and were equipped with Standard-Steel metal propellers, control sticks (instead of yokes used on previous R-XIII seaplanes) and SS-32 bis turrets. In Puck, those planes were put on floats. The last R-XIIIG was delivered on April

Location of a crew on the R-XIIIG no 716 that crashed in Puck on September 15, 1936. An SS-32 bis MG mount. A control stick is in the forward cockpit.

The bottom of the fuselage of the crashed R-XIIIG no 716. We can see the casing of the control system, the camera pipe and steps: two on the left and one on the right side of the fuselage.

Flight instruments of the R-XIII ter.

Flight instruments of the R-XIIIG. A control stick was in place of a yoke.

15, 1935. The price of one aircraft was 120,000 zł, which included 45,000 zł for an airframe, 28,000 zł for an engine, 20,000 zł for floats and 27,000 zł for equipment, armament and spare parts.

Equipment tests were conducted on the R-XIIIG no 718 with a wheeled chassis, which was given to the Riverine Air Escadrille in Pińsk. In 1936, they put a Vickers twin-mounted machine gun on a turret, and in 1937, they installed an Eagle III semi-automatic camera for taking serial photos. In 1937, they also tested an AVA radio station on it: 100W for radiotelegraphy and 40W for radiotelephony working on 40-90m waves and having a 3-5km range. In 1935, that plane was in use on wooden floats made by A. Kocjan Glider Workshops in Warsaw and in winter on skis.

The R-XIII no 705 crashed on June, 24, 1934. The R-XIII no 704 crashed on the sea in autumn 1934. Three R-XIII (nos 704, 710 and 713) forcibly landed on water near Piława. One of them, no 713, sank on October 23, 1934, whereas the damaged no 710 was towed by the boat to Piława and thence returned to Puck on the board of the tugboat *Ursus*. On June 17, 1936, the R-XIII no 709 crashed in a flat spin. On May 15, 1939, one R-XIII on a wheeled chassis crashed during a forcible landing in the forest near Swarzewo.

The Hanriot H-28 with Rudlicki's V-tail (1931).

J. Rudlicki and W. Szulczewski near the Hanriot H-28 with a butterfly tail.

In the mid-1930s, four R-XIII hydro appeared in *Rapsodia Bałtyku* (1935).

R-XIX 'a butterfly'

In 1930, the Institute of Aerodynamics of the Warsaw University of Technology started aerodynamic researches of a V-tail invented by Jerzy Rudlicki; they tested models with dihedral and anhedral angles. Such a configuration of the tail control surfaces is called Rudlicki's V-tail or a butterfly tail. The researches showed that in terms of aerodynamics, it could substitute the conventional tail. Rudlicki's V-tail simultaneously reduced aerodynamic drag in ⅓ and was ⅓ lighter. Moreover, it provided a better field of fire from the rear cockpit of a military aircraft.

In 1931, the aircraft factory E. Plage & T. Laśkiewicz in Lublin modified a military trainer aircraft Hanriot H-28 no 30.83 by installing Rudlicki's V-tail. In summer 1931, Władysław

The R-XIX model with a butterfly tail with an anhedral angle

The R-XIX model with a butterfly tail.

The Lublin R-XIX converted in 1932 from the R-XIII prototype with Rudlicki's V-tail.

The American sport aircraft Beech Bonanza (1946, 8,000 built) with a butterfly tail.

Szulczewski flew the plane and verified its good performance. Then it passed tests at the Institute of Aviation Technical Research in Warsaw.

After the information about flights of H-28 with Rudlicki's V-tail had been published, a British research establishment RAE in Farnborough got interested in that solution and conducted their own aerodynamic tests. The results were published in *Aircraft Engineering* of March 1932. Then Z. Zakrzewski, managing director of Me-

The French trainer aircraft Fouga Magister (1951, 940 built).

The American fighter aircraft Lockheed F-117 (1977, 65 built).

chanical Works E. Plage & T. Laśkiewicz, recommended Rudlicki to use the V-tail on the R-XIII.

The aircraft was designated R-XIX. It was completed in 1932 as the reworked R-XIII prototype (serial number 56-1) with wings with short ailerons, like those R-XIV had. It was flown in Lublin by W. Szulczewski. Then it was introduced on the Mokotów Field in Warsaw to the representatives of IBTL and the Aviation Department by W. Szulczewski and Col. J. Kossowski who demonstrated aerobatic manoeuvres (a spin, a loop, a wingover). The plane's handling qualities were good and the field of fire from the rear cockpit was highly beneficial. However, the chief of the Aviation Department, L. Rayski, who did not trust the new idea, commanded to stop testing the airframe and disassemble the aircraft and return it to the factory. Since that example was initially to be written off, its life ended soon.

Rudlicki's idea of a tail of this kind came into use around the world – among others, in series production of the American Beech Bonanza (8,000 examples), French Fouga Magister (800 examples) and American F-117 (59 examples).

R-XIIIC with a lowerable tail

In 1935, Jerzy Teisseyre and August Zdaniewski developed a vertical tail that could be moved downwards during the flight to expand the field of fire for a rear gunner. The configuration was implemented at the Podlasie Aircraft Factory on one of serial R-XIIICs. In 1936,

The lowerable vertical tail on the rebuilt R-XIIIB in up- and mid-positions.

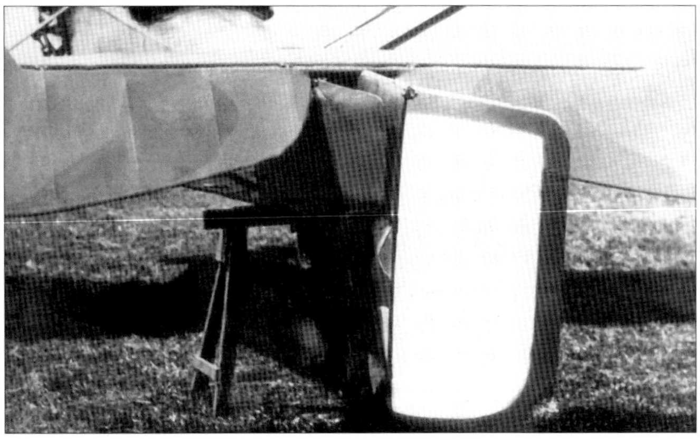

The lowerable vertical tail in a down position, which facilitated firing.

The R-XIIIE prototype no 56-100 during the tests, with a measuring probe under its wing.

the aircraft successfully passed tests conducted by the factory and the Technical Institute of Aviation. Such a tail allowed very smooth recovery from a spin. Later, it was designed for the LWS-3 *Mewa*.

R-XIIIE

Since the Aviation Department wanted to equip the R-XIII with a 340/410hp engine G-1620A Mors A produced in Poland, J. Rudlicki developed an R-XXI variant of that aircraft, in December 1932. That project entered the contest for the R-XIII's successor, in which it competed with two projects introduced by the Podlasie Aircraft Factory and the winning RWD-14 project. In September 1932, the Aviation Department ordered two R-XIII prototypes with Mors engines; those were designated R-XIIIE and R-XIIIF. Then it was decided to equip the R-XIIIE with Gnôme-Rhône 7K Titan, a 360hp seven-cylinder engine, and Gnôme-Rhône metal propeller no 93. The construction of the R-XIIIE prototype (serial no 56-100) started in July 1933 and ended on January 24, 1934. The plane's

The R-XIIIE prototype.

The R-XIIIE prototype.

empty weight constituted 1,080 kg. It received no armament but just a turret. Its fuselage was much more rounded than fuselages of serial R-XIIIs. In 1934, it passed tests at IBTL but was only used for comparison testing as the R-XIIIF had a Mors engine of Polish origin. Reportedly, 4 racks for 50kg bombs were installed on the R-XIIIE. The designer used a slotted engine cover comprised of three rings with apertures on their edges as that would reduce the resistance in his view. The tests revealed that such a covering did not have any advantages.

They also tried a 220kW (300hp) Algol 9Na engine with a compressor, which considerably increased the plane's service ceiling. The tests of its climb and service ceiling measurements were conducted in mid-May 1934, on a warm day. The crew composed of pilot J. Rzewnicki and Engr. Janiszewski, an observer, came lightly dressed; the observer only had a summer flight suit on. Because of the compressor, the aircraft rose to 6,500 m, where it was very frosty. The pilot got his neck frostbitten. When the observer's frozen cheek was touched, a wound stretching over it appeared.

R-XIIIF

In July 1933, they also started constructing a prototype of the R-XIIIF (serial number 56-101) with an engine designed by Engr. Stanisław Nowkuński from the Polish Škoda Factory – 340hp G-1620 Mors. Since that was a prototype engine, fixing its drawbacks took quite long so its construction dragged on. In 1934, they started manufacturing of 50 Mors A engines intended for 25 serial R-XIIIFs ordered. The R-XIIIF prototype was ready on November 3, 1933. It had the metal propeller Letov HA no 212. After the Mors engine had caught fire during a flight of August 28, 1934, in 1935 they decided to install a 220hp Wright engine. On September 5, 1934, they started series production of 25 R-XIIIFs the numeration of which began from no 58-1. Those planes received Szomański wooden propellers; they did not have Townend rings around their engines and sides of their fuselages were rounded like in the R-XXI project. The bottoms of their vertical stabilizers were rounded too and their rudders did not have horn balances. By the contract no 163/34 of 1934, the ordered num-

The Lublin R-XIIIF 58-8 with a Whirlwind engine in the Air Force Officer Cadet School in Dęblin. The plane has rounded fuselage sides and rounded vertical stabilizer.

The Lublin R-XIIIF no 19-D from the Air Force Officer Cadet School in Dęblin without an engine case.

The Lublin R-XIIIF no 02 without a ring engine case.

The Lublin R-XIIIF no 89 from the Air Force Officer Cadet School in Dęblin.

ber of R-XIIIFs grew to 50. The first serial R-XIIIF (no 58-1) was completed on July 22, 1935.

The aircraft was sent for tests to the Institute of Aviation Technical Research on August 6, 1935. The institute gave a critical opinion – they had reservations about the plane's flight characteristics as it tended to enter a flat spin. On September 11, 1935, they made a recommendation to redesign the horizontal tail. The plane was returned to the factory; upon completion the amendments, they sent it to IBTL on September 21, 1935. In the course of tests, ruptures of various engine components were found: that was the engine manufacturer's fault, not the airframe manufacturer's. At the end of the testing, they concluded that the aircraft would

The Lublin R-XIIIF Aerolog no 58-23 do meteorological measurements with a enclosed cockpit.

The enclosed cockpit of the R-XIIIF no 58-23 Aerolog upon the removal of its covering.

become usable after fixing the flaws: its tail was too 'heavy' and it was needed to add a steel plate that would balance its elevators; moreover, excessive tail vibration and resilience of the rudder and ailerons control system were found. The first two R-XIIIFs passed flight tests in the Air Regiments nos 3 and 6 in 1935. They found defects in the report-picking devices. Considering those flaws, the Aviation Department issued another bad review of the plane, which they had planned in advance. Then, in order to push the factory into bankruptcy, they cancelled the order for the R-XIIIF. By November 21,1935, the factory provided 7 R-XIIIFs. The rest 18 examples under construction were priced as scrap. At the end of 1934, the Works went bankrupt and was acquired by the state. The nationalised firm received the name Lublin Aircraft Works (LWS). At the beginning of 1936, the Aviation Department renewed the order for the R-XIIIF and the factory could continue operating without any financial losses. Apart from 18 airframes Mechanical Works Plage & Laśkiewicz had been commissioned to produce, LWS built 32 more R-XIIIFs in 1936-1938 so the total number was 50. Those planes had numbers from 58-8 to 58-57. In total, 58 R-XIIIFs (including prototypes) were built. Since only 50 G-1620A Mors I engines were produced, some planes had to be powered by Wright J-5 engines. The examples nos 58-46 and 58-47 passed additional tests at the Technical Institute of Aviation on August 10,

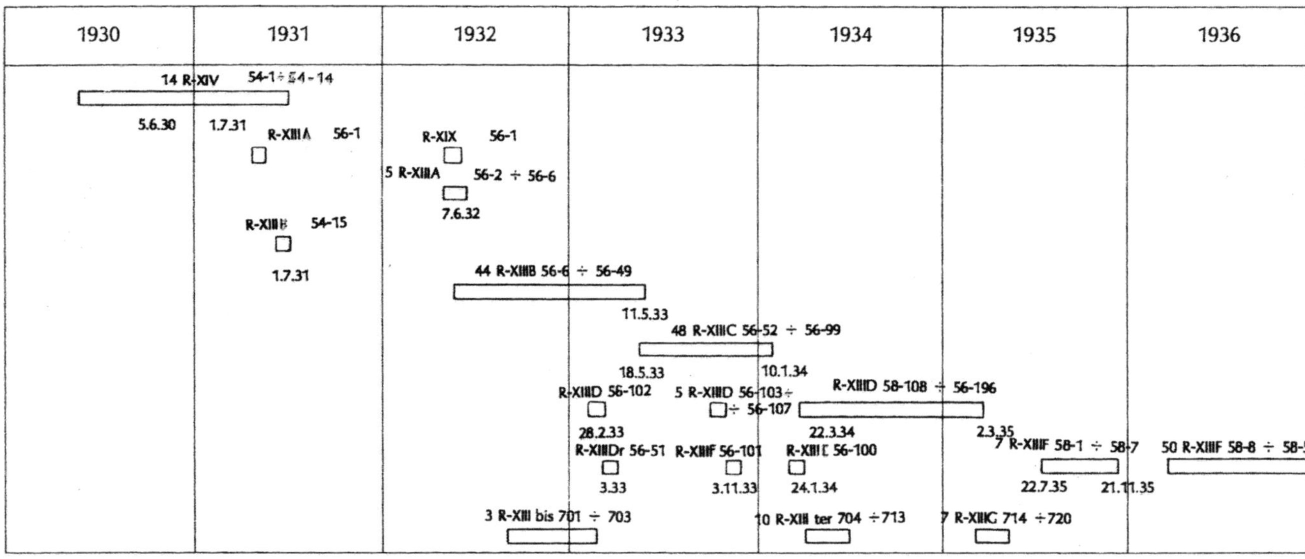

Production of R-XIVs and R-XIIIs.

1938. R-XIIIF aircraft were used for training, e.g. in Dęblin, and, being disarmed, they also functioned as so-called staff planes – among others, in the 5th Staff Escadrille (in the aerial reserve of Air Command) of the 1st Air Regiment stationed at the Mokotów aerodrome.

No 58-23 with military markings, on account of its big service ceiling, was intended for measurements taken by the meteorological station of LOT Polish Airlines in the Okęcie neighbourhood in Warsaw. Since measuring at high altitudes at very low air temperatures was difficult, it was decided to build an enclosed cockpit on the plane. In spring 1939, PZL WP-1 (Polish: Wytwórnia Płatowców No 1 – the Airframe Works No 1) located in Okęcie-Paluch was commissioned to execute that task. The plane received the designation R-XIIIF *Aerolog* (*Aerologist*). It was equipped with a radio station for correspondence, a radio station for zero visibility landings and position lights. Both cockpits had glass shields. The changes were made in summer 1939. When the war broke out, the aircraft was still at the factory and was captured by Germans.

Overall evaluation and production

R-XIII, colloquially called 'Er' or 'grasshopper' (Polish: pasikonik), was a successful liaison-observation plane in terms of the early-1930s. It was able to take off and land shortly and had good handling qualities. In 1933-1939, it was the main aircraft in observation escadrilles.

In total, 288 R-XIII and R-XIV were produced, which included 15 R-XIVs, 20 R-XIII floatplanes and 253 R-XIII landplanes (244 of them had 220hp engines). Those were military planes and only few were used in sport aviation.

R-XIII aircraft were intended to carry out liaison and observation missions for the infantry and artillery. As they were not equipped with cameras, they could only be used for visual reconnaissance and making sketches from observation. The results could be transmitted via radio, however, only some of the aircraft had radio stations (just transmitting). After changing the wavelength for land forces in the late 1930-s, such transmission of visual information became impossible. Army cooperation aviation was to obtain new radio stations working on the same wavelengths as radio stations used by land forces but that did not happen before the war outbreak. The main means of communication with land units were dropping of weight reports (i.e. in bags with small weights attached), picking up reports from the ground, interpretation of signs composed of signal cloths on the ground, transmitting information from a plane and the ground using coloured light-smoke flares as well as landing near land units or on the own airfield while a report would be carried by an observer on a motorcycle.

When a flood occured in July 1934, four R-XIIIs were used in rescue operations in the upper Vistula basin area. At the turn of July and August 1934, two R-XIII squadrons took part in manoeuvres for the first time. Upon completion of manoeuvres in Pomerania in September 1937, the coordinator, Col. Władysław Kalkus, found that with an adversary's active anti-aircraft defense, R-XIIIs were not suitable for flights over the battlefield. However, his opinion did not impact the conception of using R-XIII planes in September 1939.

Use in the military aviation before the war

In 1932-1936, 33 liaison platoons, each composed of 3 aircraft, were created. In autumn 1937, those aviation units were reorganised by merging two platoons into a squadron and simultaneously dissolving some of them. In 1937-1938, 18 squadrons featured R-XIII planes: the 13th, 16th and 19th Observation Escadrilles of the 1st Air

Użycie samolotów R-XIII w eskadrach w latach 1931–1939

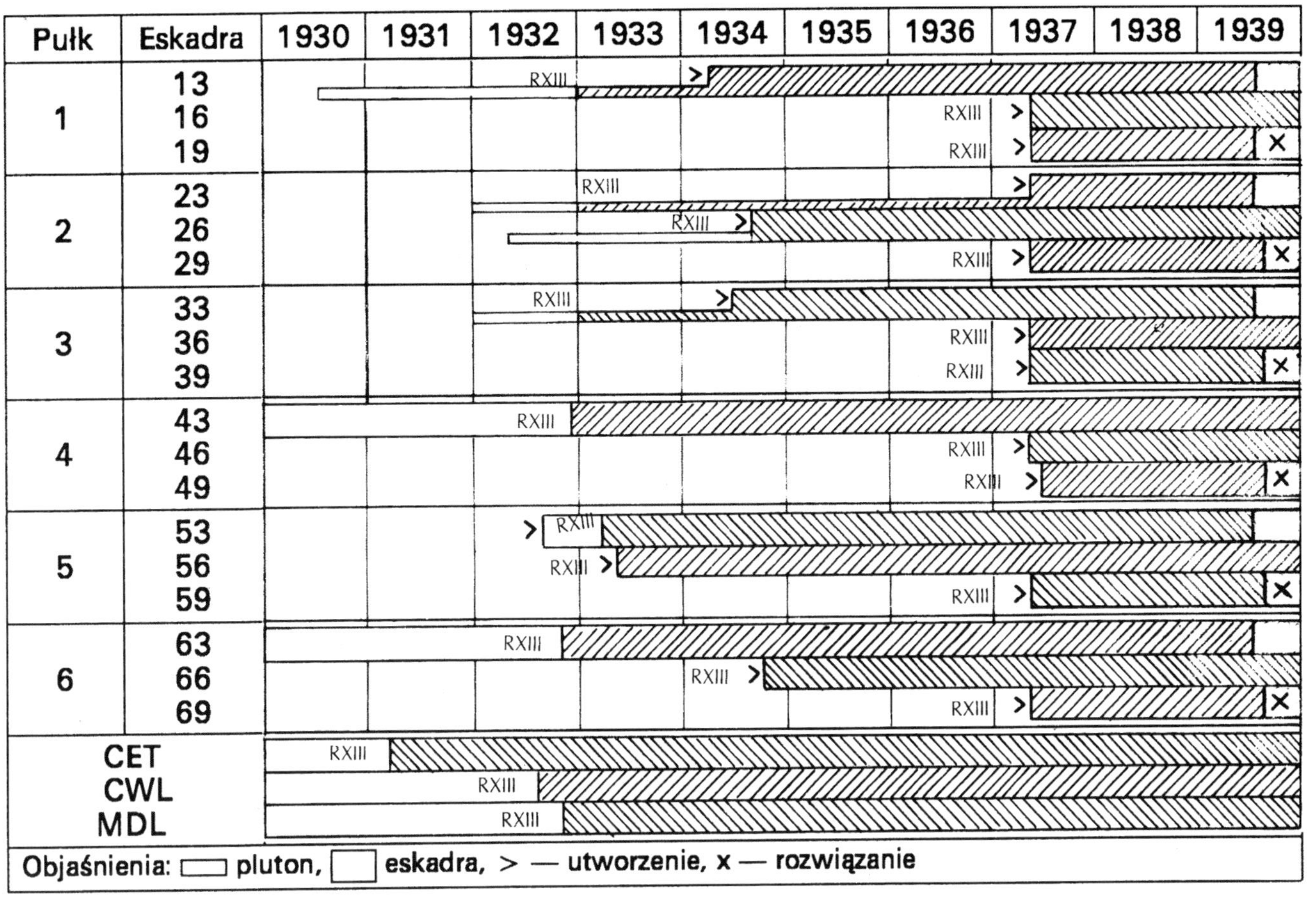

Use of R-XIII aircraft in squadrons in 1931–1939.

Regiment in Warsaw; 23rd, 26th and 29th Escadrilles of the 2nd Air Regiment in Kraków; 33rd, 36th and 39th Escadrilles of the 3rd Air Regiment in Poznań; 43rd, 46th and 49th Escadrilles of the 4th Air Regiment in Toruń; 53rd, 56th and 59th Escadrilles of the 5th Air Regiment in Lida and 63rd, 66th and 69th Escadrille of the 6th Air Regiment in Lviv. During that time, the combat aviation used 225 R-XIII including training and reserve planes. Since 1936, R-XIIIs was to be gradually replaced with RWD-14 *Czapla* planes. Due to the delay in production of the *Czapla*, only five R-XIII squadrons were converted to *Czapla* units – only in 1939. In the same year, the first LWS-3 *Mewa* planes, intended to substitute all the R-XIIIs in squadrons, were produced.

R-XIII/hydro seaplanes in the Naval Air Squadron in Puck were primarily used for training flights, sometimes for reconnaissance flights.

The proportion of accidents on R-XIIIs was close to other types of military aircraft. 15 accidents happened on the R-XIII (273 planes), which constituted 6%; for instance, on the PZL Ł.2 this proportion was 10%. Only one accident happened on the R-XIV. Among those 15 R-XIIIs, three R-XIIIter seaplanes (nos 704, 705 and 709) crashed. As many as 10 R-XIII crashed due to mistakes in pilotage and a few more crashed because of bad atmospheric conditions.

In 1935, when several accidents happened on R-XIIIs during long flights, the Institute of Aviation Technical Research conducted additional tests of the aircraft as they suspected it entered a flat spin when its centre of gravity was shifted due to fuel exhaustion. In the course of testing at IBTL, the plane was navigated by Engr. Jerzy Rzewnicki, whereas Kazimierz Dzwonkowski who weighed 85 kg was chosen as an observer. The aircraft was made enter a flat spin after moving the horizontal stabilizer to the 'heavy to tail' position. To recover it from the spin, the observer had to use a parachute, which would relieve the tail. However, the centrifugal force turned out to stop him from leaving the cockpit. The plane lost 200 m in height, the pilot moved the stabilizer letting it recover from the spin. When the crew reported on that flight, pilot K. Kazimierczuk acknowledged that the information on the impossibility of leaving the cockpit in a spin was false. Rzewnicki took another flight with Kazimierczuk who was unable to jump out of the plane and, in an attempt to leave the cockpit, strained his diaphragm so he could not fly for a few weeks.

Use in September 1939

In 1939, the Polish Air Force used up to 150 Lublin R-XIII that included 50 R-XIIID and R-XIIIC in combat units, 30 in training, 40 in the reserve

Position of R-XIIIs in combat units and losses in September 1939.

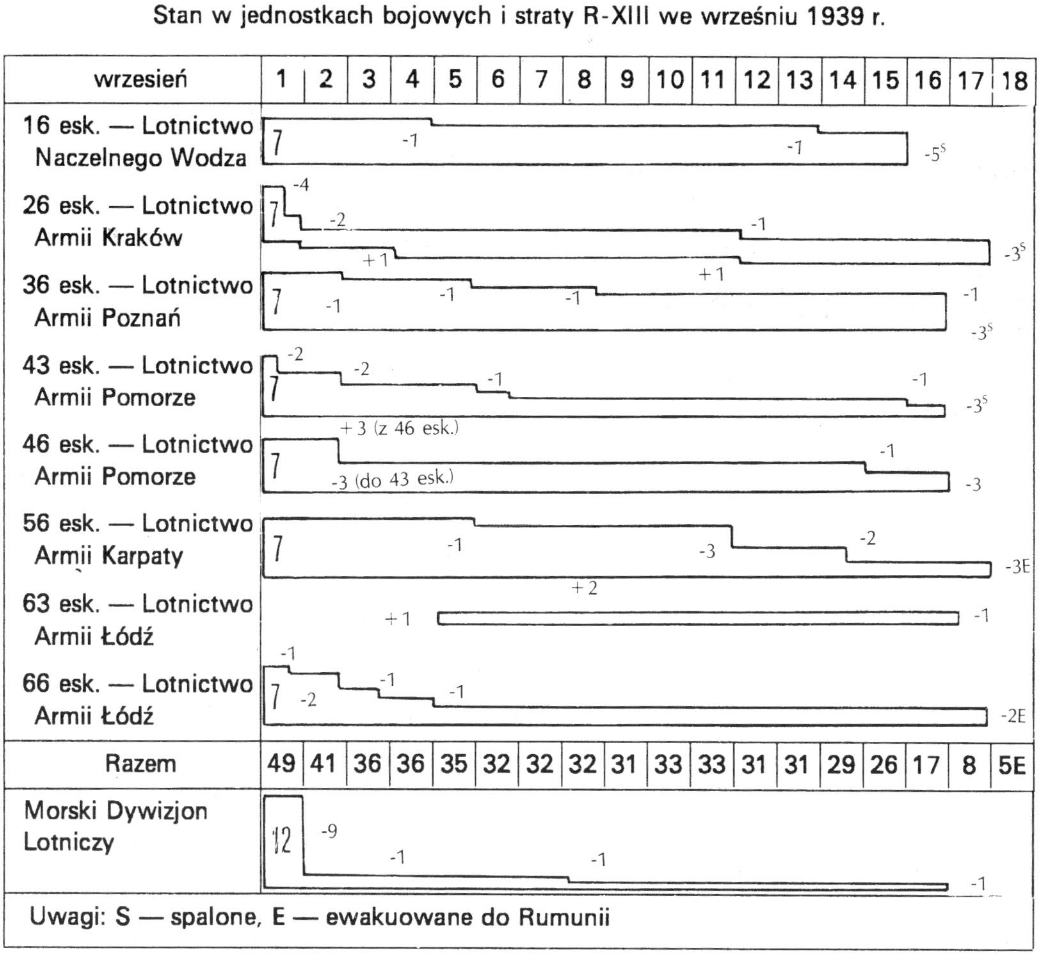

The Lublin R-XIIID with its registration SP-AMG painted over and its 'chessboard' cut off, crashed in September 1939 at Okęcie.

and around 40 were being repaired. That year, escadrilles nos 13, 23, 33, 53 and 63 were substituted with Czapla planes, whereas escadrilles nos 19, 29, 39, 49, 59 and 69 were dissolved. In September 1939, the 16th Observation Escadrille was part of the liaison aviation, which formed the aerial reserve of the Commander in Chief together with the Pursuit Brigade (Polish: Brygada

Pościgowa) and Bomber Brigade (Polish: Brygada Bombowa). The rest of squadrons were part of the military aviation: the 26th Escadrille was in the army aviation of Kraków, 36th Escadrille in the army of Poznań, 43th and 46th Escadrilles in the army of Pomerania, 56th in the Carpathian army and 66th Escadrille in the army of Lodz.

During the September Campaign of 1939, R-XIII aircraft performed observation of the battlefield and its facilities and were used for communications. In the course of war operations, 5 R-XIIIs arrived as a reinforcement, thus, 55 landplanes of this type participated in battles. They performed 474 combat (observation) and 107 liaison flights as well as one leaflet. In the defense of Warsaw, on the Mokotów aerodrome, 2 R-XIII were shot down by Germans and R-XIIIs that were part of the

The Lublin R-XIII D no 65 with its marks painted over in September 1939.

The R-XIIID no 409-S from the 6th Air Regiment crashed in September 1939 near Tarnów, destroyed by Germans. Its 'chessboards' are chopped off as a war trophy.

The R-XIIID masked with branches in September 1939. The marks are painted over.

The R-XIIID no 2, no 17-K from the 23rd Escadrille of the 2nd Air Regiment destroyed at Rakowice.

Skeletons of R-XIIIs at Rakowice.

The R-XIIID 56-110 from the 13th Escadrille from Warsaw captured by Germans in Dęblin.

An R-XIIID destroyed in September 1939 at Rakowice in Kraków.

The skeleton of the R-XIV without covering, destroyed in September 1939.

An R-XIIIC with its engine casing extended and an exhaust manifold, captured by Germans in September 1939 in Lviv.

Technical Exhibition at the Air Force Officer Cadet School (Polish: Szkoła Podchorążych Lotnictwa) had to be put to operation. Those planes performed combat flights. 24 R-XIII endured till September 16, 19 of them were broken, burnt or destroyed on September 16-18. 50 out of 55 R-XIII involved in the September Campaign were destroyed (around 7 of those were shot down by disoriented Polish troops) and 5 were withdrawn to Romania. On September 16, 1939, one R-XIIID (serial no 56-158) landed near Yampil, the USSR, another one in Slovakia and one in Hungary. The German Air Force captured more than a dozen R-XIIIs yet did not put those to use. Together with aircraft from training squadrons, 26 R-XIII were in Romania including 1 R-XIIIA, 10 R-XIIIB, 4 R-XIIIC, 7 R-XIIID, 2 R-XIIIF and 1 air ambulance R-XIIIS (no 56-134) as well as 1 R-XIV. They were used in 1940-1944 by the Royal Romanian Air Force. One plane, captured by the Soviet Army, was demonstrated at the exhibition of captured equipment in Kyiv in 1945.

The R-XIIIC no 56-77 captured by Germans atop the wagon in Legnica.

An R-XIII seaplane destroyed in September 1939 near the Hel Peninsula.

The R-XIII bis no 702 with a Townend ring around its engine, destroyed in September 1939 near the Hel Peninsula.

An R-XIII seaplane destroyed in September 1939.

The Lublin R-XIIID taken by the Romanian Royal Air Force.

A Romanian R-XIII at the exhibition of captured equipment Kiev in 1945.

The replica of the R-XIIIG no 714 in Puck.

The rear view of the replica R-XIIIG no 714.

In September 1939, the R-XIII G/hydro from the Naval Air Squadron that participated in the defence of Hel only performed two combat flights. Lieutenant J. Rudzki and lieutenant Juszczakiewicz, an observer, performed a reconnaissance flight on the R-XIII no 714 in the night of September 6-7 and another one in the night of September 7-8, when they were shooting Germans celebrating the capture of Westerplatte in Gdańsk. On September 8, 1939, R-XIIIs from the Naval Squadron were bombarded near Jurata.

Replica of the Lublin R-XIII G/hydro

In Spring 2013, a group of enthusiasts and lovers of the Puck Region history and Baltic naval aviation, brought to life the Historical Association of the Naval Air Squadron in Puck. They set ambitious goals, such as creating the Muzeum MDLot in an old local seaplane base, forming a team of reconstructors wearing a sailor uniform and building replicas of seaplanes that were in use back in time. As the first, they chose a floatplane variant of the most known Polish liaison-observation aircraft – Lublin R-XIII.

A project for building a full-size replica of the seaplane Lublin R-XIIID no 714 was sent to the contest in the North Kashubian Local Fishing Group and got on the list of ventures for financing. That became possible thanks to the great commitment of Mikołaj Czub, Ireneusz Makowski and Zdzisław Jaroni. Andrzej Doroszewicz, an experienced aviator among whose works there was a copy of the RWD-13, undertook the construction of the plane. He also chose his team. With the remarkable support from employees of the Central Military Archives in Warsaw, the Polish

The R-XIII seaplane and its finder Jacek Dzienisiuk.

Aviation Museum in Kraków, the State Archive in Lublin and Polish Naval Museum in Gdynia, the documentation was prepared. Besides, Andrzej Olejko, Marek Trojanowicz, Mariusz Konarski and Jarosław Wróbel shared their collections.

A truss fuselage framework and, later, a rudder were first introduced in Puck in November 2014. Next, the completed replica was launched within the *Aerial Puck* Historical Festival on July 31, 2016. It currently is an attraction at various events.

A valuable exhibit of the MDL Museum in Puck is a float of the R-XIII excavated from the sea near Hel by Capt. Jacek Dzienisiuk from LOT.

The design

The R-XIII was a two-seated liaison-observation (so-called accompanying) aircraft of mixed construction, laid out as a monoplane with braced high wings of the parasol type. The R-XIV was a two-seated trainer (so-called trainer-aerobatic) aircraft.

The truss fuselage was welded from steel pipes covered with linen canvas. Its top and front were skinned with a duralumin plate. The forward section of the fuselage framework was braced with pipes and the rear one with wires. A small turret for mounting panels and side pyramids for fixing the landing gear and struts were joined with the fuselage lattice. Flight instruments were different for particular variants; among other things, they included a Badin flight controller with a speedometer, turn and sleep indicator and inclinometer, two altimeters, a heading indicator, an artificial horizon, oil and fuel gauges, an oil temperature indicator and timer.

Control wheels were in both cockpits and a removable control stick was in the rear cockpit. The seats accommodated seat parachutes, the cockpits were open. The forward (pilot's) cockpit was protected with a windscreen. The rear (observer's) cockpit on the R-XIII was equipped with a turret type R-1, TO-7, R-2 (modified TO-7), KZA F-13 or SS-32 bis produced by W. Stelmaszyk Airparts Factory (Polish: Wytwórnia Części Lotniczych W. Stelmaszyka) in Lublin; a turret had a raised-up lifting bail made of a pipe – a machine gun was mounted on it, which facilitated firing upwards and downwards. Some aircraft had an RKL/D or Ava N2L/0 radio station in the rear cockpit, a camera for taking vertical-oriented photos and a K-28 gun camera. Some planes had a retractable report-picking device under the fuselage; it was composed of pipes or a cable with an anchor. There was a trunk in front of the cockpit. They also had a 300W wind generator.

The two-wheeled main landing gear had the 2,54m spacing, three legs and oleo struts. The wheels were 750x125 mm, with conical or convex shields (PZL), interchangeable with wooden skis. The tailskid was self-adjusting, with a rubber shock absorber.

In a seaplane variant, the undercarriage was made of steel pipes and it had two Short metal floats with rudders or wooden floats manufactured by A. Kocjan Glider Workshops.

An engine casing on the R-XIIID, ter i G.

A generator with a single-blade propeller.

The wings were rectangular-elliptical, bipartite, wooden, two-girder, covered with plywood up to the front girder and with canvas from there, installed on a pyramid of steel pipes and supported by two pairs of oval-shaped duralumin struts, braced with profile tie rods. The plane had modified IAW-127 wings. Its ailerons had winglets. The empennage was welded from steel pipes and covered with canvas. The stabilizers were stiffened with wires. The horizontal stabilizer was in-flight adjustable. The rudder and elevators had horn aerodynamic balances.

The engine was air-cooled nine-cylinder radial Wright Whirlwind J5 made by the Polish Škoda Factory, of nominal power of 220 hp at 1,800 rpm and take-off power of 240 hp, weighing 250 kg. The R-XIIIE had a seven-cylinder radial engine Gnôme-Rhône 7K Titan Major of nominal power of 360 hp at 2,000 rpm, weighing 280 kg. The R-XIIIF had a nine-cylinder radial engine G-1620A Mors A made by Škoda Poland, of nominal power of 340 hp at 2,000 rpm and take-off power of 410 hp, weighing 242 kg. The casing of the engine and front of the fuselage was made of a duralumin plate. The propeller was permanent, two-blade wooden Szomański-Hamilton 658 of 2,7 m in diameter. A fuel tank for 200 l (fuel uplift normally was 180 l) was in the forward fuselage, behind the engine; it was riveted form dura-

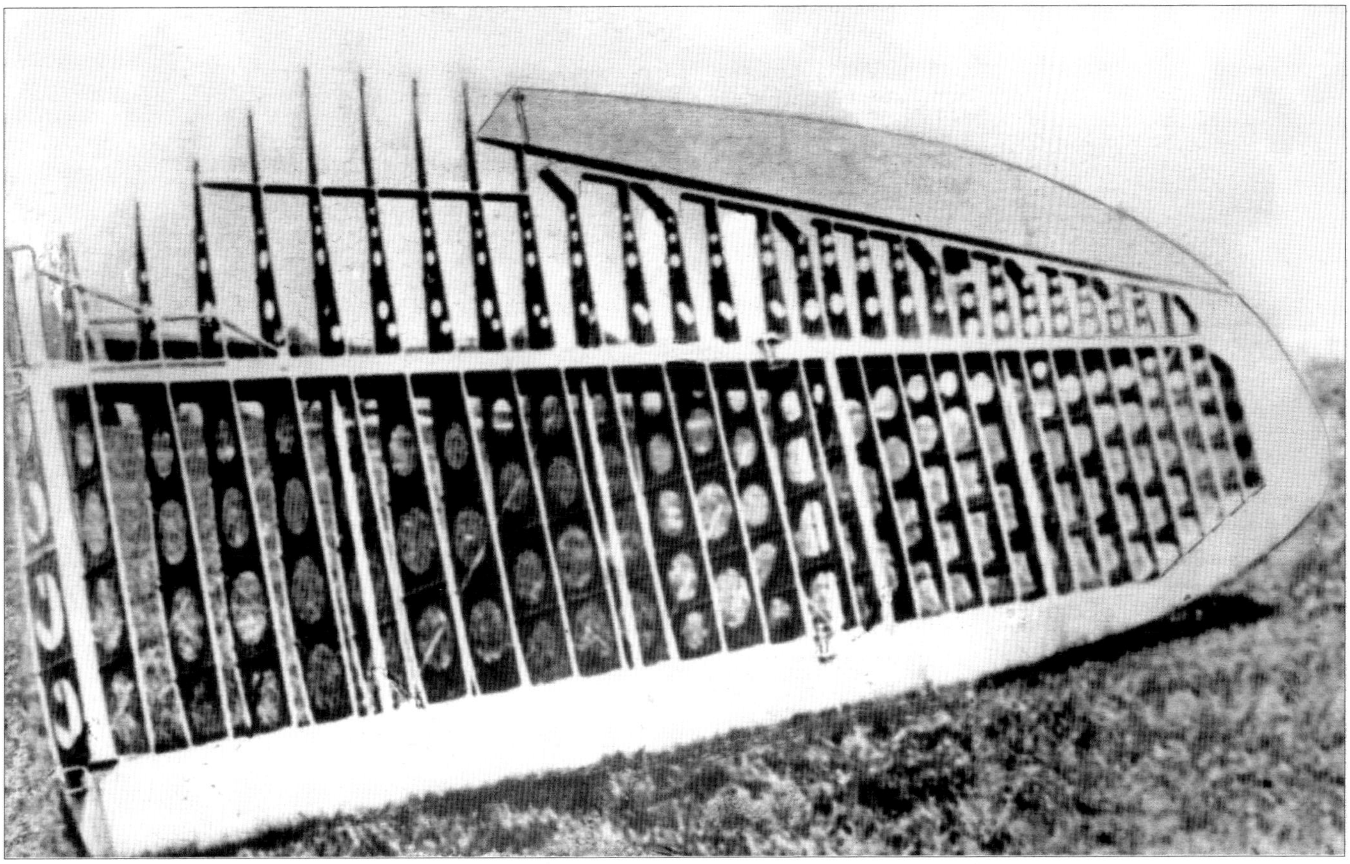

Configuration of a wing of the R-XIII.

lumin, ejectable in case of an accident. A fuel tank on the R-XIV was for 135 l. In-flight fuel consumption was 45 l/km.

Camouflage

Prototypes were painted olive green from the top and light blue from the bottom. Landplanes were painted light green, brown and dark green camouflage spots from the top and silver from the bottom. They had inscriptions 'Lublin R-XIII' on their rudders. Seaplanes were light steel grey. 'Chessboards' were drawn on R-XIII landplanes and seaplanes – big from the wing bottom and small from its top (as on rudders), put asymmetrically. Sport examples had military colours (e.g. SP-AKK at the beginning) or they were silver with red edges of their wings and tails, engine casings and stripes along their fuselages (e.g. SP-ANG and SP-AKK later). SP-AJT was painted light blue grading from dark on the engine cover to light on the rear fuselage. Swallows were painted on both sides of its fuselage; 'Polska' was inscribed on the right side of the fuselage, below the forward cockpit, and 'Zakłady Mechaniczne Plage i Laśkiewicz Lublin' on the forward fuselage. On the rudder, there were inscriptions 'Lublin R-XIIID' and 'Made in Poland' as well as the ARP mark; 'Aeroklub Rzeczypospolitej Polskiej' was inscribed on the vertical stabilizer.

Technical details

Variant	R-XIV prototype	R-XIV	R-XIII prototype	R-XIIIA/B	R-XIIIC	R-XIIID	R-XIIIDr
Wingspan, m	13,50	13,50	13,25	13,25	13,25	13,25	13,25
Length, m	8,20	8,20	8,20	8,20	8,20	8,46	8,20
Height, m	2,76	2,76	2,76	2,76	2,76	2,76	2,76
Bearing surface, m^2	25,9	25,9	24,5	24,5	24,5	24,5	24,5
Empty weight, kg	825	800	870	890-910	910	887	1063
Operating weight, kg	291	290-337	430	400-394	400	443	1091
Gross weight, kg	1116	1090-1137	1300	1290-1304	1310	1330	2154
Surface loading, kg/m^2	43,0	44,0	53,2	53,2	53,5	54,3	88,0
Power-to-weight ratio, kg/hp	5,1	5,2	5,9	5,9	5,9	6,0	9,8
Maksimum speed, km/h	195	180	185	178	180	187	196
Cruising speed, km/h	170	165	165	155	160	165	150-170
Minimum speed, km/h		75				80	86
Rate of climb, m/s	5,0	4,3	4,3	3,3	3,5	4,1	1,6
Service ceiling, m	5625	4500	4500	4100	4100	4300	1200
Range, km	500	500	600	600	600	600	2500
Takeoff distance, m				68			

Technical details

Variant	R-XIIIG landplane	R-XIIIE	R-XIIIF prototype	R-XIIIF	R-XIIIbis hydro	R-XIIIter hydro	R-XIIIG hydro
Wingspan, m	13,25	13,25	13,25	13,25	13,25	13,25	13,25
Length, m	8,20	8,46	8,46	8,46	9,13	9,13	9,13
Height, m	2,76	2,76	2,76	2,76	3,08	3,08	3,08
Bearing surface, m²	25,9	25,9	24,5	24,5	24,5	24,5	24,5
Empty weight, kg	948	1080	970	1033	998	1031	1094
Operating weight, kg	394	440	430	512	402	394	331
Gross weight, kg	1342	1520	1400	1545	1400	1425	1425
Surface loading, kg/m²	56,7	62,5	57,1	63,0	57,1	58,2	58,2
Power-to-weight ratio, kg/hp	6,1	4,2	4,1	4,6	6,4	6,5	6,5
Maksimum speed, km/h	185	200	215	208	170	175	175
Cruising speed, km/h	165	180	190	185	150	155	155
Minimum speed, km/h			86		86	86	86
Rate of climb, m/s	3,5	5,8	6,2	6,0	3,3	3,2	3,2
Service ceiling, m	4000	6100	6600	6300	3900	3800	3800
Range, km	500				450	450	450

Variants of the R-XIII and R-XIV

No	Variant	Serial numbers	Number of examples	Notes
1	R-XIV	54-1 to 54-14	14	including the prototype R-XIII no 56-1
2	R-XIV (S)	54-11	(1)	staff (liaison) SP-AFD
3	R-XIII	54-15	1	the prototype of R-XIIIB
4	R-XIII	56-1	1	the prototype of R-XIIIA
5	R-XIIIA	56-2 to 56-6	(5)	converted to R-XIIIB
6	R-XIIIB	56-2 to 56-50	49	a series including R-XIIIA rebuilt
7	R-XIIIS	56-12, -13, -20, -48	(4)	liaison, fmr R-XIIIB SP-AFD, SP-AND, SP-ANF, SP-AKK
8	R-XIIIt	56-10, -22, -34, -35, -37, -41, -44, -47	(8)	'deer flies', fmr R-XIIIB
9	R-XMIDr	56-51	1	sport, fmr R-XIIIB, SP-AJT
10	R-XIIIC	56-52 to 56-99	48	a series
11	R-XIIIC(t)	56-56, -57, -58, -59	(4)	'deer flies'
12	R-XIIIC(h)	56-89	(D)	a tow-plane
13	R-XIIIE	56-100	1	experimental prototype
14	R-XIIIF	56-101	1	a prototype
15	R-XIIID	56-102	1	a prototype
16	R-XIIID	56-1 03 to 56-1 96	94	a series
17	R-XIIID	56-1 72 to 56-1 96	(25)	with an exhaust manifold
18	R-XIIID(S)	56-127	(1)	liaison (staff), SP- AMG
19	R-XI1ID(S)	56-145, 56-148	(2)	liaison, SP-ANE, SP-ANG
20	R-XIII bis	701 – 703	3	hydro, a series
21	R-XIII bis (t)	702	(D)	hydro, 'a deer fly'
22	R-XIII bis		...	on a wheeled chassis
23	R-XIII ter	704 – 713	10	hydro, a series
24	R-XIII ter			on a wheeled chassis
25	R-XIIIG	714 – 719	5	hydro, a series
26	R-XIIIG	720	1	a landplane
27	R-XIX	56-1	(1)	'butterfly', a prototype
28	R-XIII experimental	56-..	(1)	with a lowerable tail, fmr R-XIIIC
29	R-XIIIF	58-1 to 58-57	57	a series
30	R -XIII F *Aerolog*	58-23	(1)	for aerological purposes

Legenda: (x) – numbers of reconstructed aircraft included in numbers without parentheses; fmr – former

Turrets on the R-XIII

Turret type	R-XIII variant	Characteristics
R-1	R-XIIIA	– half-turnable (a bow-shaped handle); – a rubber compensator; – an 8-position lock
TO-7 (and R-2)	R-XIII (54-15) R-XIIIB R-XIIIC	– a bow-shaped handle; – a rubber compensator; – a 15-position lock; – a dial was outside the ring mount
KZA R-13	R-XIIIB R-XIIIC R-XIIID R-XIIIE R-XIII bis R-XIII ter	– rounded-rectangular handle; – a rubber compensator; – a 4-position lock; – a dial was outside the ring mount
SS-32 bis	R-XIIID R-XIIIF R-XIIIG	– a bow-shaped handle; – a spring compensator; – a 6-position lock; – a dial was on the ring mount

Examples of marks on the R-XIV and R-XIII

Variant	Serial No	Unit	Symbol	Side number	Call sign (under-wing)	Call sign colour
R-XIV	54-..	2 PL	—	2	—	—
R-XIV	54-..	CET 1 PL	—	3	—	—
R-XIII	56-1	CET 1 PL	cT	1	..Z	black
R-XIII A	56-3	—	—	—	—	—
R-XIII B	54-15	CET 1 PL	—	—	89Z	black
R-XIII C	56-..	43 ET	a beetle	—	52T	black
R-XJII C	56-..	53 ET	—	1	—	—
R-XIII C	56-..	56 ET	a bear	4; 7; 9; 10	—	—
R-XIII C	56-..	59 ET	a bee	3	—	—
R-XIII C	56-..	63 ET	a square	—	— .	—
R-XIII C	56-89	CET	a shield	3	— -	—
R-XIII D	56-110	13 ET	a cricket	—	N..	black
R-XIII D	56-179	13 ET	a cricket	—	N 27	black
R-XNI D	56- (126)	26 ET	a wasp	E	(15K)	black
R-XIII D	56-...	26 ET	a wasp	5		
R-XIII D	56-...	29 ET	a spider	6		
R-XIII D	56-169	36 ET	a dragonfly	6	14F	black
R-XIII D	56-159	36 ET	a dragonfly	8	—	—
R-XIII D	56-...	53 ET	St. Christopher	7, 8, 9		
R-XIII D	56-...	63 ET	a mosquito			
R-XIII D	56-27	66 ET	a chameleon			
R-XIII t	56-..	4PL	a pentagon	—	—	
R-XIII t	56-..	WSP	—	8	08U	black
R-XIII t	56-..	LSSiB	LSSiB	6		
R-XIII t	56-..	WSP	—	2, 3	..U	white
R-XIN F	58-..	CWL	—	89, 146		
R-XIII F	58-..	SPRL	—	02	02R	black
R-XIII F	58-..	CWL-SPL	—	19	19D	black

Legenda:
PL (pułk lotniczy) – air regiment
CET (Centralna Eskadra Treningowa) – Central Training Squadron
ET (eskadra towarzysząca) – army cooperation squadron
CWL (Centrum Wyszkolenia Lotniczego) – Aviation Training Centre
LSSiB (Lotnicza Szkoła Strzelania i Bombardowania) – Aviation School of Shooting and Bombardment
SPL (Szkoła Podchorążych Lotnictwa) – Air Force Officer Cadet School
SPRL (Szkoła Podchorążych Rezerwy Lotnictwa) – Aviation Reserve Officer Cadet School
WSP (Wyższa Szkoła Pilotażu) – Higher Pilotage School
() – presumed information

Jerzy Rudlicki

Rudlicki Jerzy Stanisław (March 14, 1893, Odesa – August 18, 1977, Fort Lauderdale, Florida) was a mechanical engineer, aircraft designer and creator of a butterfly tail. He was the son of Walery, an engineer, and Teresa from the Urbańskis.

Rudlicki graduated from a classical gymnasium in Odesa. In 1907, he designed an amateur spark-gap transmitter-receiver telegraph station with letter notation. In 1908, he won the second prize of the Imperial Academy of Arts at the All-Russia Exhibition of School Drawings in Saint Petersburg for his tables of insects and plants. In 1909-1911, Rudlicki designed and built seven gliders on which he performed aerotows by attaching them to horses by ropes. For the latest of them, he received a diploma with honours from the Odesa Department of the Imperial Polytechnic Community, moreover, gliders of his construction were purchased by a representative of the Shah. His next design was an aircraft he started to build in 1914 together with his colleague S. T. Dobrowolski.

During World War I, Rudlicki served as an observer in the Air Squadron of the 8th Russian Air Force Corps on the South-Western Front. For his photos of the front and Dubno fortress, he was awarded with the Cross of Saint Vladimir with Swords. In Simferopol, he completed a course on pilotage and returned to the front. He was shot and wounded two times. He got to Polish units that were being formed in Minsk, Lithuania; on their order, he went to Harbin in 1918, thence via Suez to Marseille, where he joined aviation divisions of Gen. J. Haller's army in France. There he was re-trained to navigate the Breguet 14. In January 1919, he was sent with a mission to to Istanbul on the board of *Chachuła* which sank in the Strait of Messina. Rudlicki survived and returned to France.

In spring 1919, along with Haller's army, he came to Poland and in September, being a flying captain, became a commander of the 16th Reconnaissance Escadrille, with which in 1920 he took part in the Kiev expedition, offensive in Grodno and operations of Gen. L. Żeligowski's Army of the Central Lithuania. After that, he moved to France, where he studied

Jerzy Rudlicki

at the École Superieure d'Aéronautique in Paris (1921-1922) and received an engineer degree. In 1922-1925, he worked at the Polish Military Sales Mission in Paris by obtaining engines for aircraft ordered for the Polish Air Force. In 1925, Rudlicki returned to Poland and started working at the Institute of Aviation Technical Research (IBTL). In 1926, he took the position of chief engineer at the Mechanical Works Plage & Laśkiewicz in Lublin. In accordance with his project, in 1928, they constructed a reconnaissance bomber Lublin R-VIII built as a series of 5 examples and later used by the Polish Navy. His next development was a bomber variant of an airliner Fokker F.VIIb/3m, which was being built in Lublin under the licence. A two-seated liaison aircraft designed by Rudlicki Lublin R-X (10 serial examples built) was flown non-stop from Poznań to Barcelona (1,800 km) by Engr. W. Makowski in 1929. In 1931, Capt. S. Karpiński and Engr. J. Suchodolski took a trip around Europe of a total length of 6,450 km. In 1932, a crew of S. Karpiński and mechanic W. Rogalski flew it to Africa and Asia, a total length of 14,390 km.

The aircraft constructed by Rudlicki and produced in the biggest number of exemplars was liaison-observation plane Lublin R-XIII (270 built) and its trainer variant R-XIV (15 built). The naval (floatplane) variant of that aircraft was used by the Polish Navy. On the R-XIIIDr, S. Karpiński and W. Rogalski took a trip from Warsaw to Siam in 1935. The other R-constructions – the R-IX, R-XI and R-XIV – were prototypes of airliners, whereas the R-XII was a prototype of a sport plane. The R-XVIb was the first Polish air ambulance aircraft. It won first place in the contest of air ambulance aviation in Madrid in 1933. The prototype of a seaplane R-XX was the biggest aircraft built in interwar Poland (its wingspan was 25,4 m).

Rudlicki also experimented. His patented idea was a tail called Rudlicki's V-tail or a butterfly tail. It was studied at the Institute of Aerodynamics in Warsaw and used on the Hanriot H-28 and, in 1933, on the R-XIX. The Ministry of Military Affairs forbade tests with that tail as they did not see any advantages of it. Later, it was used on aircraft in several countries (900 Magister in France and 8,000 Bonanza in the USA). At the end of 1935, as the Lublin factory was nationalised, he got relegated from work in the aerospace industry.. 1936-1939 he spent farming on the Olbięcin estate near Kraśnik: he volunteered and, in cooperation with the Ministry of Agriculture, conducted many agrarian experiments.

In 1939, upon the outbreak of World War II, he was summoned to the 4th Air Regiment. In the course of evacuation through Romania, Yugoslavia and Italy, he escorted the vehicle column of PLL LOT with Polish aviation personnel to France. In February 1940, in Paris, thanks to his study acquaintances, he managed to get 74 LOT employees hired by the SNCAN (Potez) works in Casablanca, where, under his leadership, Polish mechanics assembled and repaired 200 American aircraft Curtiss Hawk and Martin Maryland. When France capitulated, the British evacuated the entire team headed by Rudlicki to Great Britain, and, since September 1940, employed them at the Burtonwood Repair Depot.

During the war, he developed a few more inventions and patents: an alarm sounder towed by a plane for communication with scattered land units, a sound transmitter for aerial bombs, a project of a jet-powered flying wing with blown ailerons and rudders (1941), towed gyroglider (and its control system) for anti-aircraft defence, electric bomb ejector rack, barometric leaflet rack (1942), flare (fusee) ejector to use in defence from night bombardments (1943). He also developed projects on installing machine guns on aircraft for assault missions, reconfigured bomb doors on the Marauder. On

February 1, 1943, he relocated to the workshops of the American branch of the Lockheed aerospace company at the 3rd Base Air Depot of the U.S. Air Force in Belfast, Northern Ireland. There he designed a bomb slip for carpet bombing (simultaneous dropping of 300 10kg bombs) for four-engined bombers Boeing B-17 Flying Fortress; he improved the automatic control system of gun turrets and developed a non-freezing hydraulic control system of gun turrets (1943). In 1944, he developed a conception of a tiltwing aircraft (a vertical take-off and landing (VTOL) aircraft with double flaps directing the slipstream downwards).

On April 23, 1945, as he was acquainted with the engineer Alexander Kartveli, chief designer of the Republic Aviation Corporation, since his student times, Rudlicki started working for that company. He worked for 16 years, improving aircraft and spacecraft designs and developing new inventions. Among others, he invented controlled discharge nozzles for a jet engine General Electric J85 in 1956; they allowed deflection of the engine's thrust vector and were intended for vertical take-off jet aircraft. In 1961, he retired and settled in Florida. There he continued working on concepts of VTOL and jet aircraft of arrangements that were not used till now.

Around 1925, he married Jadwiga d'Aystetten (by her first married name), with whom he had a son, Jerzy (b. 1926, died as a pilot in England in 1944) and a daughter, Teresa (b. 1938, married name Budaszewska). In the USA, he married Zofia from the Szukiewiczes, Surmacka by her first married name.

Among other awards, Rudlicki received the Cross of Valor, Gold Cross of Merit and French Legion of Honour.

He was buried in the USA, in in Częstochowa, Doylestown, New Jersey.

Bibliography

Akta Zakładów Mechanicznych Plagę i Laśkiewicz *(Files of the Mechanical Works E. Plage & T. Laśkiewicz)*. Archiwum Wojewódzkie w Lublinie

R. Bartel: Przemysł lotniczy i zaopatrzenie w sprzęt lotniczy *(Aerospace industry and supply of aviation equipment)*. W: Z historii polskiego lotnictwa wojskowego. Warsaw, 1978

W. BĄCZKOWSKI: Samolot towarzyszący Lublin R-XIII *(Army cooperation plane Lublin R-XIII)*. Warsaw, 1980

J. Cynk: Le Lublin R-XIII. Le Fana de l'Aviation, 1985, No 191, 192,193

J. Cynk: Siły lotnicze Polski i Niemiec – Wrzesień 1939 *(Polish and German air forces – September 1939)*. Warsaw, 1989

A. Glass: Lublin R-XIII. Warsaw, 1994

A. Glass: Polskie konstrukcje lotnicze 1893-1939 *(Polish aviation constructions 1893-1939)*. Warsaw, 1976

A. Glass: Polskie konstrukcje lotnicze do 1939 r. t.I. *(Polish aviation constructions before 1939, Vol. I)*. Sandomierz, 2004

M. KONARSKI: Rzeczna Eskadra Lotnicza Flotylli Pińskiej *(Riverine Air Escadrille of the Pińsk Flotilla)*. Gdynia, 1992

T. KRÓLIKIEWICZ: Polski samolot i barwa *(Polish aircraft and colouring)*. Warsaw, 1990

G. Labuda: Festiwal historyczny – Lotniczy Puck 29-31. VII.2016 *(Historical Festival – Aerial Puck)*. Historie Puckie No 8/2016

M. W. Majewski: Przemysł lotniczy w Lublinie 1919-1939 *(Aerospace industry in Lublin 1919-1939)*. Warsaw, 2005

W. Mazur: Samolot Lublin R-XIII (*Lublin R-XIII plane*). Warszawa 2014

A. MORGAŁA: Polskie samoloty wojskowe 1918-1939 *(Polish military aircraft 1918-1939)*. Warsaw, 1972

A. MORGAŁA: Samoloty wojskowe w Polsce 1924-1939 *(Military aircraft in Poland 1924-1939)*. Warsaw, 2003

A. Olejko, Morski Dywizjon Lotniczy *(Naval Air Squadron)*. Pruszków 1992

A. Olejko, Morski Dywizjon Lotniczy *(Naval Air Squadron)*. Uzupełnienia, 1993

Opis płatowca Lublin R-XIII. Warsaw, 1932

J. Pawlak: Polskie eskadry w latach 1918-1939 (*Polish squadrons in 1918-1939)*. Warsaw, 1989

J. Pawlak: Polskie eskadry w wojnie obronnej 1939 *(Polish squadrons in the defensive war 1939)*. Warsaw, 1982

J. Rozwadowski: Morski Dywizjon Lotniczy 1918-1939 *(Naval Air Squadron 1918-1939)*. Albany, New York, 1973

Wodnosamolot obserwacyjny Lublin R-XIII hydro *(Reconnaissance plane Lublin R-XIII hydro)*. Historie Puckie No 6/2015

Lublin R XIII D

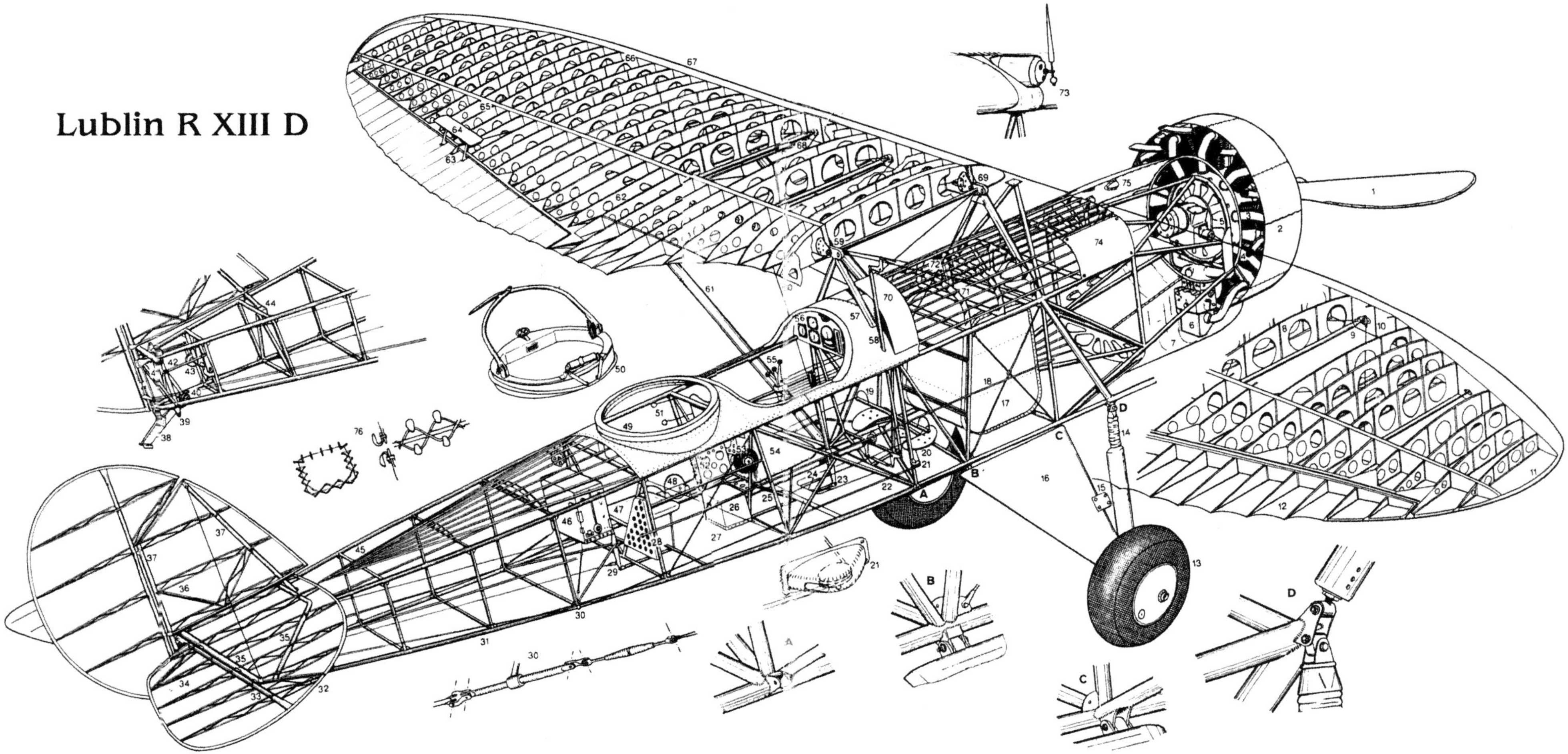

Explanations to the perspective drawing.

1. A Szomański wooden propeller – Hamilton 658.
2. A Townend ring.
3. Suction manifolds on a Wright Whirlwind J-5Ab engine manufactured by PZŠkoda.
4. Exhaust pipes of the engine. The lowermost one is connected to a carburettor heater.
5. Engine ring mount joined with the fuselage.
6. A Zenith 50TJ carburettor.
7. The lower aluminium casing of the forward fuselage.
8. Plywood ribs of the wing.
9. Tubular struts and wires stiffening the wing construction.
10. The forward girder.
11. The edge of the wing.
12. An aileron with a trailing edge made of a wire.
13. A PZL weel 750x125 mm.
14. A PZL oleo strut.
15. Fittings on the landing gear.
16. Plywood skinning of the landing gear legs.
17. An ejecting 200l fuel tank.
18. A mechanical screed on the fuselage.
19. The pilot's rudder bar.
20. Supports for cockpit steps.
21. A roller of the rudder steering cables.
22. The floor in the pilot's cockpit.
23. A tappet of the elevator.
24. A torsional pipe of manual control wheels.
25. The observer's rudder bar connected with the pilot's rudder bar via cables.
26. A casing of the rear control stick mount (the stick is removed).
27. The floor in the observer's cockpit.
28. A tray for signal flares.
29. A lever of the elevators drive system.
30. A slide rod of the rudder drive system.
31. The longeron (made of a steel pipe) of the fuselage framework.
32. The elevators with horn balances.
33. A rudder girder made of a steel pipe.
34. Ribs of the rudder welded from steel pipes.
35. Pipe girders of the horizontal stabilizer.
36. Ribs of the vertical tail.
37. Pipe girders of the vertical stabilizer and rudder.
38. The tailskid made of a riveted plate.
39. A boom stop of the tailskid.
40. A shock absorber on the tailskid – a rubber compensator.
41. A lever of the elevator.
42. A tappet of the elevator.
43. A bearing of the lever of the elevator drive system.
44. A fitting for mounting the vertical stabilizer.
45. Plates skinning the top of the rear fuselage.
46. An RKL/D radio station.
47. A folding observer seat.
48. Handles for ammunition chargers.
49. A ring mount for a machine gun turret.
50. An SS-32 bis turret.
51. Levers of thrust and air-fuel ratio – rods topped with circles.
52. A control box for the radio station.
53. An ammunition charger for 96 cartridges.
54. The aluminium riveted pilot seat.
55. A lever of thrust, air-fuel ratio and carburettor heater.
56. The flight instruments.
57. The rear wing pyramid mount.
58. A tappet of the ailerons and a lever.
59. The rear fitting of the wings.
60. A handle on the wing for easier getting inside.
61. The rear strut of the wing made of a duralumin profil pipe.
62. A rib of the wing.
63. A lever of the aileron drive system.
64. An aerodynamic winglet balancing ailerons.
65. The rear wing girder.
66. The front wing girder.
67. Plywood covering of the wings.
68. Tubes and lines stiffening the wing structure.
69. The front fitting of the wings mounted to the front pyramid.
70. The hatch cover.
71. Plywood frames and wooden stringers forming the top of the front fuselage.
72. A fuel fill on a tank.
73. Pipes supporting the generator mount, the generator with an SD (Stefan Drzewiecki's) propeller.
74. The covering of the inspection opening.
75. The upper aluminium casing of the forward fuselage.
76. An inspection opening on the rear fuselage side and its lacing.

A. The fitting joining the fuselage with the rear strut of the wings.
B. The fitting joining the fuselage with the rear chassis leg.
C. The fitting joining the fuselage with the front chassis leg.
D. The fitting joining the landing gear pyramid with the shock absorber and front strut of the wings.

Drawings of construction details.

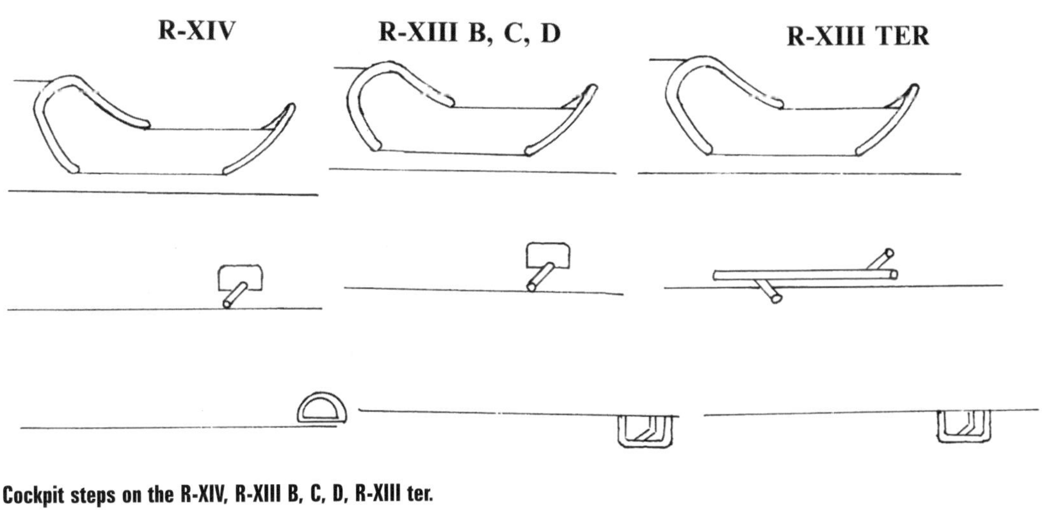

Cockpit steps on the R-XIV, R-XIII B, C, D, R-XIII ter.

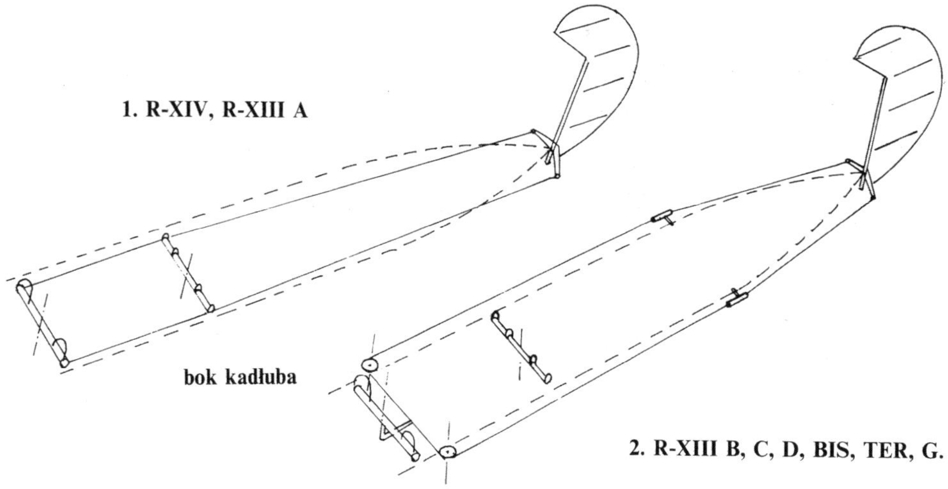

Rudder control:
1. On the R-XIV and R-XIIIA to the inside of the fuselage, 2. On the R-XIII B, C, D, bis, ter, G to the outside of the fuselage.

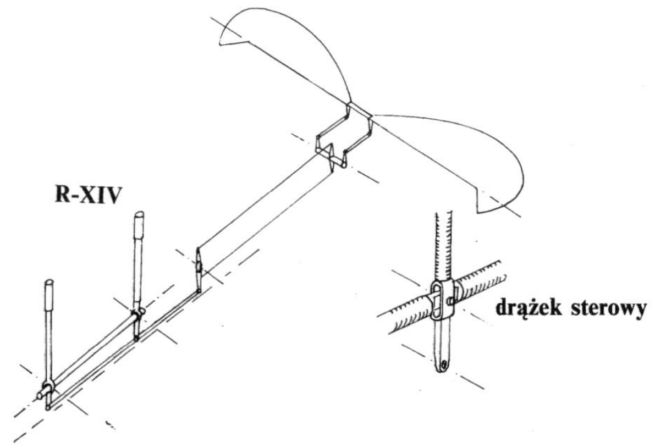

R-XIII A, B, C, BIS, G

The elevators control system: the R-XIV, R-XIII A, B, C, bis, G.

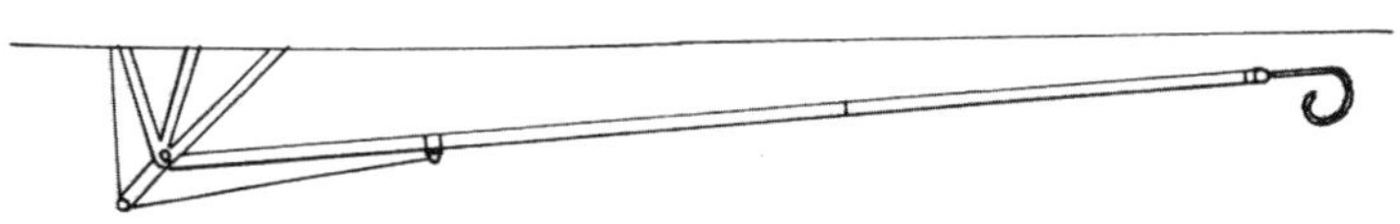

A report-picking device on the R-XIIIB.

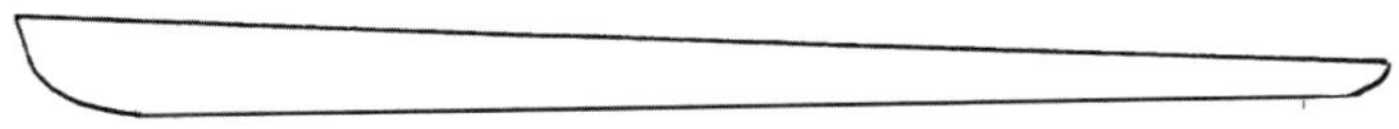

A fairing of the ventral rod of the elevator on the R-XIIIF and some of R-XIIID.

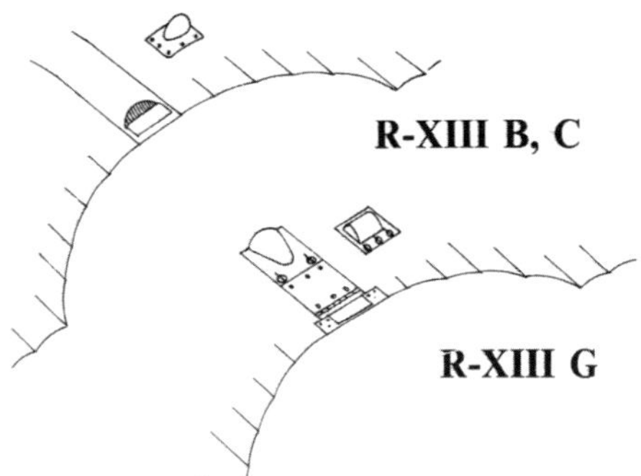

A handle on a wing above the cockpit and casing of a tappet of the ailerons: R-XIIIB, C, R-XIIIG.

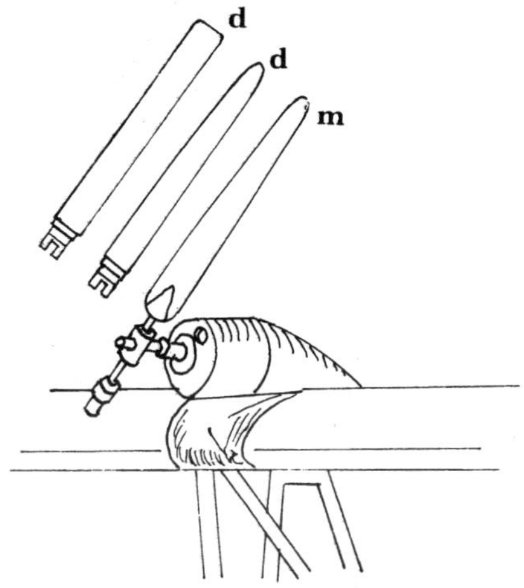

Blades of the generator: d – wooden, m – metal

Position lights on the R-XIII A, D, ter, SP-AJT, SP-AMG.

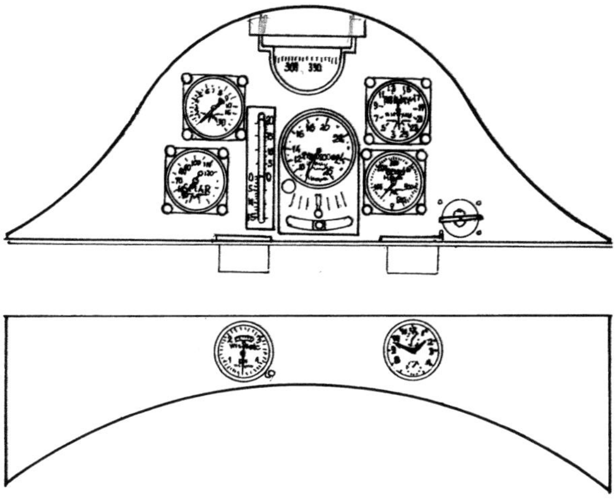

Flight instruments:

R-XIIIB
1. an oil gauge,
2. an oil temperature indicator,
3. a longitudinal inclinometer,
4. a Zürn-Kolberg Z-6 heading indicator,
5. a speedometer with a transverse inclinometer,
6. a tachometer,
7. a boost gauge,
8. an altimeter 0-5,000 m,
9. a timer.

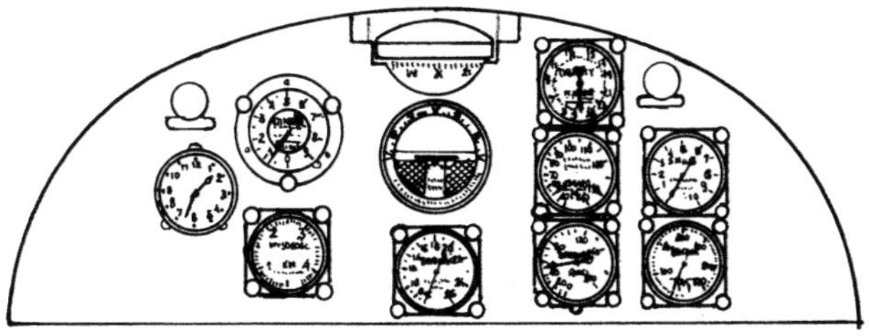

R-XII ter
1. a timer,
2. an altimeter 0-1,000 m,
3. an altimeter 0-5,000 m,
4. a heading indicator,
5. an artificial horizon,
6. a speedometer,
7. a tachometer,
8. an oil temperature indicator,
9. a boost gauge, 10. an oil gauge, 11. a fuel gauge.

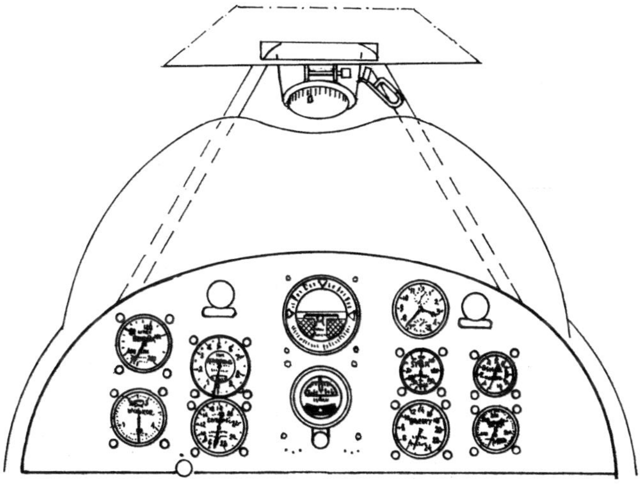

R-XIIIG
1. a fuel gauge,
2. an altimeter 0-5,000 m,
3. an altimeter 0-1,000 m,
4. a speedometer,
5. a heading indicator,
6. an artificial horizon,
7. a heading indicator with an inclinometer,
8. a timer,
9. an oil temperature indicator,
10. a tachometer,
11. an oil gauge,
12. a boost gauge.

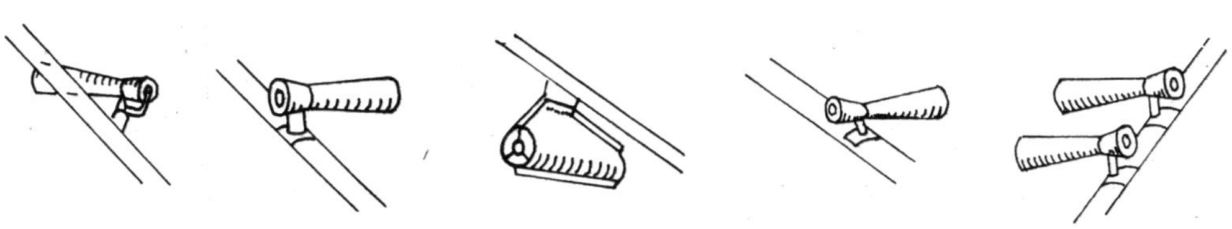

Venturi tubes on the R-XIII A, B, C, bis, D and SP-AMG and on the R-XIIIter iG.

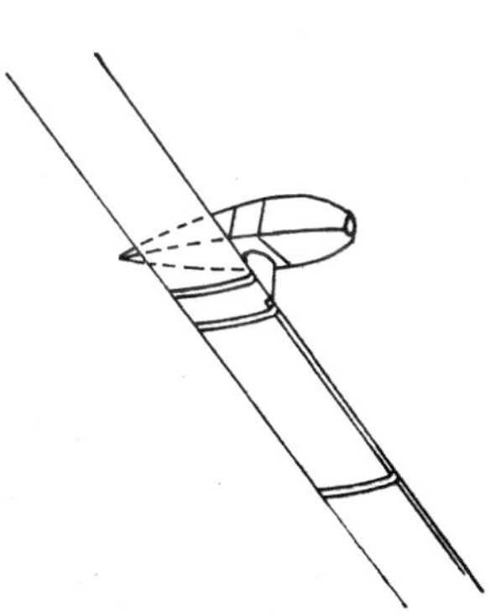

A. A K-28 gun camera.

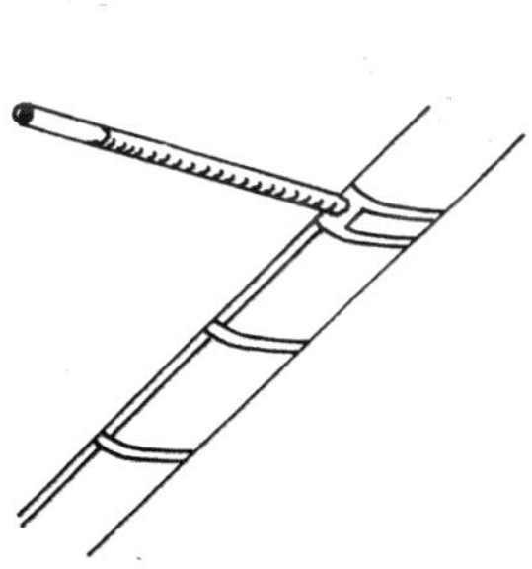

B. A Pitot tube to measure airspeed.

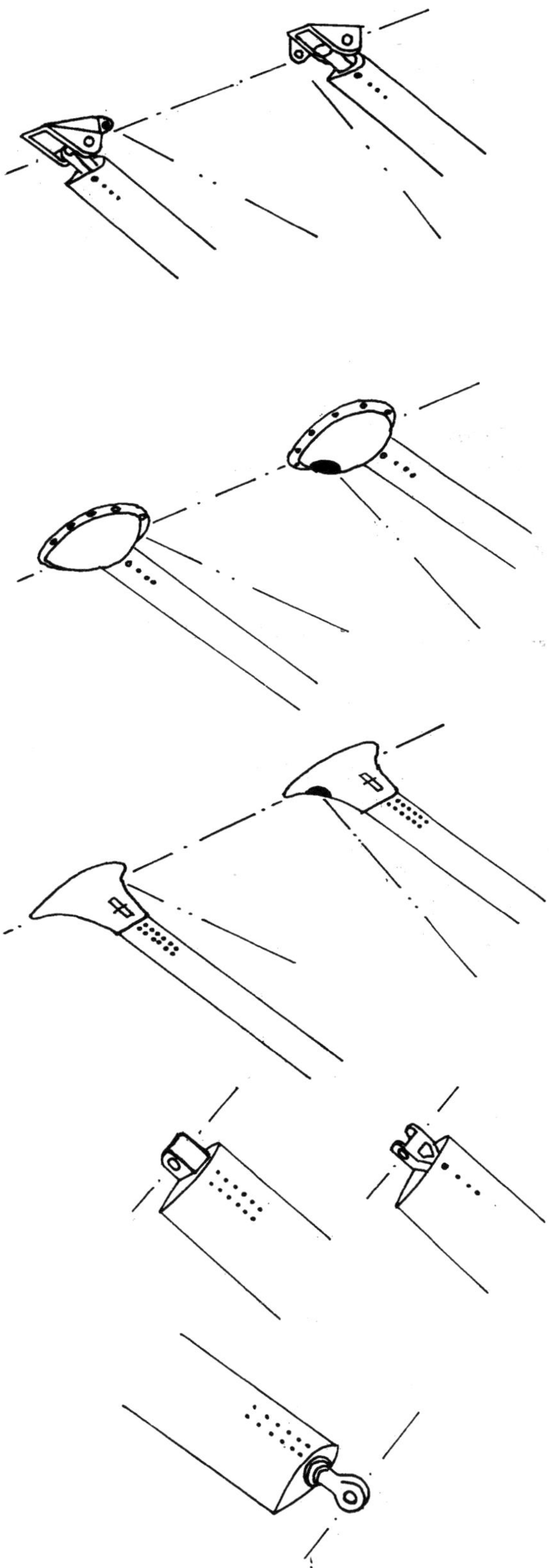

Fittings and fairings of the struts.

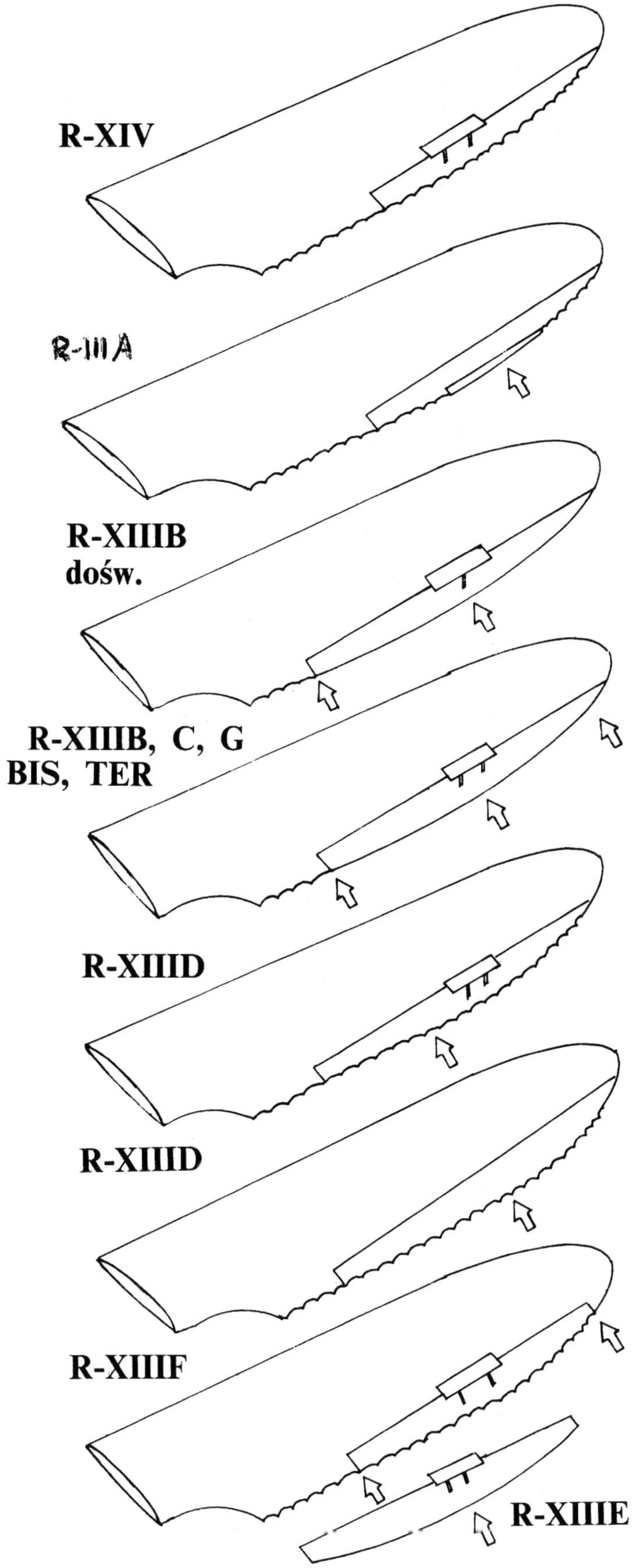

Types of wings and ailerons.

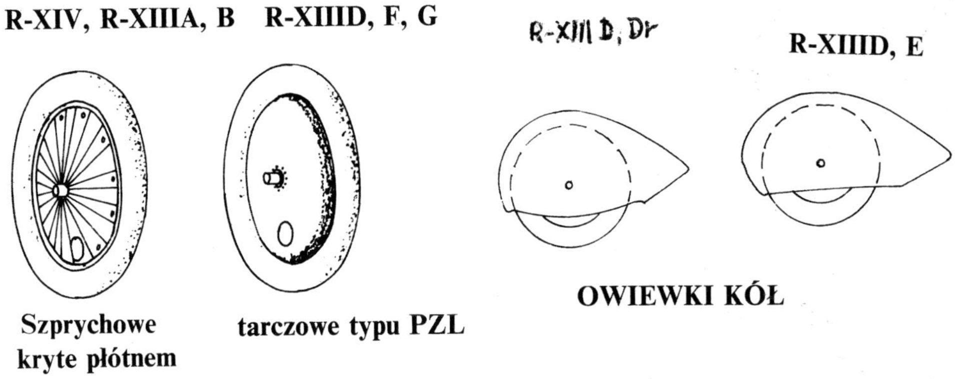

Wheels and wheel fairings.

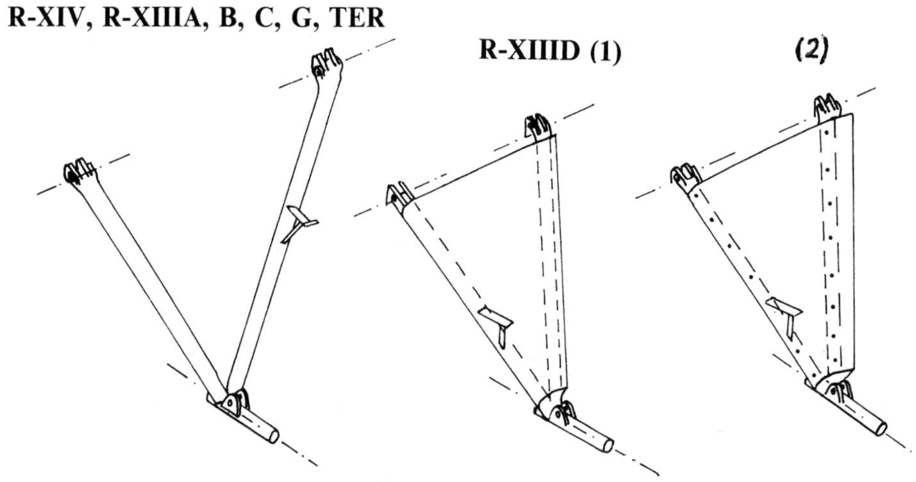

Landing gear legs: without casing on the R-XIV, R-XIIIA, B, C, G, ter; with permanent casing on the R-XIIID; with removable casing on the R-XIIID.

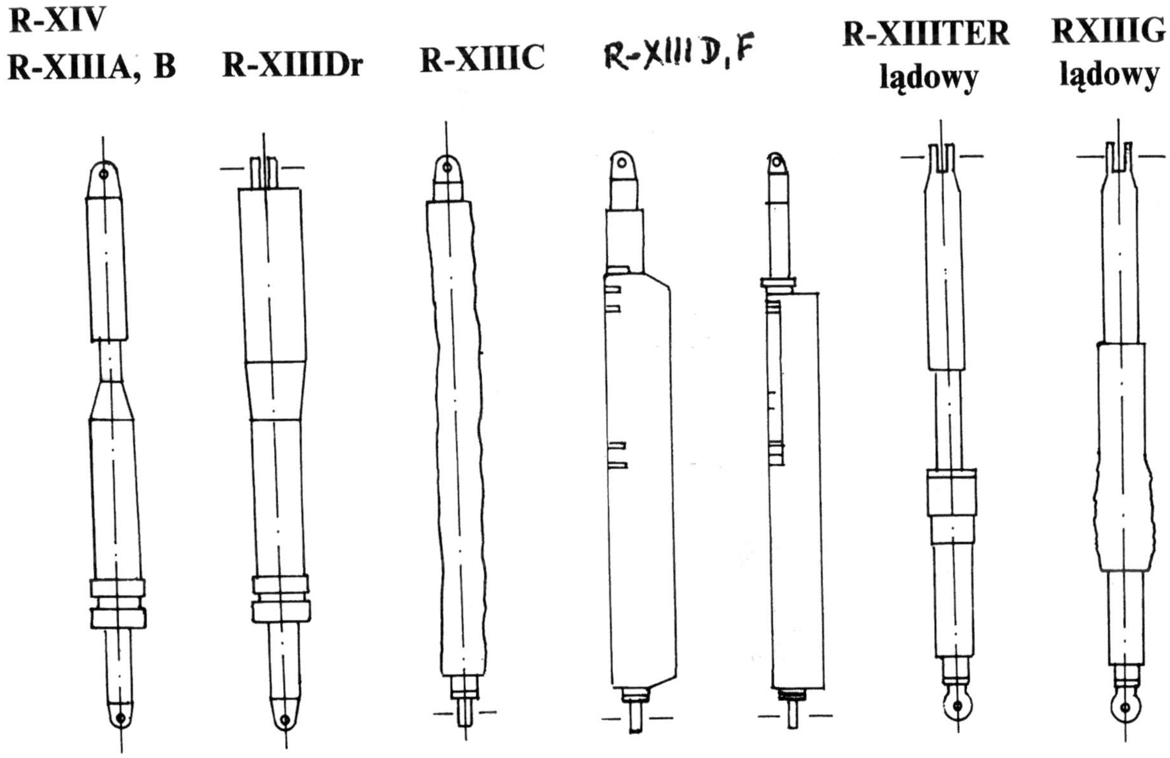

Shock absorbers of the main landing gear on the R-XIV, R-XIII A, B, R-XIIIDr, R-XIIIC, R-XIII D, F, R-XIII ter landplane and R-XIIIG landplane.

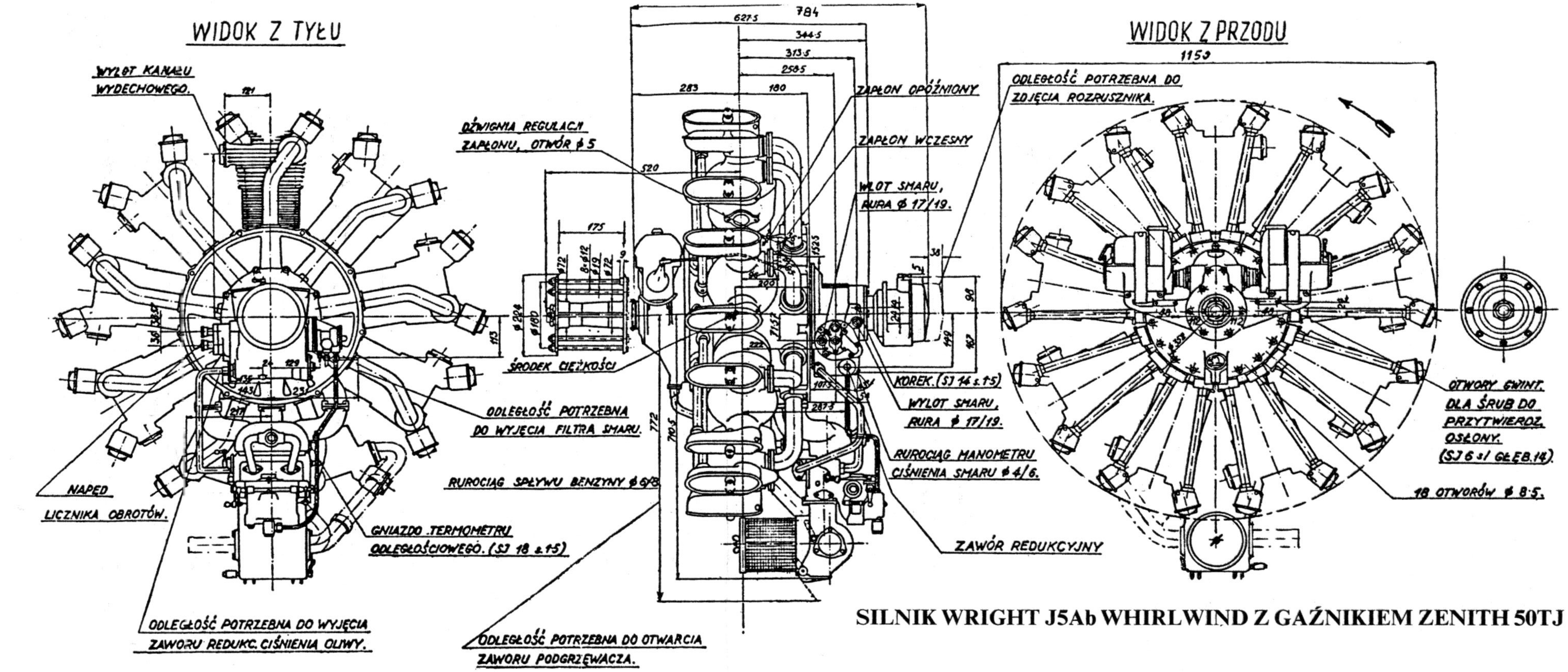

SILNIK WRIGHT J5Ab WHIRLWIND Z GAŹNIKIEM ZENITH 50TJ

A nine-cylinder radial engine Škoda-Wright Whirlwind J-5Ab.

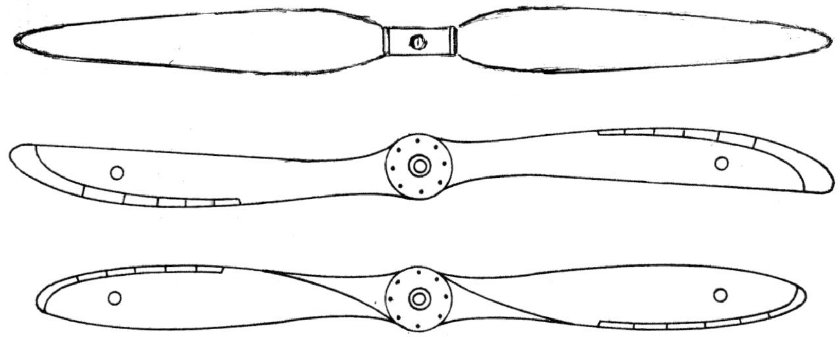

Propellers: metal for a Whirlwind engine, Szomański-Hamilton 658 2,7 m in diameter for a Whirlwind engine, Szomański CB-06 2,2 m in diameter for a G-1620A engine.

Inscriptions and letterings.

Napisy na ustrzeniu

Lublin R XIV — 0,2 m — RXIV

Lublin R XIII — 0,2 m — RXIII A, B

Lublin R XIII — 0,15 m — RXIII SP-AFD

LUBLIN R XIII D — 0,06 m — 0,1 m

№ 56-116 — 0,09 m

1234567890 — 0,09 m

Znak firmowy na śmigłach W. Szomańskiego

LUBLIN R XIII TER — 0,06 m — 0,1 m — R-XIIITER

Znak warsztatów 4 pułku lotniczego

№ 712 — 0,1 m

1234567890 — 0,1 m

LUBLIN R XIII D — 0,06 m — 0,12 m — SP-AJT, SP-ANG, SP-AMG

LUBLIN R XIII D F — 0,06 m — 0,1 m

№ 56-178 № 58-8 — 0,08 m

1234567890 — 0,08 m

Oznaczenia na kadłubie w pułkach

3 — 0,45 m — 11234556678 90 — 0,6 m

IE

Oznaczenia pod skrzydłami w pułkach

N27 — 1 m — 14F52TSZ — 1,2 m

89Z — 1,6 m

Oznaczenia w pułkach na stateczniku

3 — 0,2 m — cT — 0,45 m

Oznaczenia na kadłubie (0,5 m) i pod skrzydłami (0,85 m) w CWL

1234567890 — 0,5 m — DRU — 0,85m

Oznaczenia na kadłubie w MDL (0,45 m)

70231234567890 — 0,45 m

714 — 0,15 m

TU UNOSIĆ TU PODPIERAĆ — 0,04 m

Numery ewidencyjne na kadłubie

54-14 56-1 58-23 — 0,2 m

1234567890- — 0,2 m

Instalacja elektryczna Tabl. XI

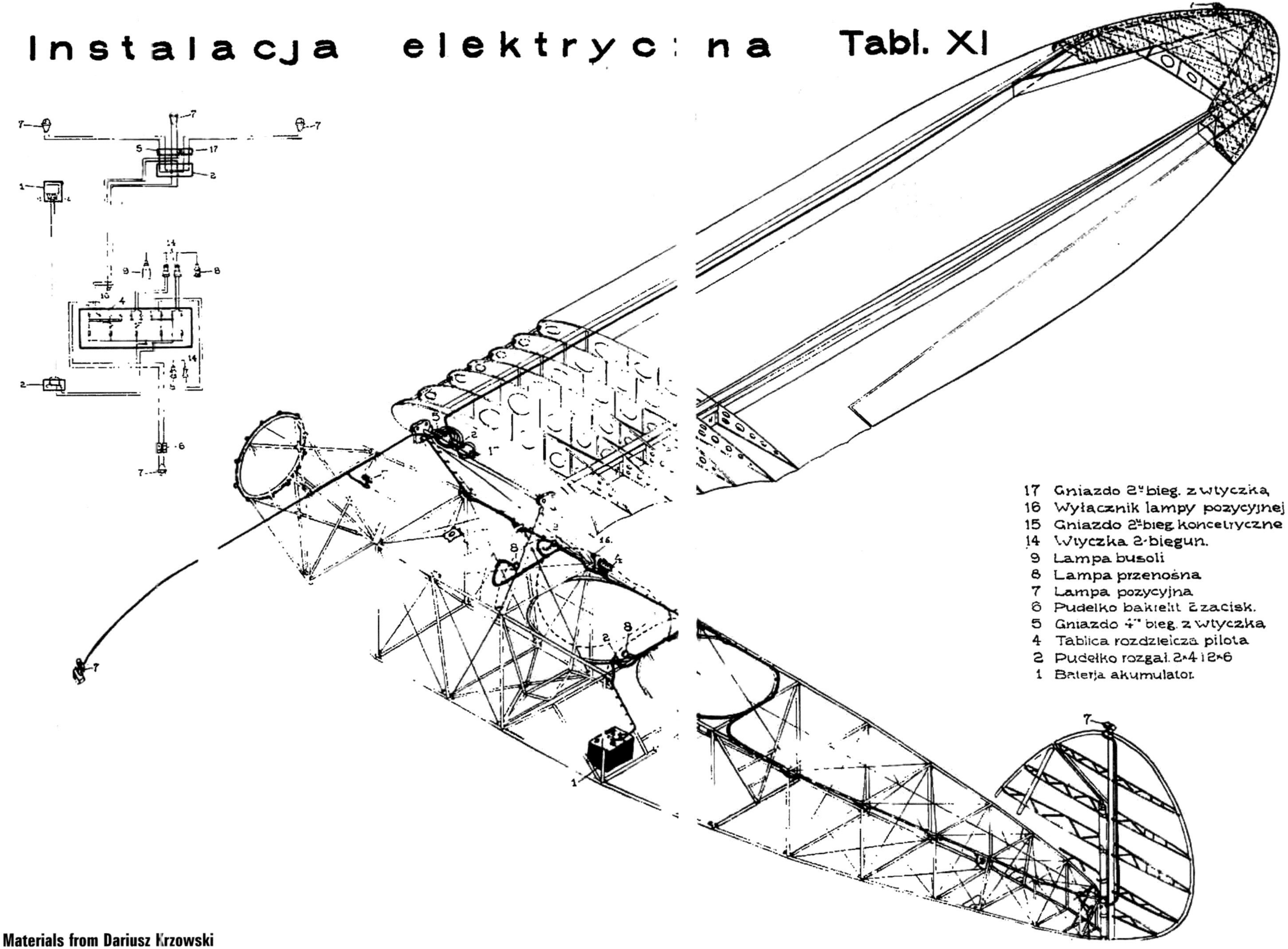

17 Gniazdo 2" bieg. z wtyczką
16 Wyłącznik lampy pozycyjnej bald.
15 Gniazdo 2" bieg. koncentryczne
14 Wtyczka 2-biegun.
9 Lampa busoli
8 Lampa przenośna
7 Lampa pozycyjna
6 Pudełko bakielit. z zacisk.
5 Gniazdo 4" bieg. z wtyczką
4 Tablica rozdzielcza pilota
2 Pudełko rozgał. 2×4 12×6
1 Bateria akumulator.

Centralne smarowanie

Tabl. IX

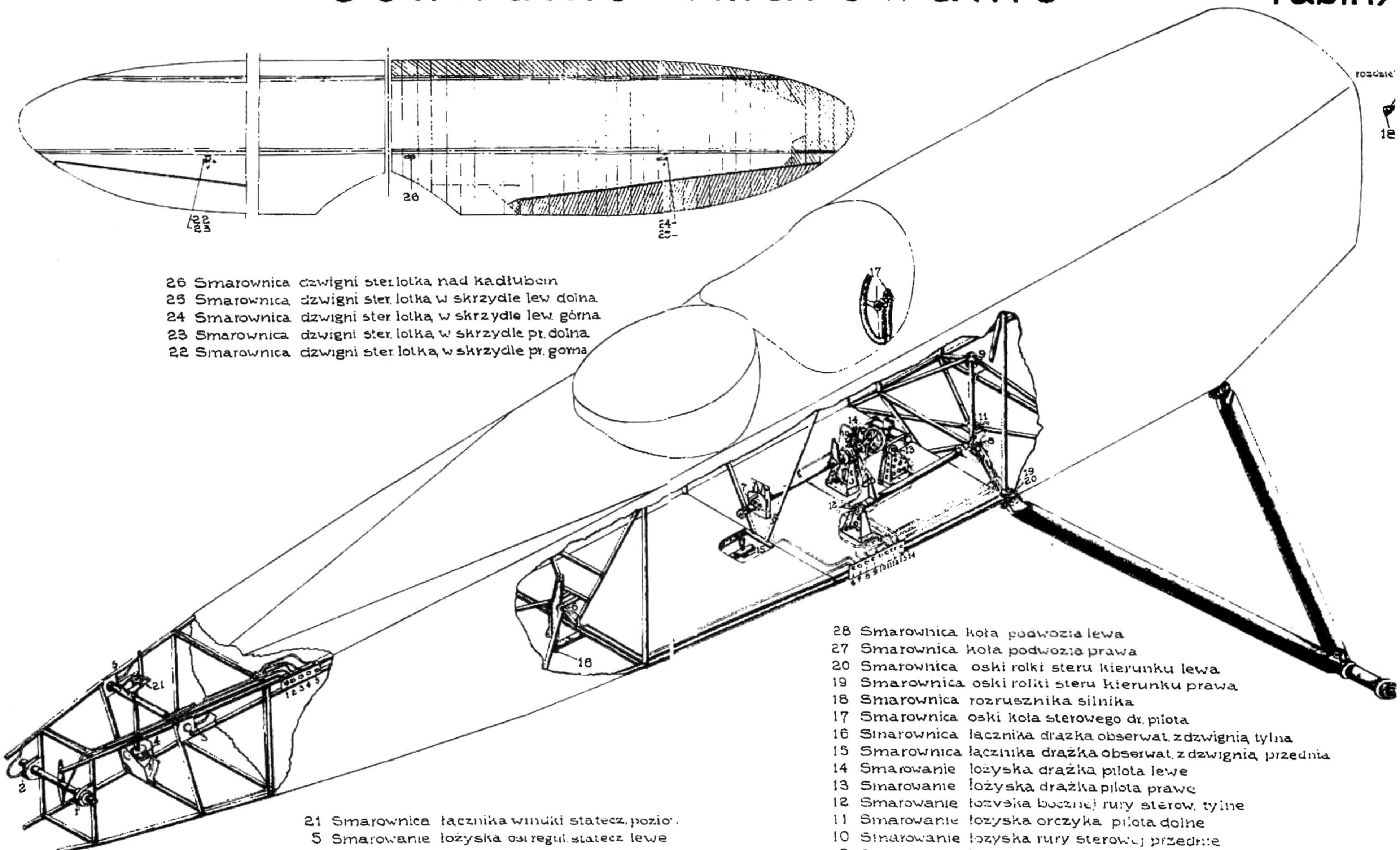

26 Smarownica dzwigni ster. lotka nad kadłubem
25 Smarownica dzwigni ster. lotka w skrzydle lew. dolna
24 Smarownica dzwigni ster. lotka w skrzydle lew. górna
23 Smarownica dzwigni ster. lotka w skrzydle pr. dolna
22 Smarownica dzwigni ster. lotka w skrzydle pr. górna

28 Smarownica koła podwozia lewa
27 Smarownica koła podwozia prawa
20 Smarownica oski rolki steru kierunku lewa
19 Smarownica oski rolki steru kierunku prawa
18 Smarownica rozrusznika silnika
17 Smarownica oski koła sterowego dr. pilota
16 Smarownica łącznika drążka obserwat. z dźwignią tylna
15 Smarownica łącznika drążka obserwat. z dźwignią przednia
14 Smarowanie łożyska drążka pilota lewe
13 Smarowanie łożyska drążka pilota prawe
12 Smarowanie łożyska bocznej rury sterow. tylne
11 Smarowanie łożyska orczyka pilota dolne
10 Smarowanie łożyska rury sterowej przednie
9 Smarowanie łożyska orczyka pilota górne
8 Smarowanie łożyska bocznej rury sterow. przednie
7 Smarowanie łożyska rury sterowej tylne
6 Smarowanie łożyska dźwigni środ. steru głębokości

21 Smarownica łącznika windki statecz. poziom.
5 Smarowanie łożyska osi regul. statecz. lewe
4 Smarowanie przyrządu regulow. statecznikiem
3 Smarowanie łożyska osi regul. statecz. prawe
2 Smarowanie łożyska dźwigni steru głęb. lewe
1 Smarowanie łożyska dźwigni steru głęb. prawe

Materials from Dariusz Krzowski

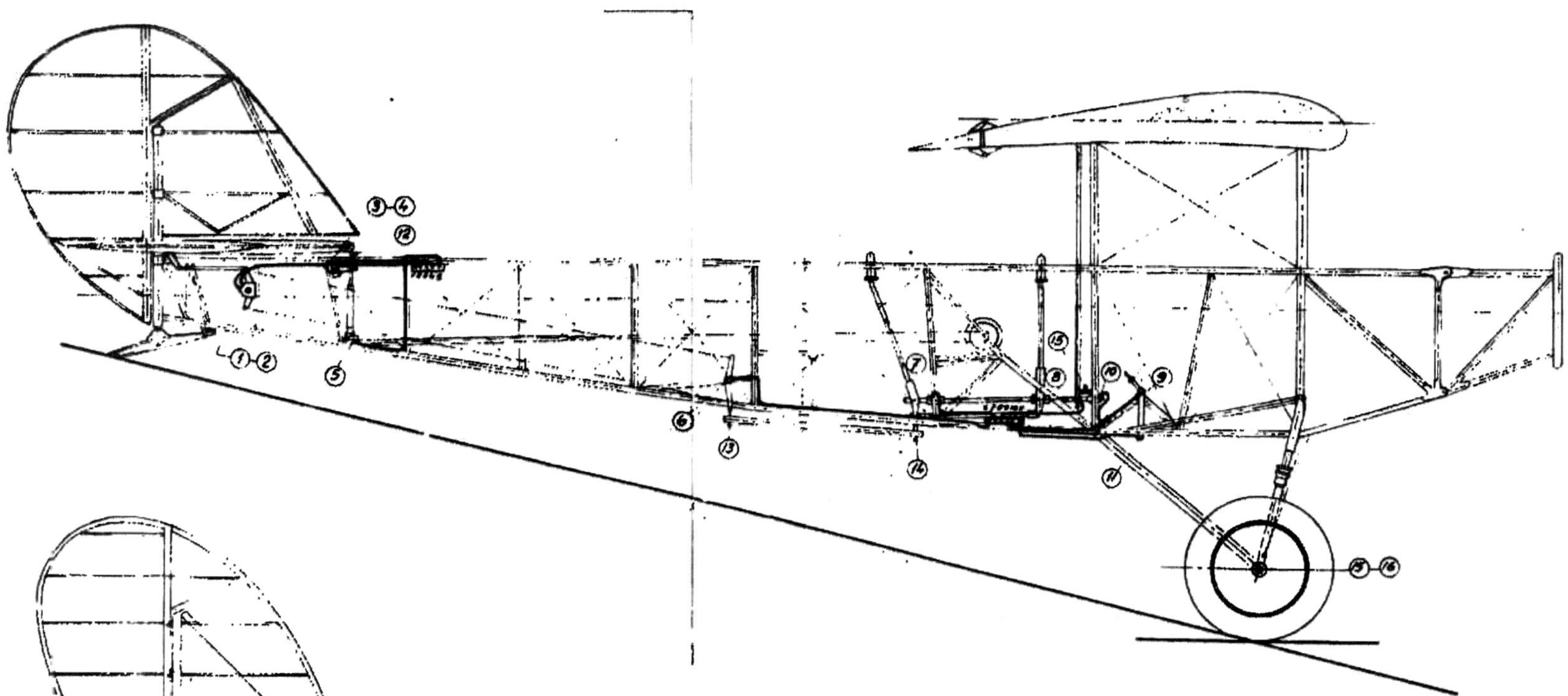

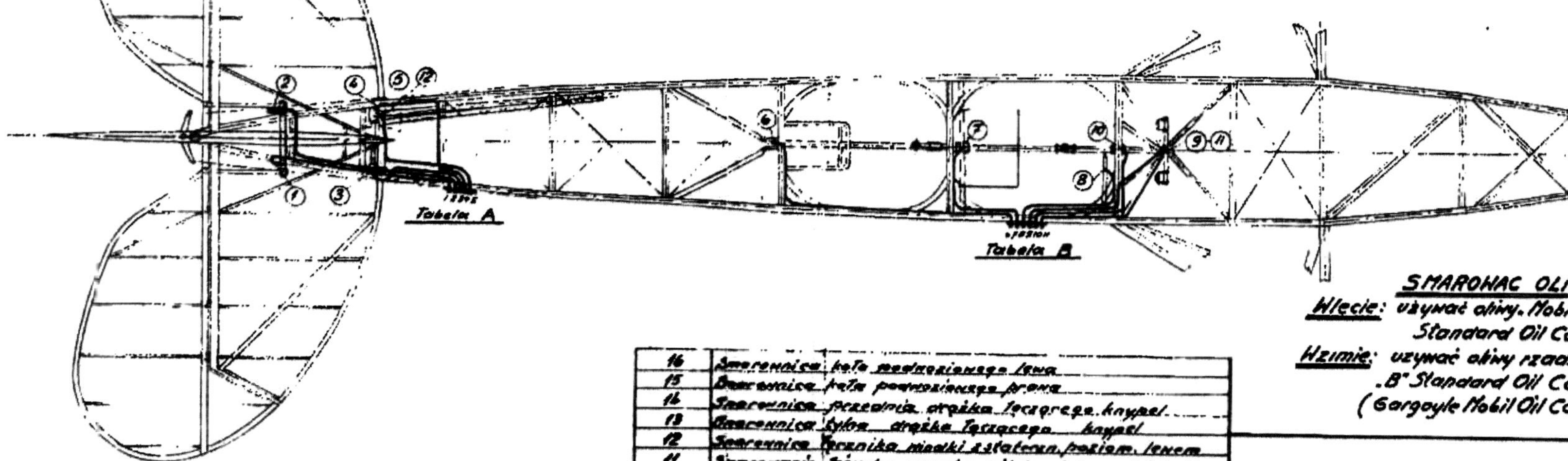

SMAROWAĆ OLIWĄ

W lecie: używać oliwy „Mobil Grais" Standard Oil Co.

W zimie: używać oliwy rzadszej np. „B" Standard Oil Co. (Gargoyle Mobil Oil Co.)

Nr poz.	OBJAŚNIENIE	
16	Smarownica	koła podwoziowego lewa
15	Smarownica	koła podwoziowego prawa
14	Smarownica	przednia drążka łączącego knypel
13	Smarownica	tylna drążka łączącego knypel
12	Smarownica	łożyska miseki z stateczn. poziom. lewem
11	Smarowanie	łożyska orczyka pilota dolnego z tab. „B"
10	Smarowanie	łożyska przedniego nogi sterowej z tab. „B"
9	Smarowanie	łożyska orczyka pilota górne z tab. „B"
8	Smarowanie	łożyska dźwigni steru lotkami z tab. „B"
7	Smarowanie	łożyska orczyka obserwatora z tab. „B"
6	Smarowanie	łożyska dźwigni steru głębok. środk. z tab. „B"
5	Smarowanie	przyrządu regul. statecznikiem z tab. „A"
4	Smarowanie	łożyska osi regul. statecznik. lewe z tab. „A"
3	Smarowanie	łożyska osi regul. statecznik. prawe z tab. „A"
2	Smarowanie	łożyska dźwigni steru głębokości lewe z tab. „A"
1	Smarowanie	łożyska dźwigni steru głębokości prawe z tab. „A"

CENTRALNE SMAROWANIE

w sam. LUBLIN R.XIII

Data	12-VII-32	ZAKŁADY MECHANICZNE E. PLAGE i T. LAŚKIEWICZ W LUBLINIE	RYS. Nº 5
Rysował	[illegible]		
Sprawdził			

SCALE DRAWINGS

by Witold Szewczyk

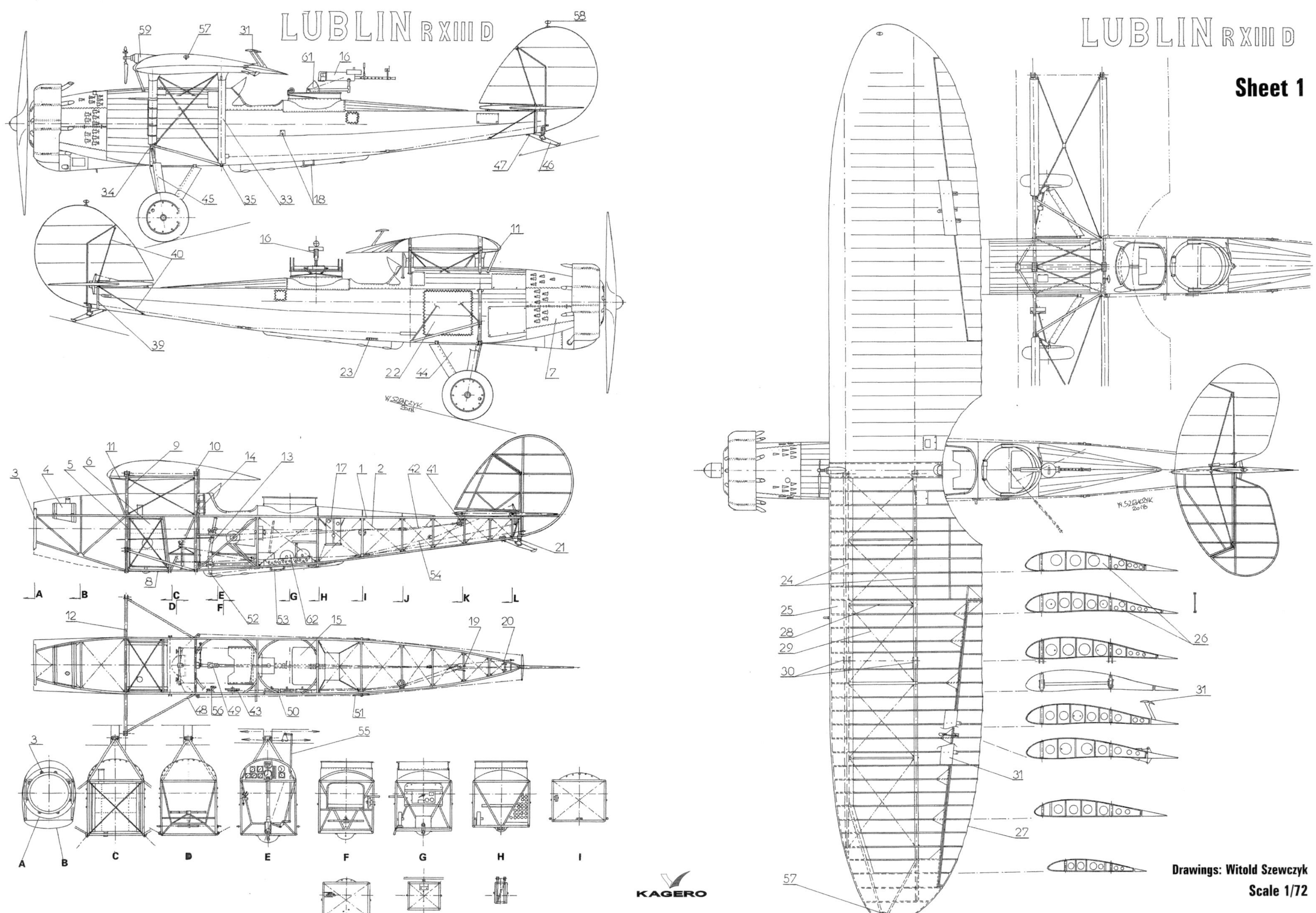

LUBLIN R XIII D
LUBLIN R XIII D
Sheet 1
A
B
C
D
E
F
G
H
I
J
K
L
KAGERO
Drawings: Witold Szewczyk
Scale 1/72

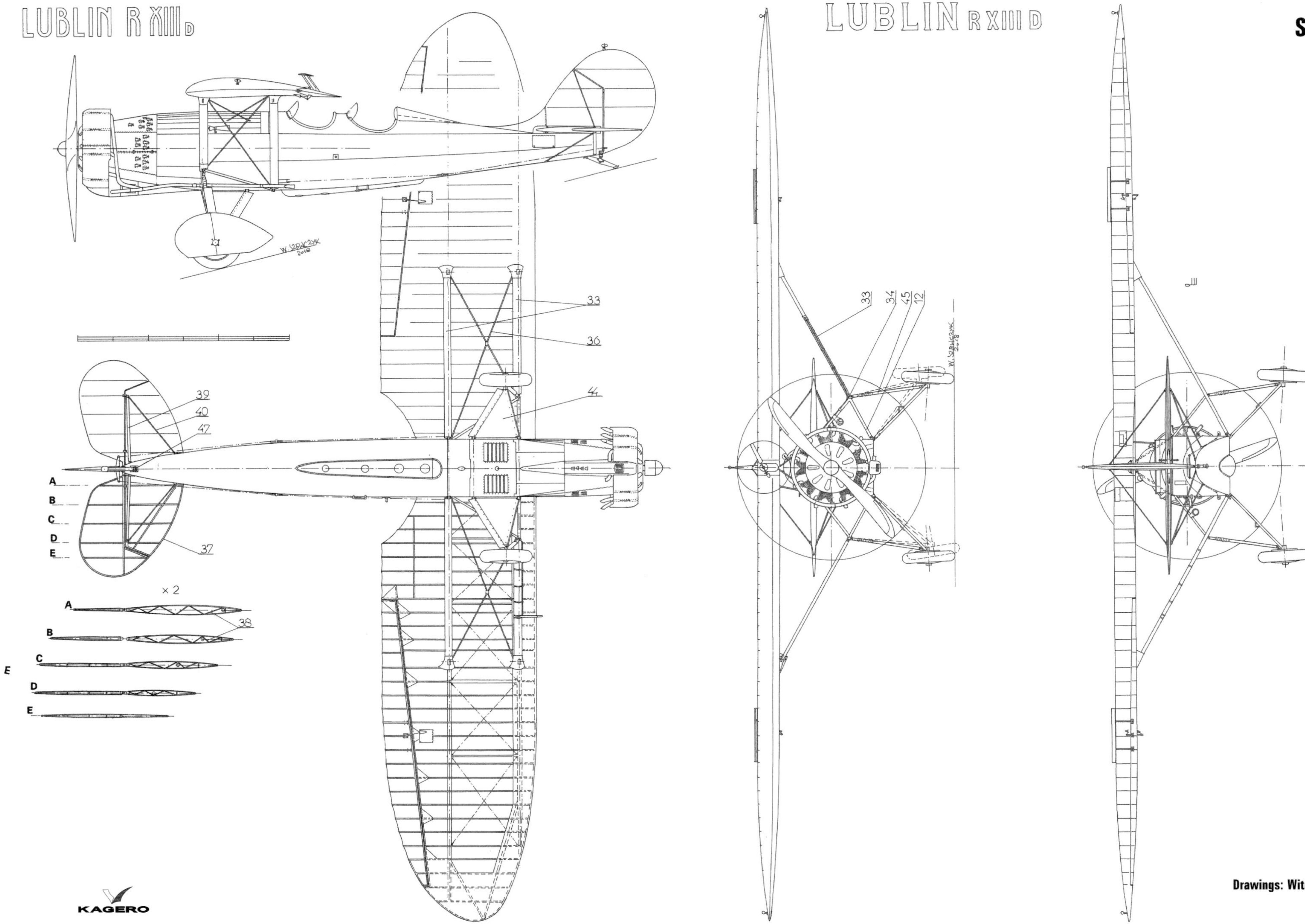

Sheet 2

Drawings: Witold Szewczyk
Scale 1/72

Sheet 3

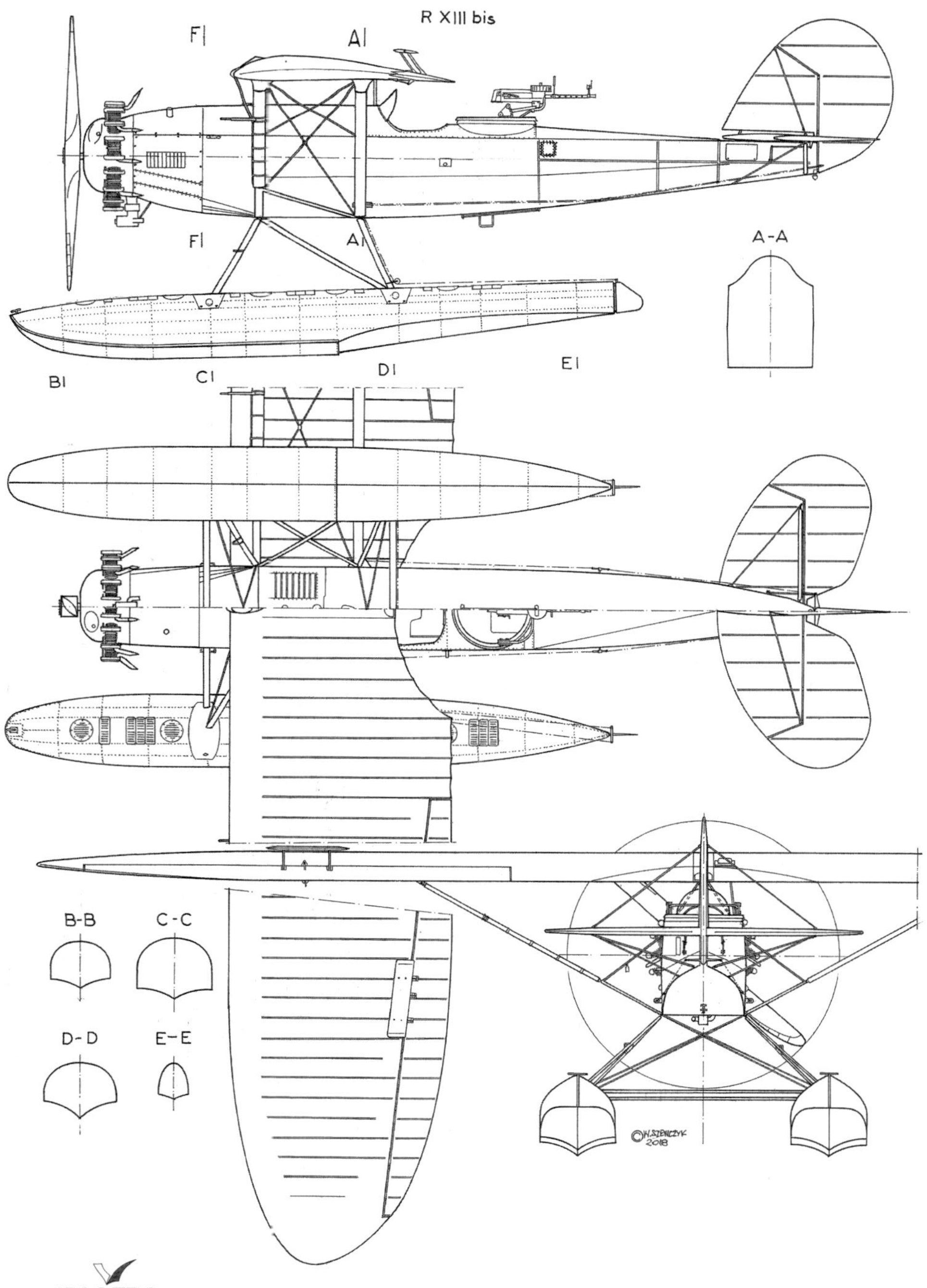

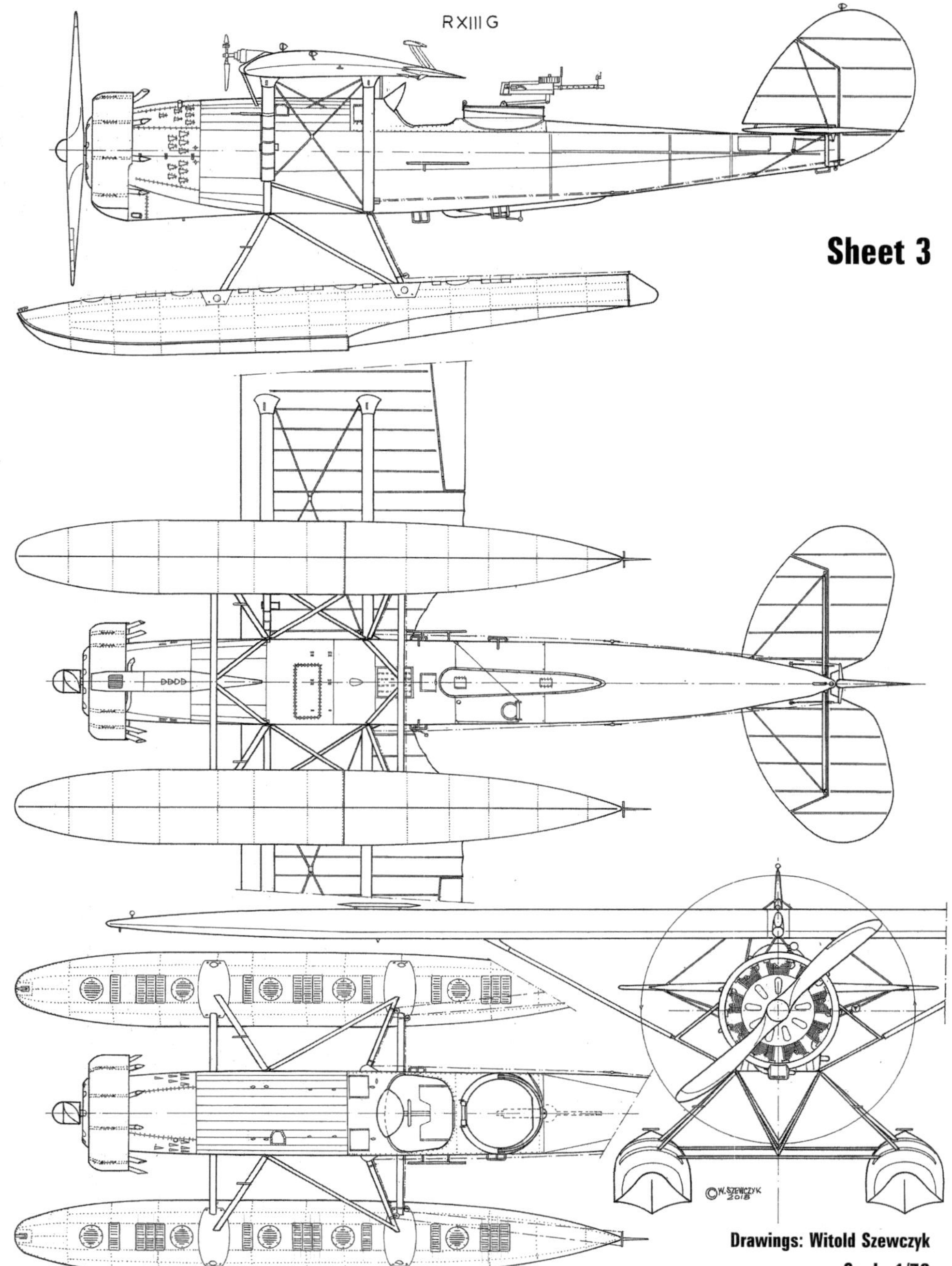

Drawings: Witold Szewczyk

Scale 1/72

KAGERO

Sheet 4

R-XIV 54-1/I

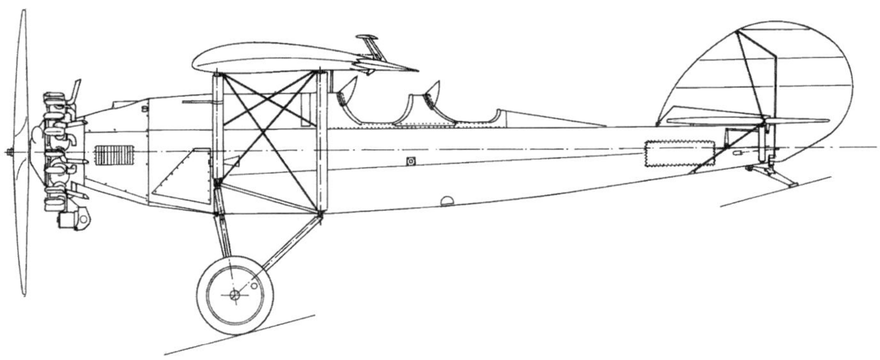

R-XIV 54-1/II

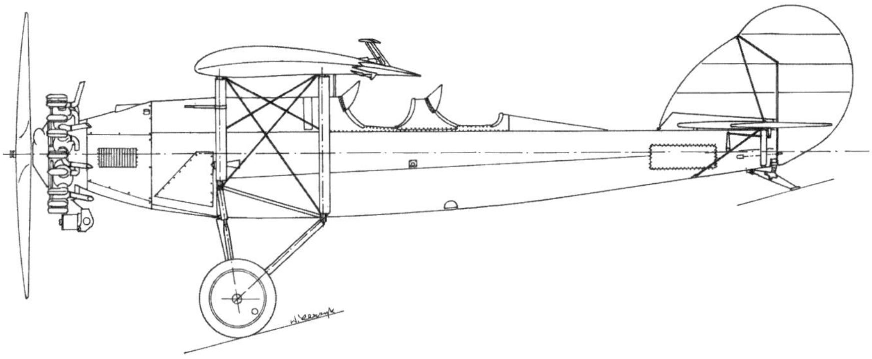

R-XIV 54-15

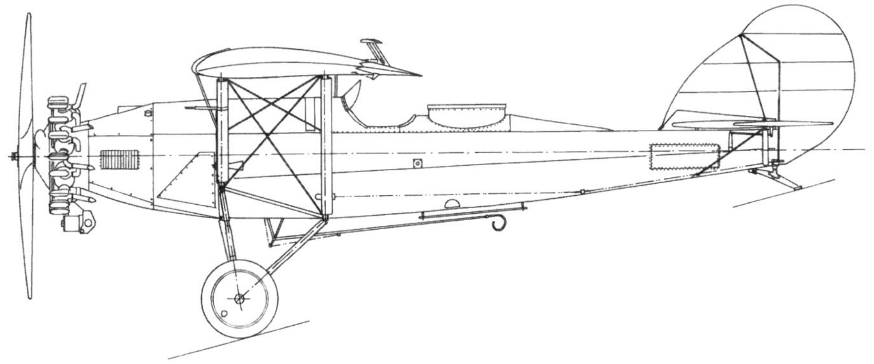

R-XIII Prototype 56-1

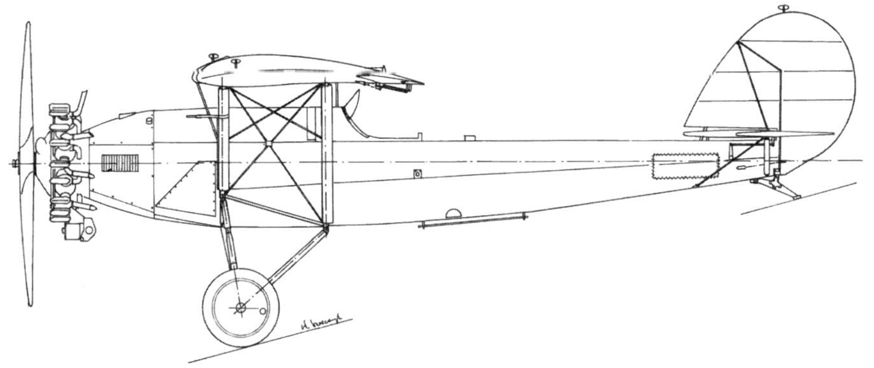

Drawings: Witold Szewczyk

Scale 1/72

Sheet 5

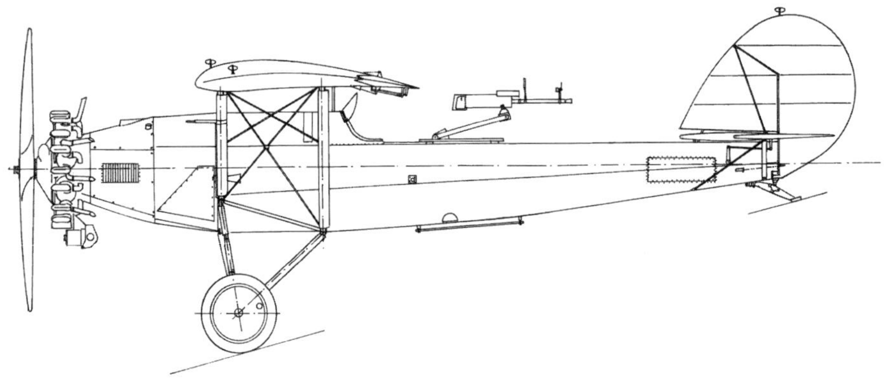

R-XIIIA 56-3

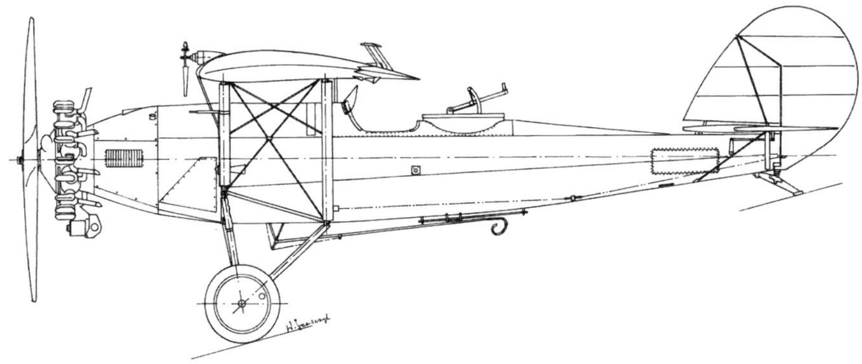

R-XIIIB

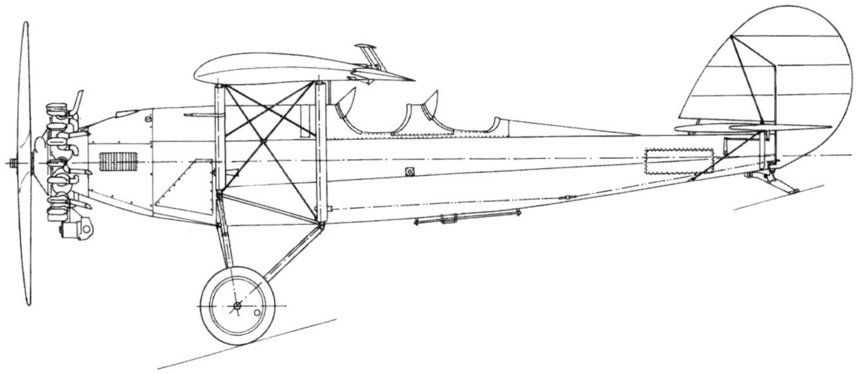

R-XIIIB 56-48 SP-AKK

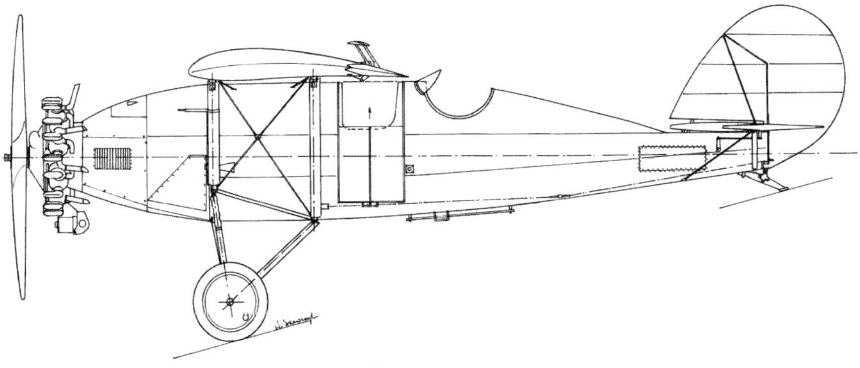

R-XIIIt 56-24

Drawings: Witold Szewczyk

Scale 1/72

Sheet 6

R-XIIIC 56-21 SP-AJT

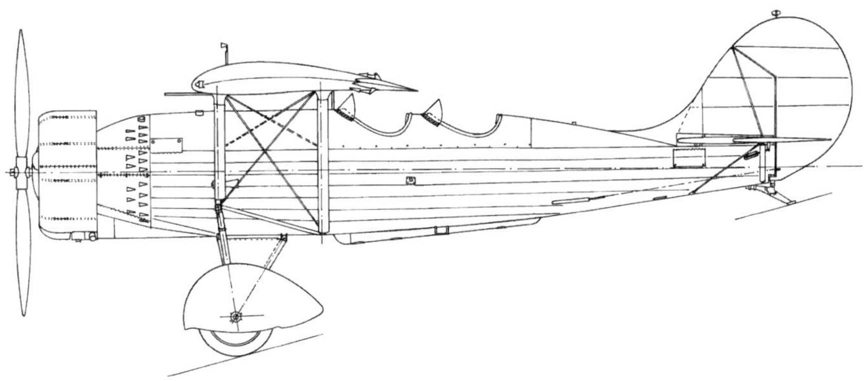

R-XIIIC

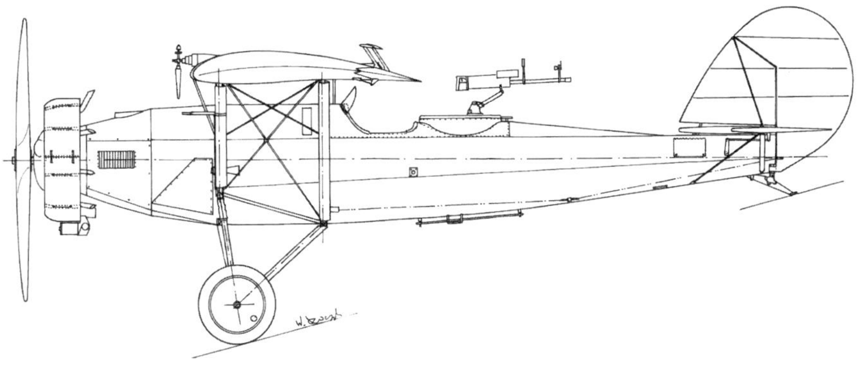

R-XIIID 56-127 SP-AMG

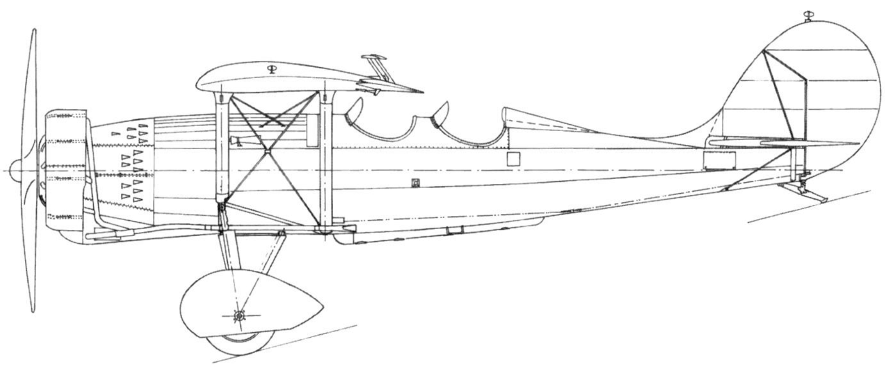

R-XIIIE 56-100

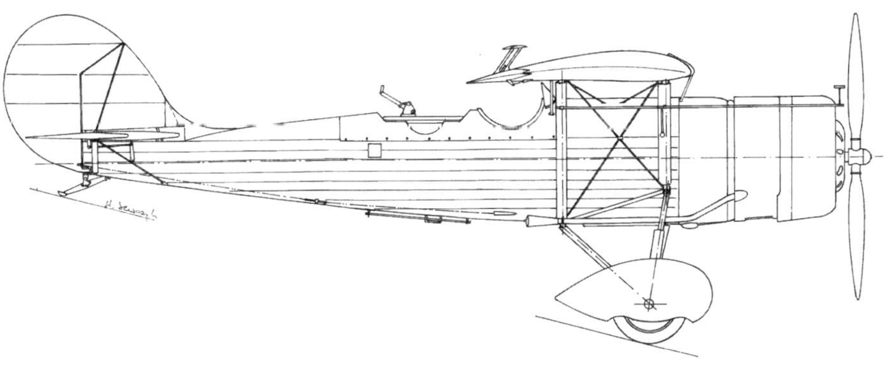

Drawings: Witold Szewczyk

Scale 1/72

Sheet 7

R-XIIIF 58-8

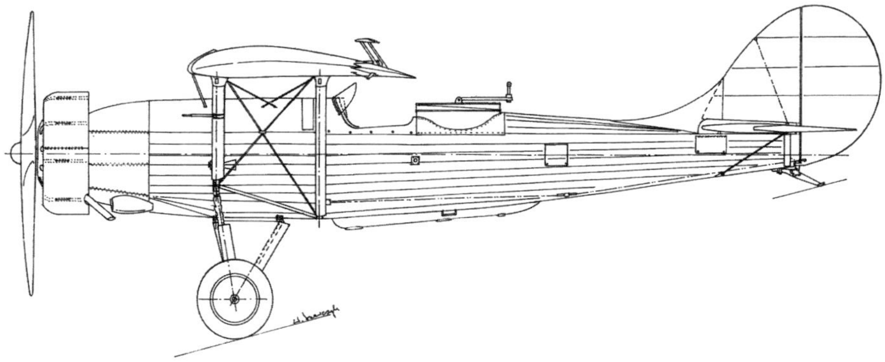

R-XIIIF 58-23

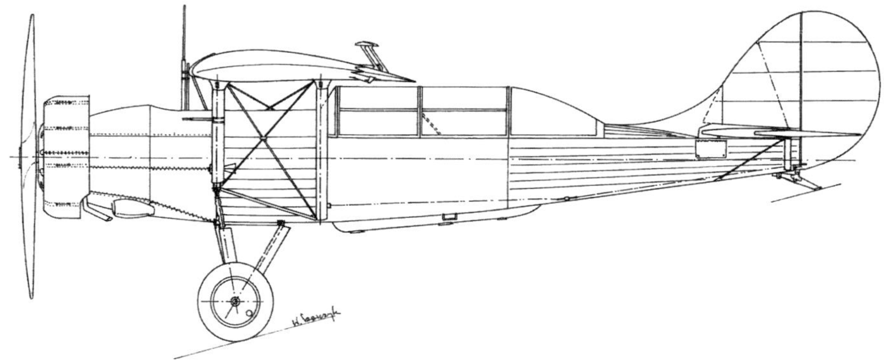

R-XIX – experimental, butterfly tail

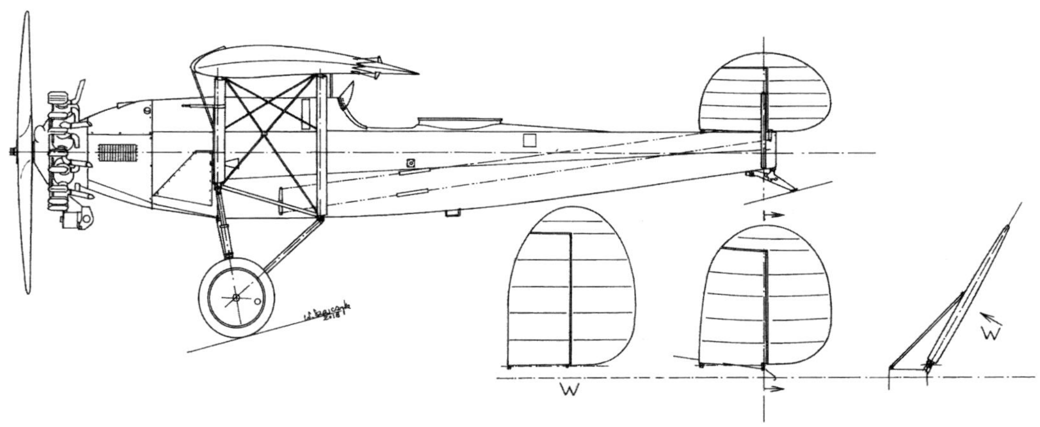

R-XIII – experimental, lowerable tail

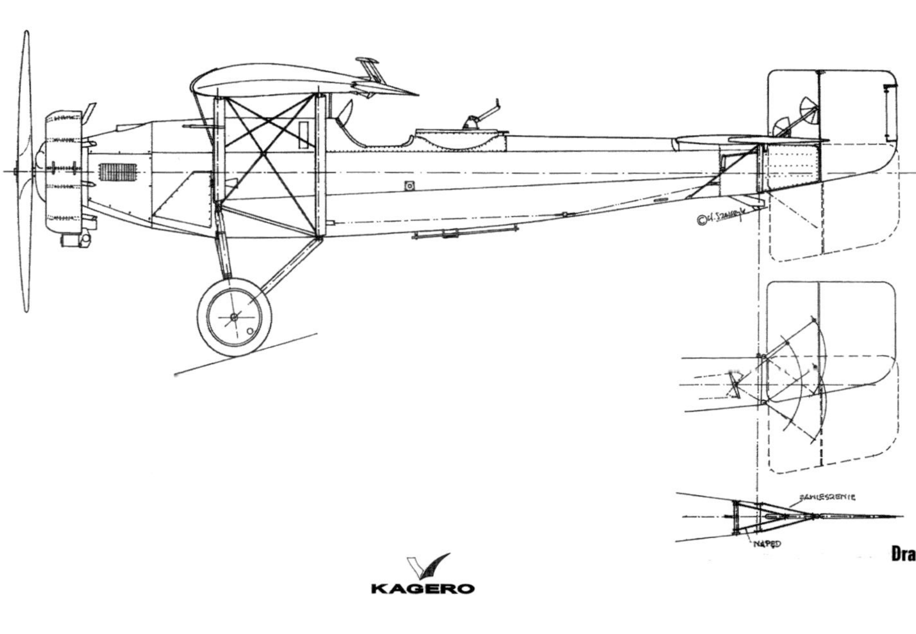

KAGERO

Drawings: Witold Szewczyk

Scale 1/72

LUBLIN R XIII D

Sheet 8

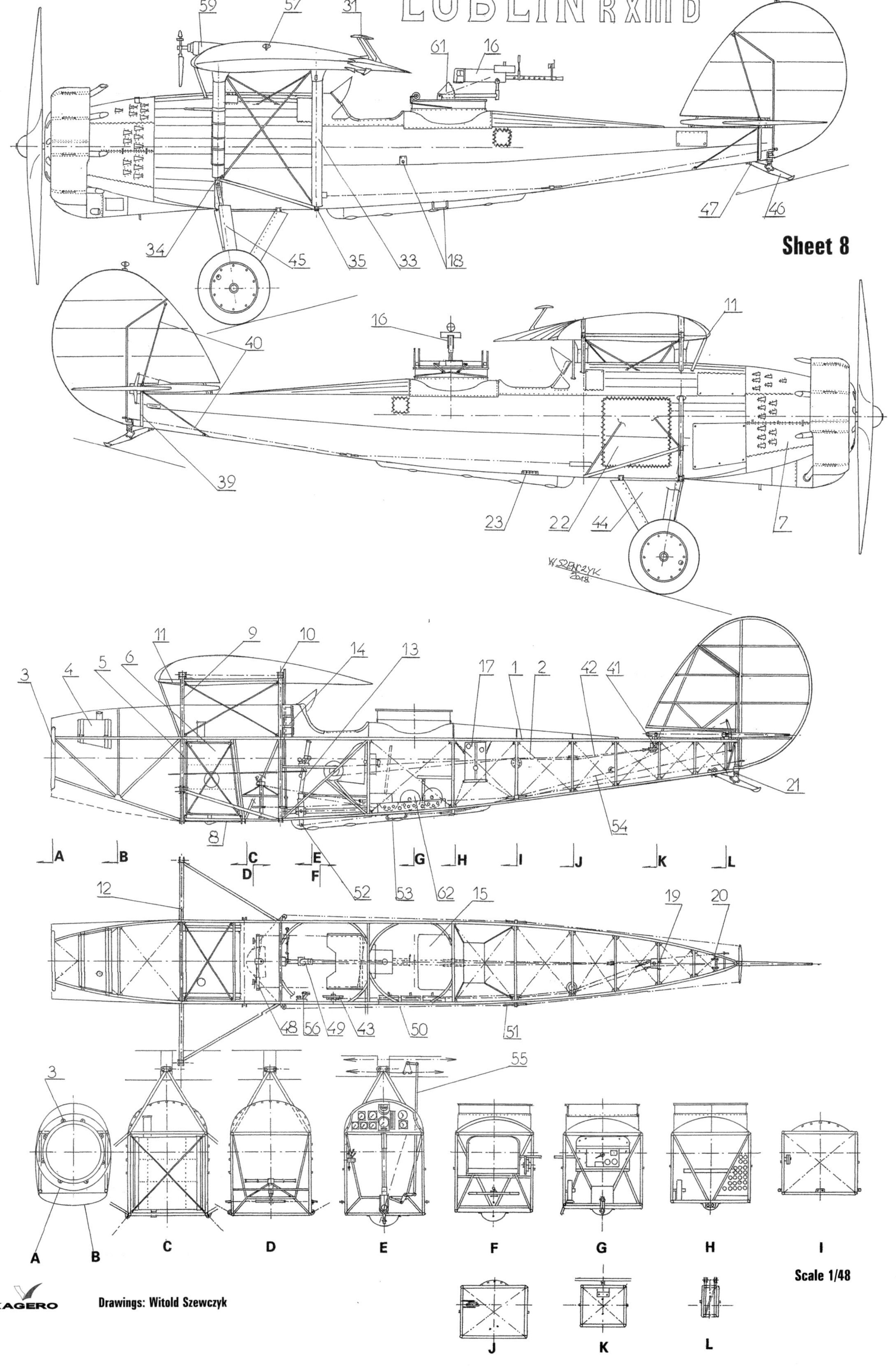

Scale 1/48

KAGERO

Drawings: Witold Szewczyk

Sheet 9

LUBLIN R XIII D

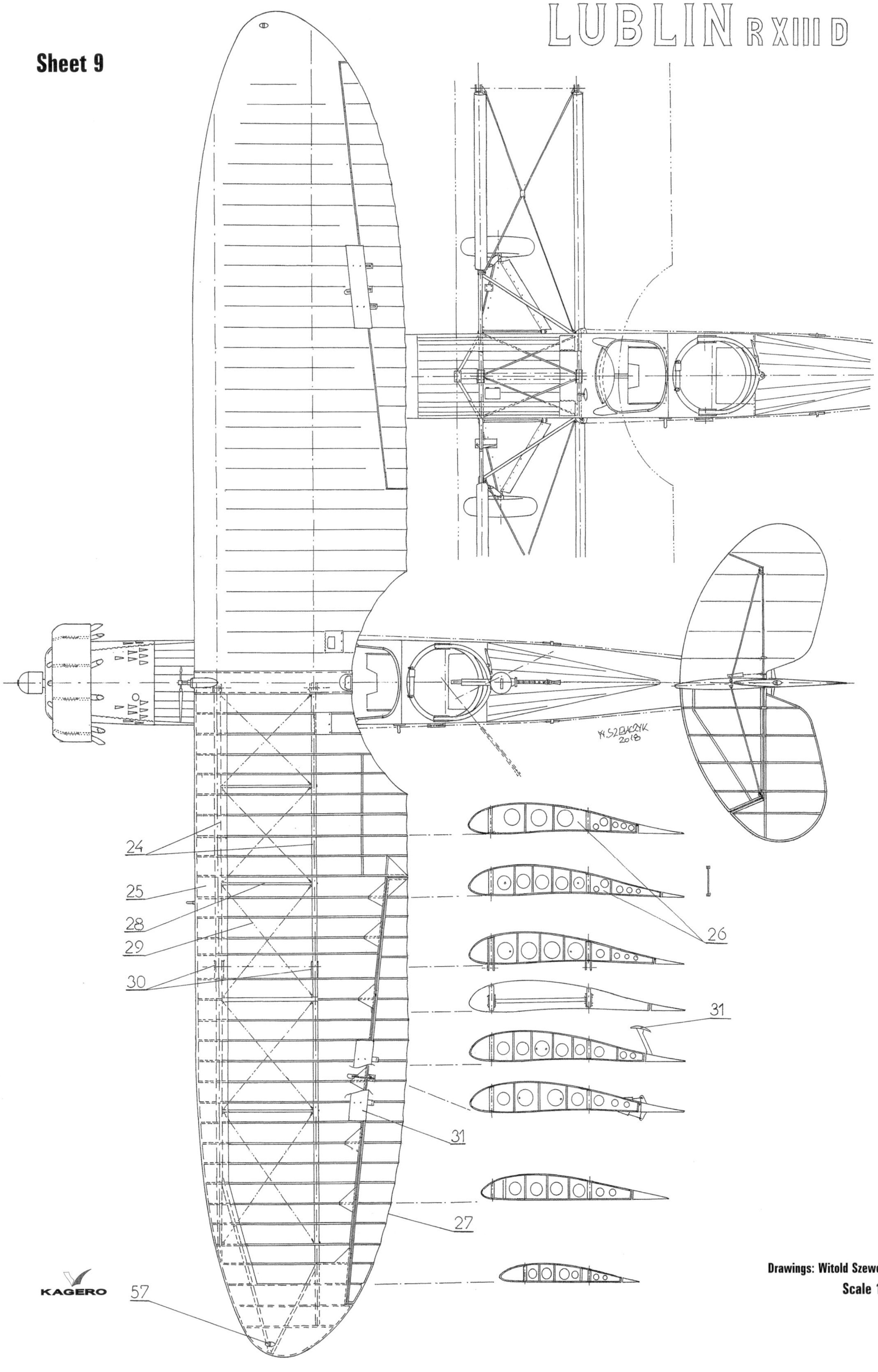

Drawings: Witold Szewczyk

Scale 1/48

KAGERO

LUBLIN R XIIId

Sheet 10

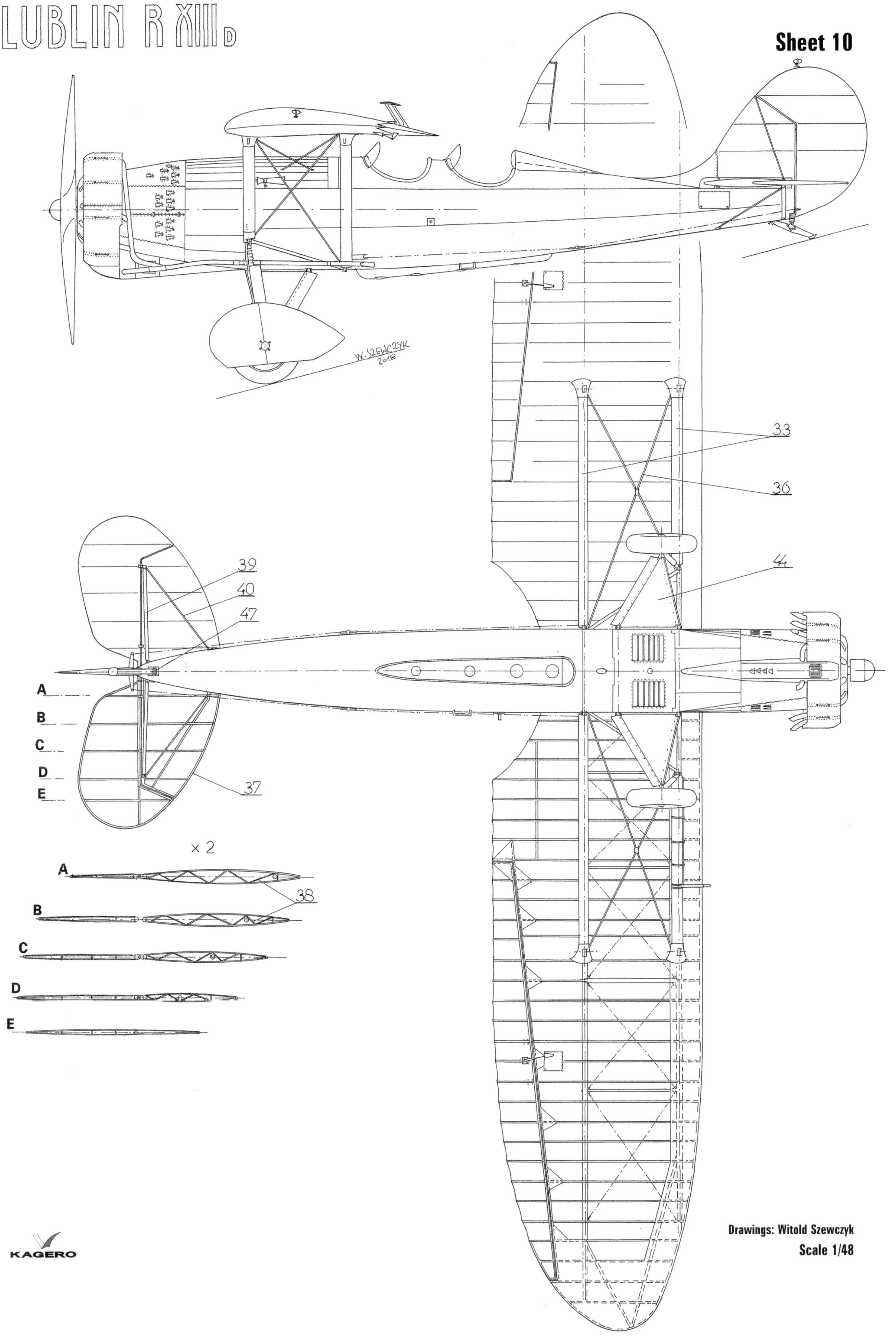

KAGERO

Drawings: Witold Szewczyk
Scale 1/48

LUBLIN R XIII D

Sheet 11

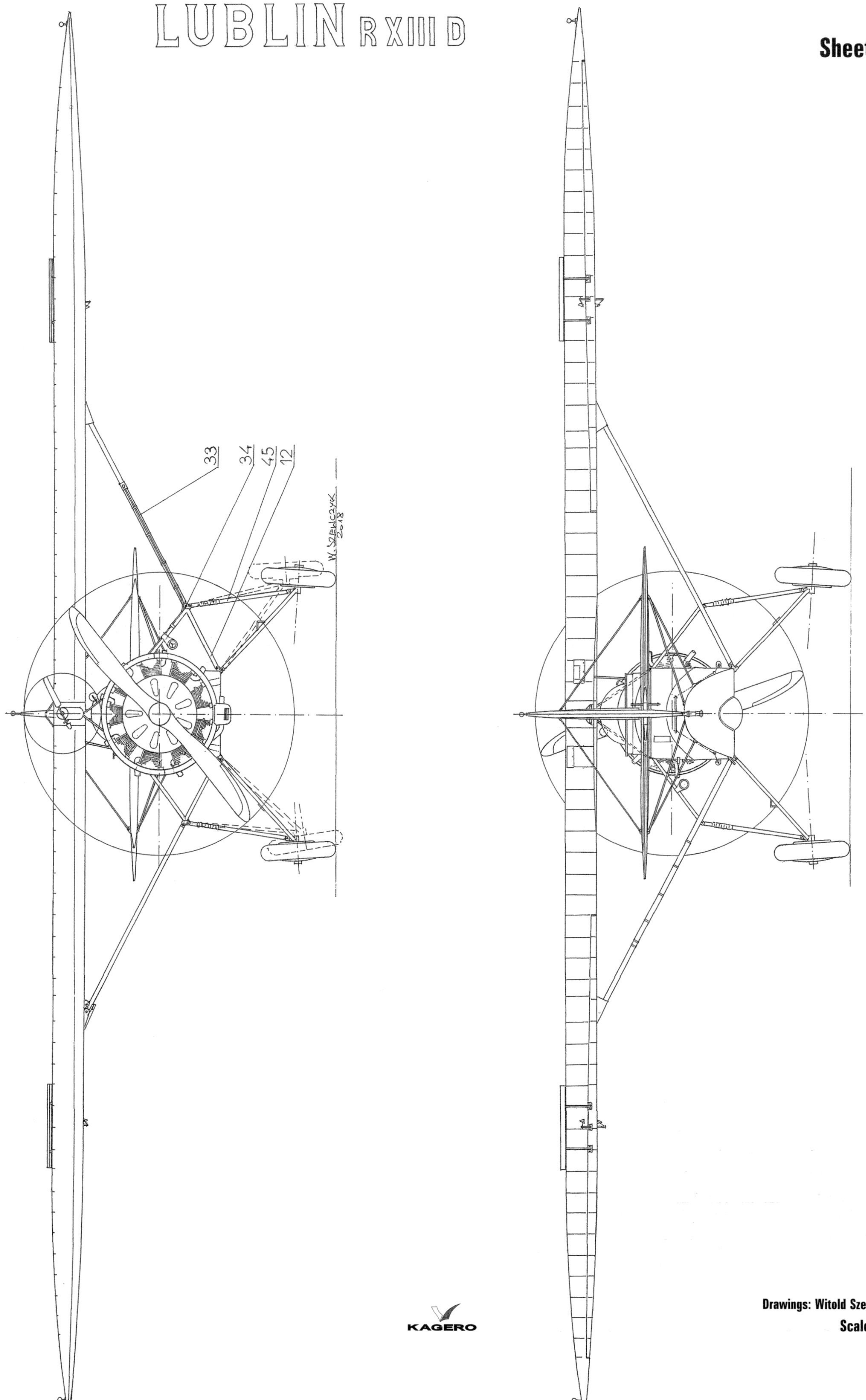

KAGERO

Drawings: Witold Szewczyk

Scale 1/48

Sheet 12

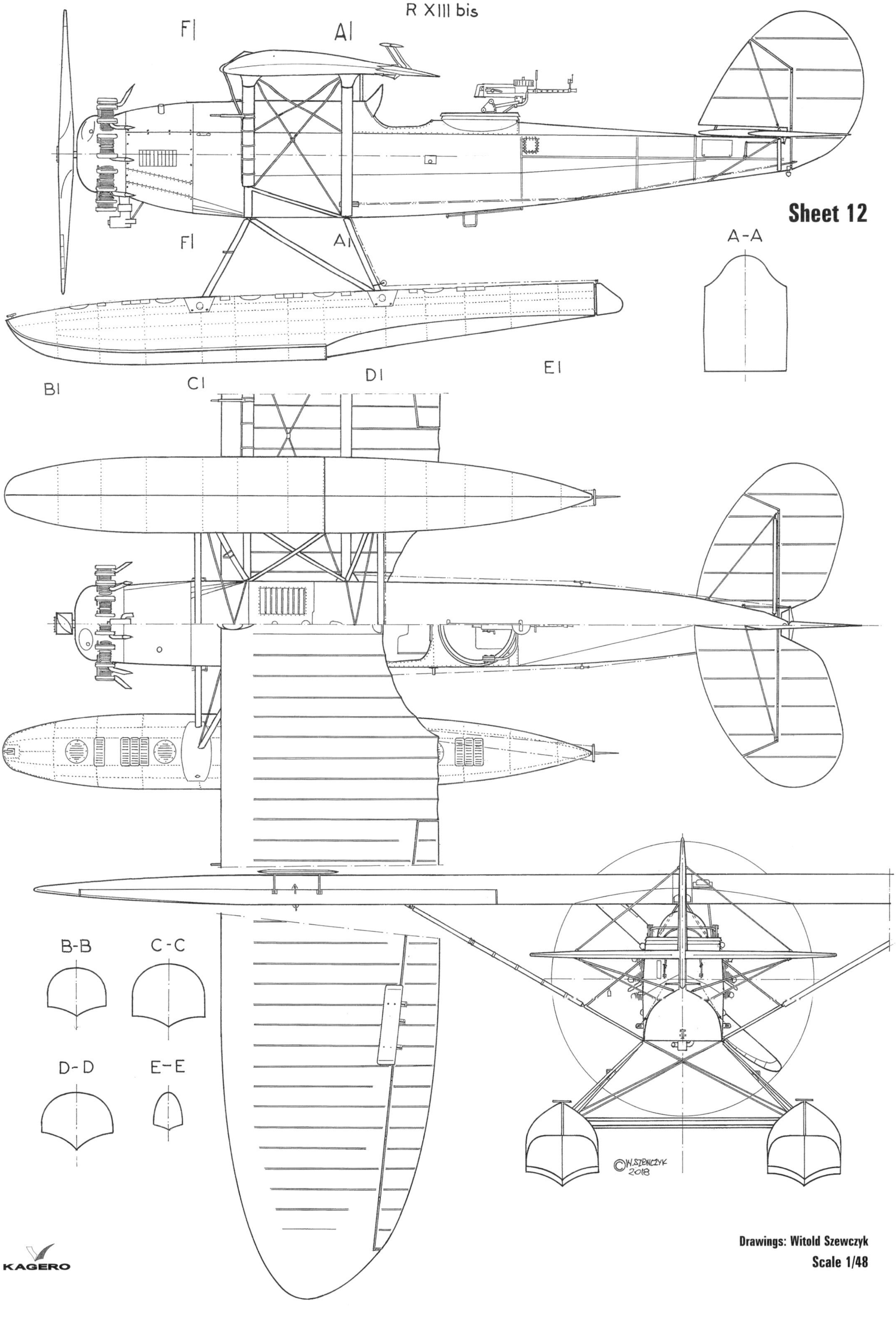

Drawings: Witold Szewczyk

Scale 1/48

KAGERO

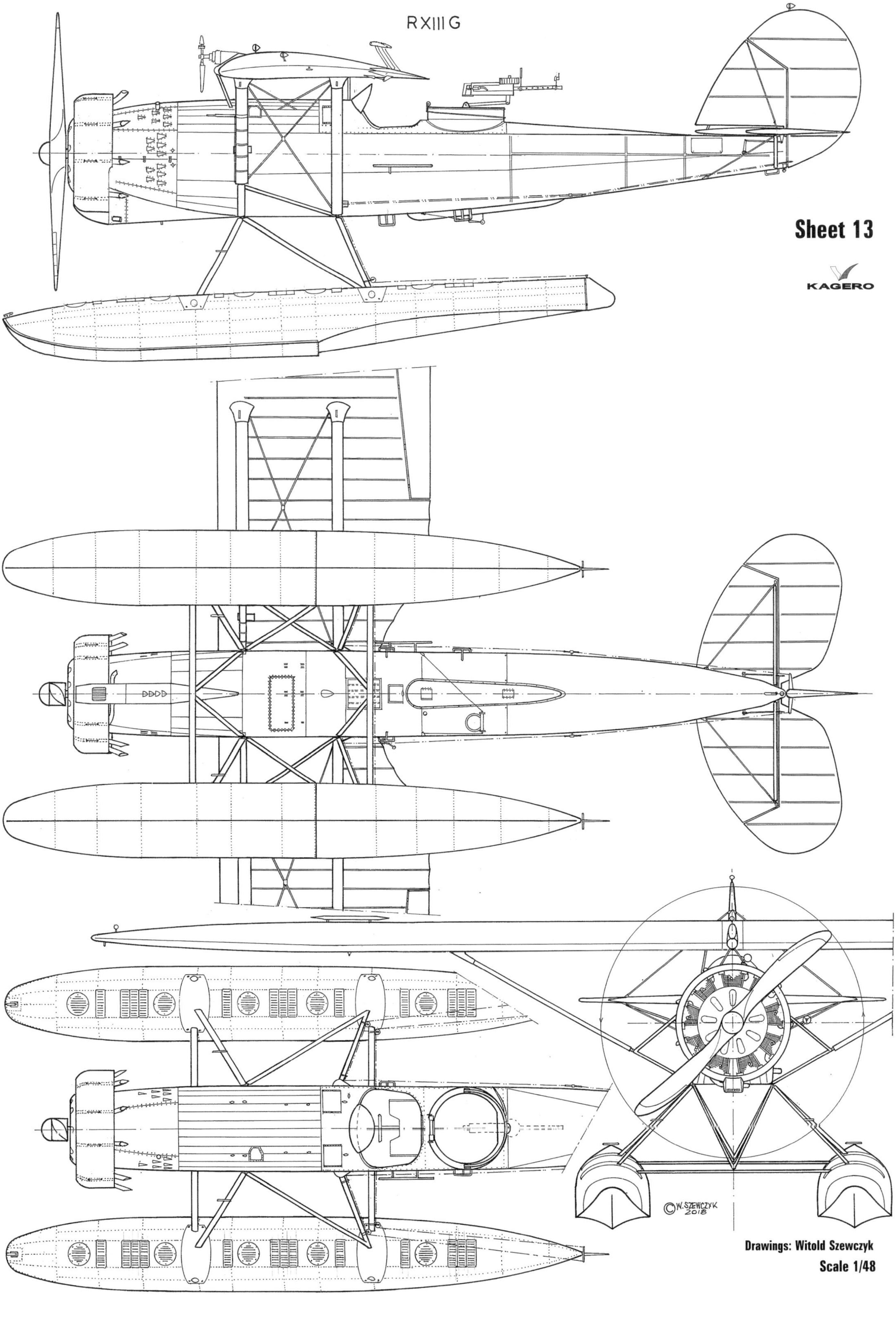

Sheet 13

KAGERO

Drawings: Witold Szewczyk

Scale 1/48

Sheet 14

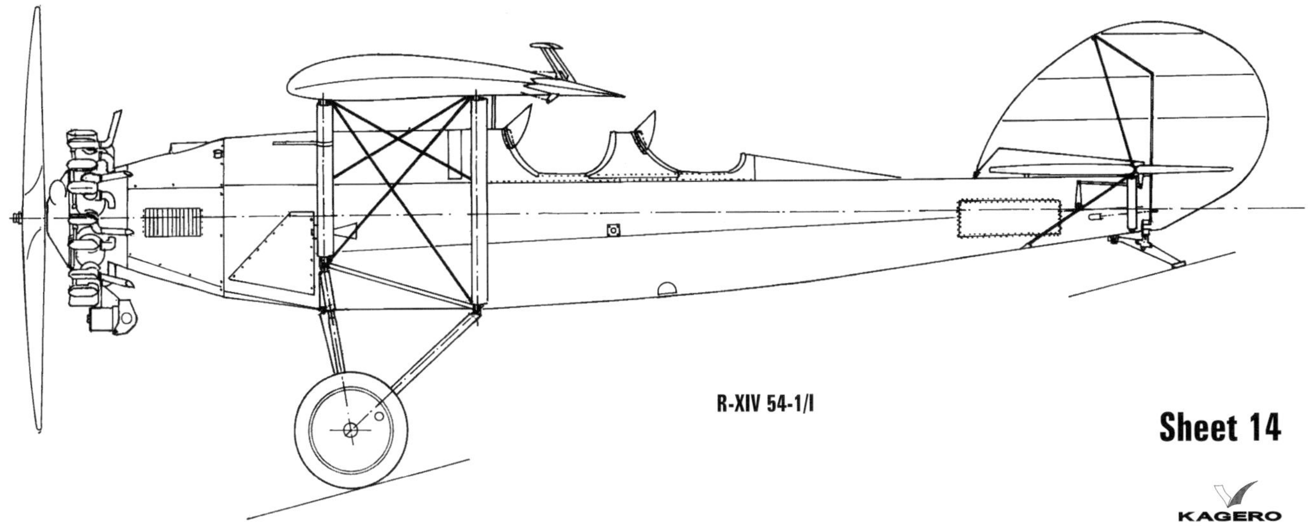

R-XIV 54-1/I

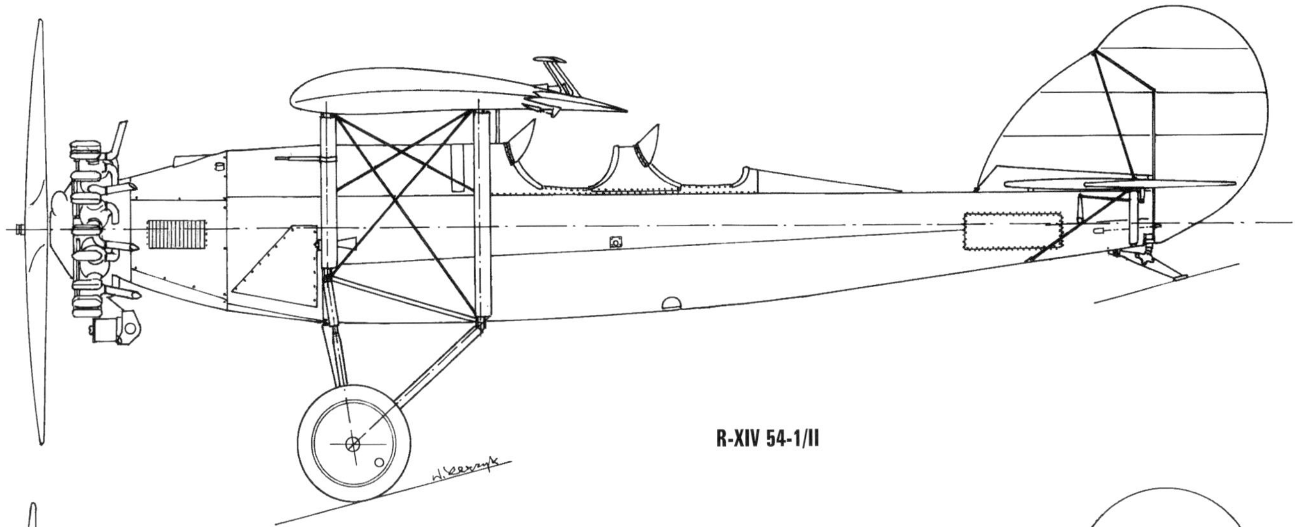

R-XIV 54-1/II

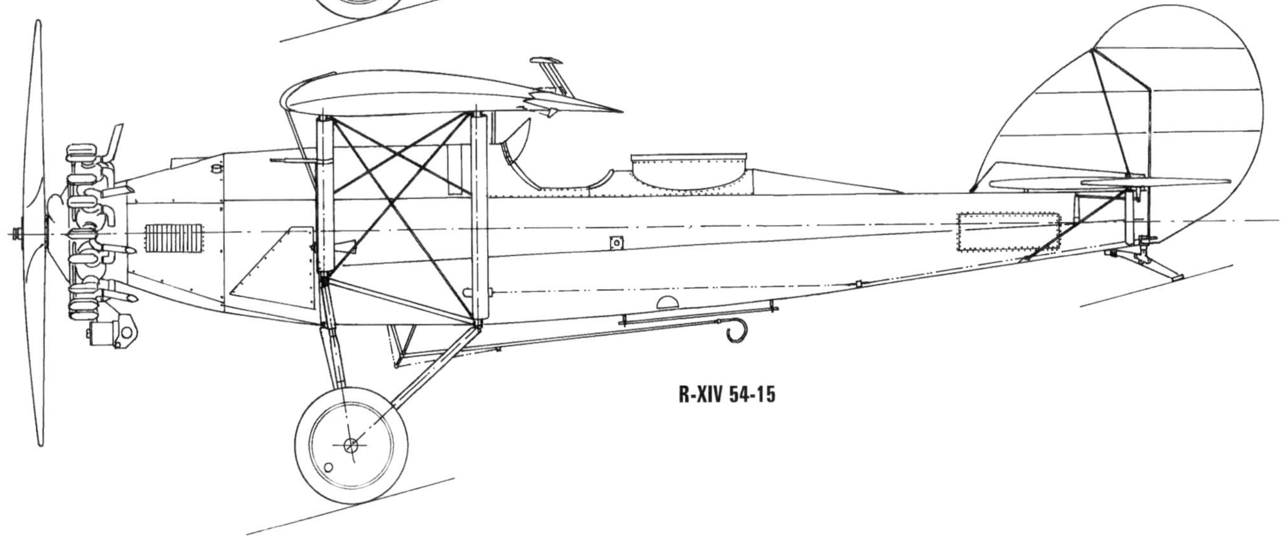

R-XIV 54-15

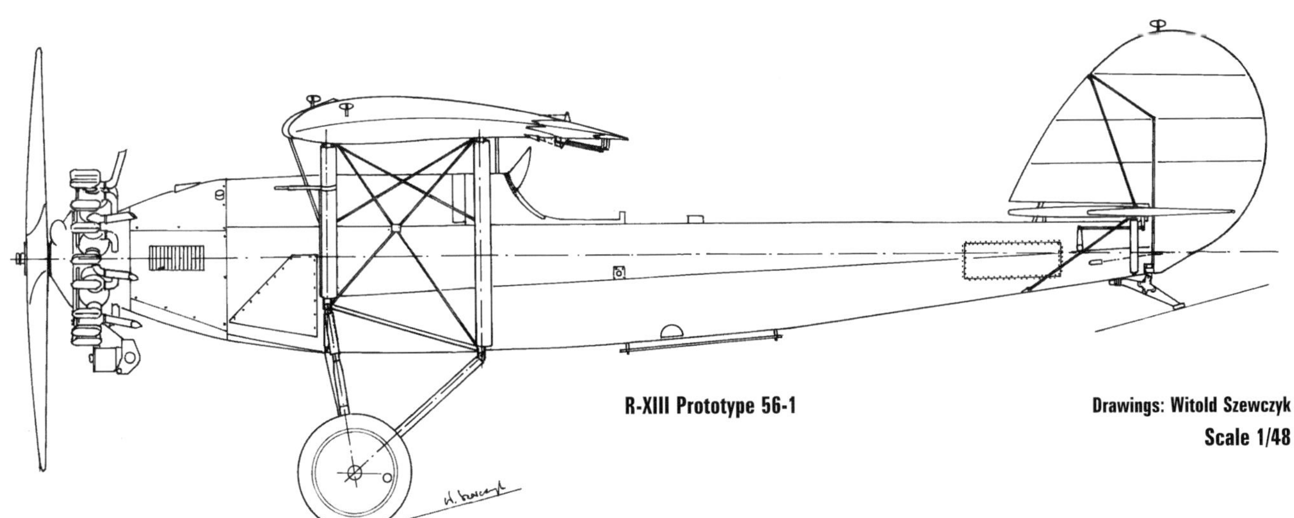

R-XIII Prototype 56-1

Drawings: Witold Szewczyk

Scale 1/48

Sheet 15

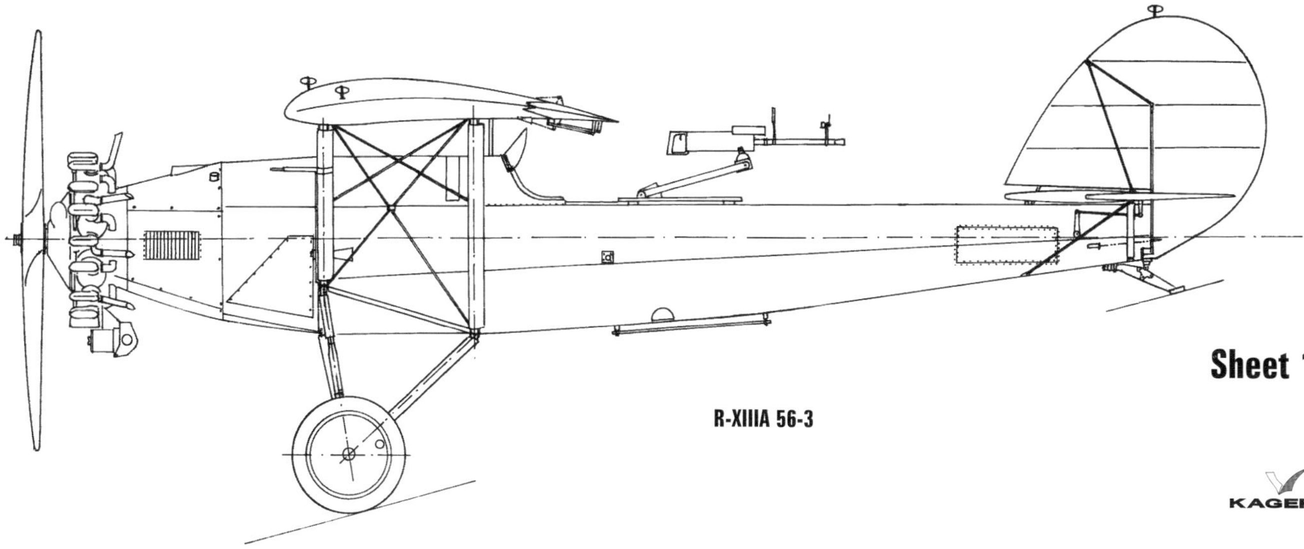

R-XIIIA 56-3

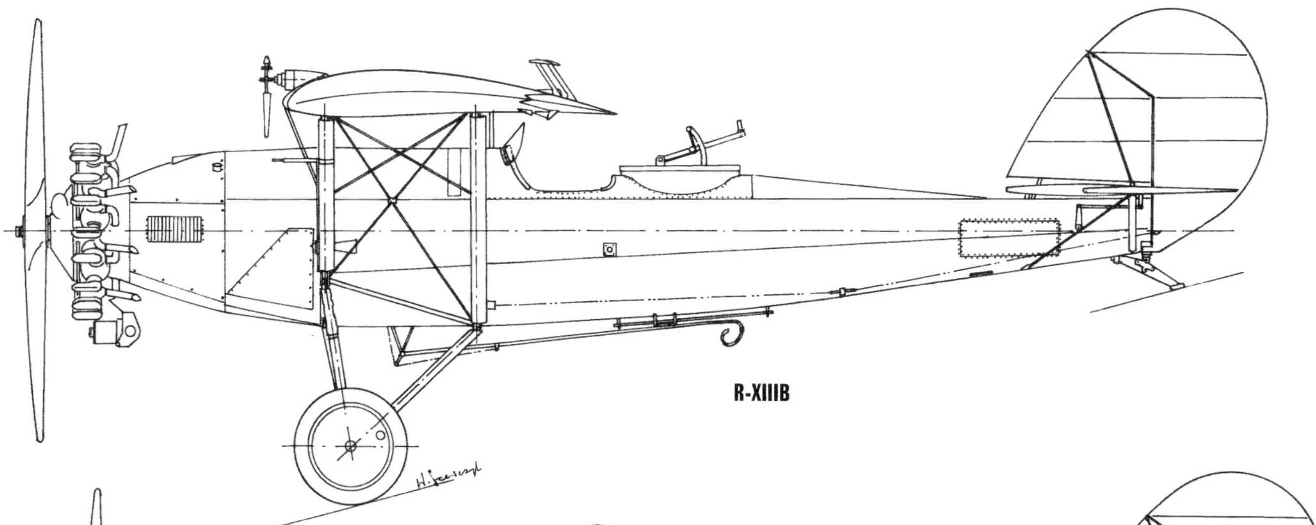

R-XIIIB

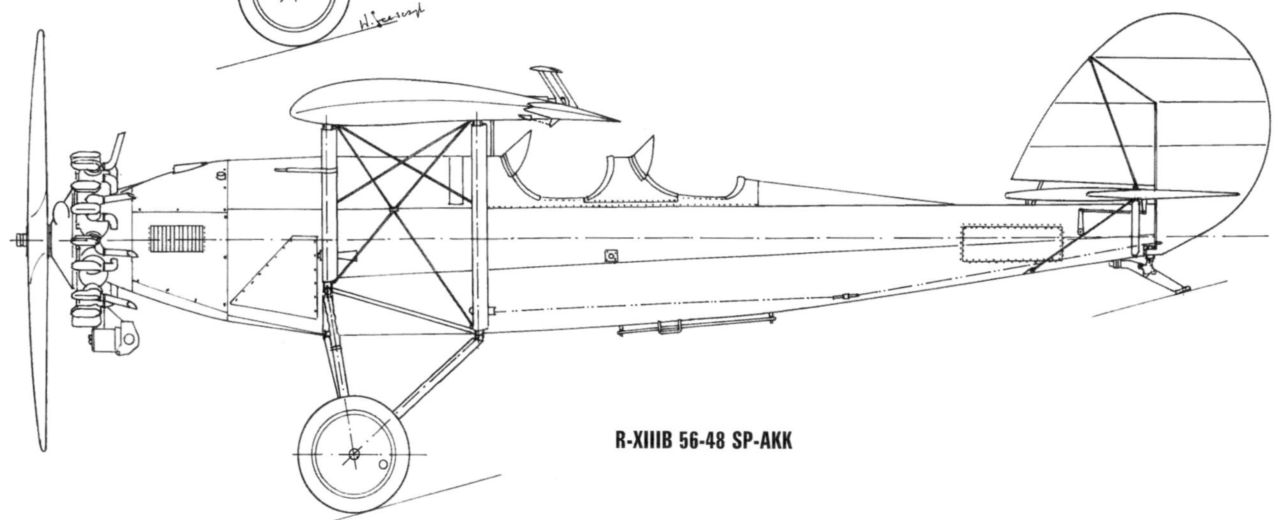

R-XIIIB 56-48 SP-AKK

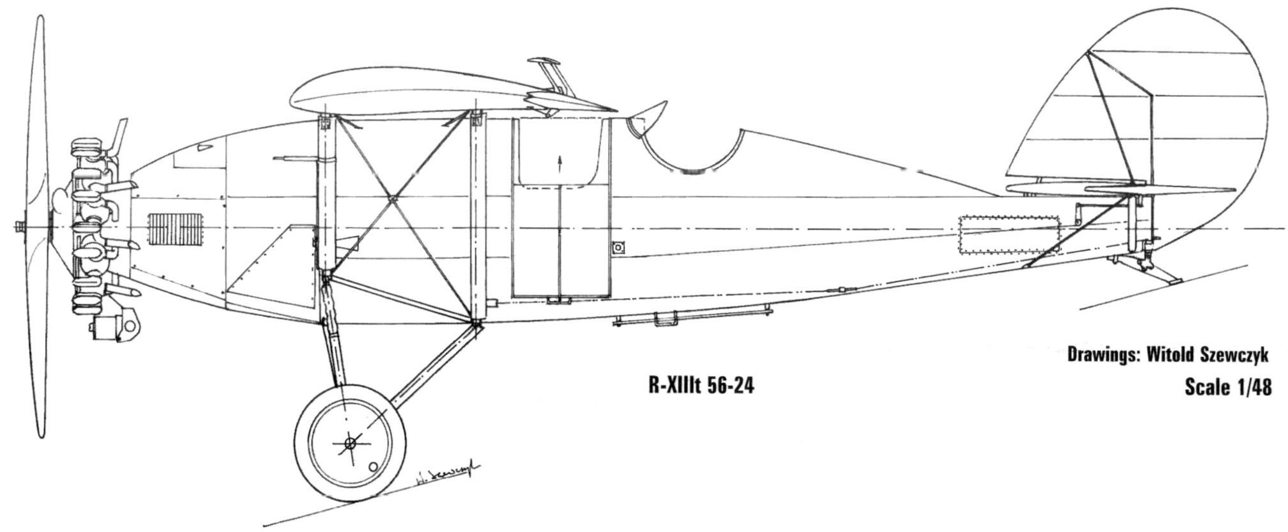

R-XIIIt 56-24

Drawings: Witold Szewczyk

Scale 1/48

Sheet 16

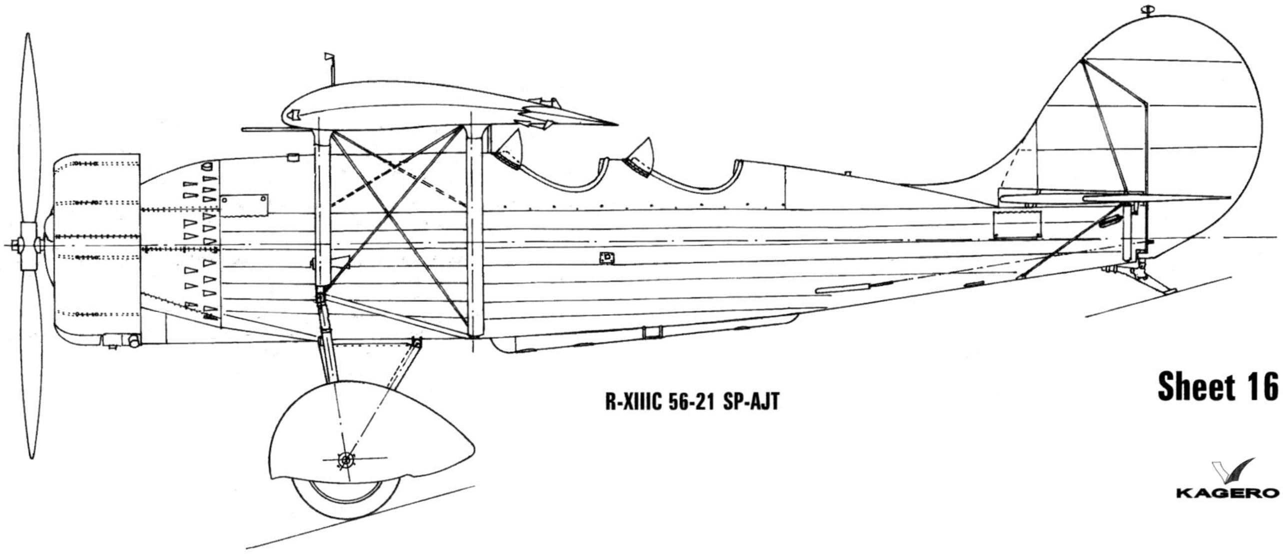

R-XIIIC 56-21 SP-AJT

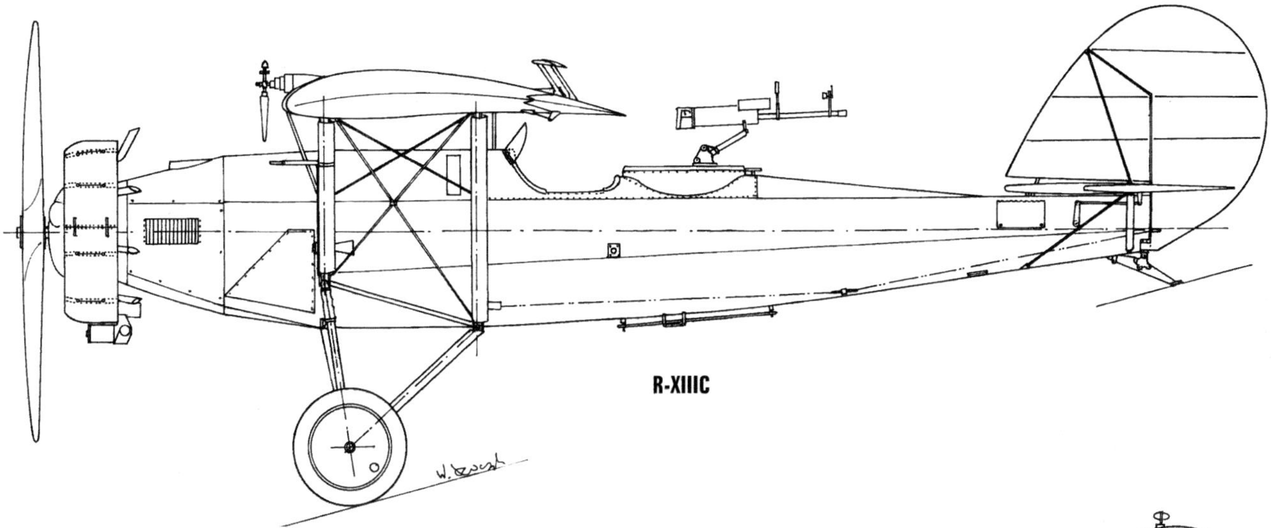

R-XIIIC

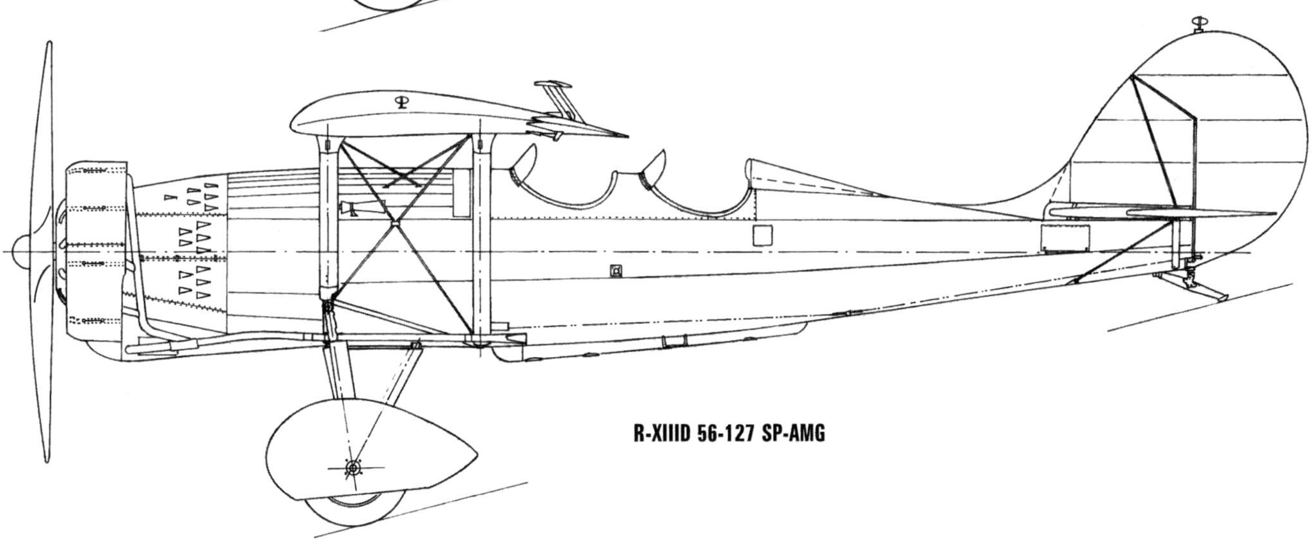

R-XIIID 56-127 SP-AMG

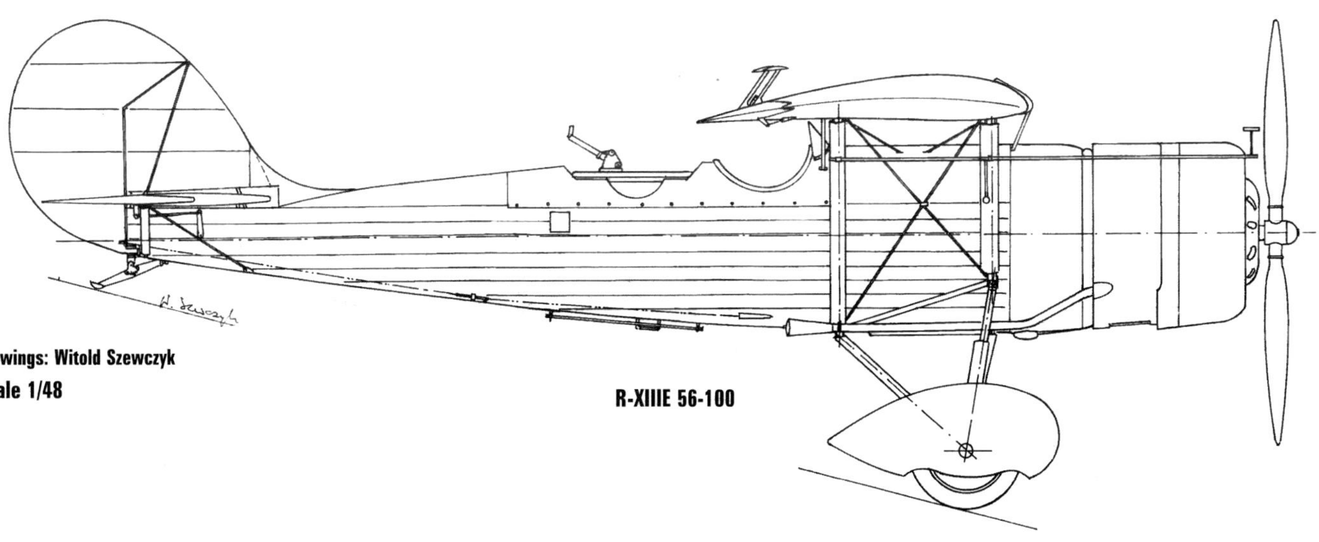

R-XIIIE 56-100

Drawings: Witold Szewczyk

Scale 1/48

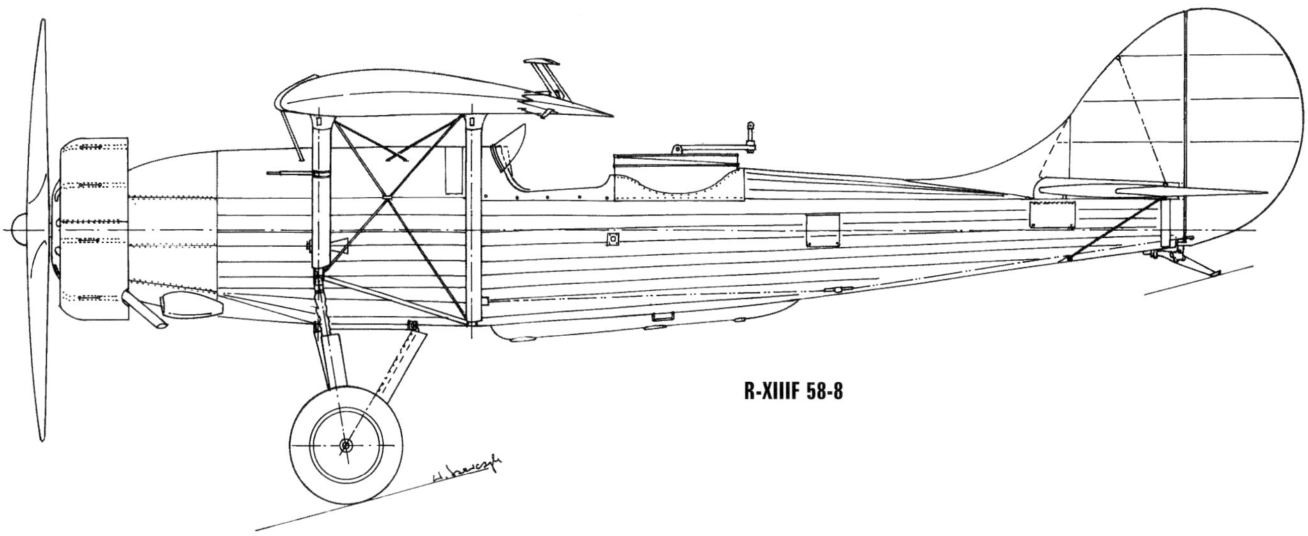

R-XIIIF 58-8

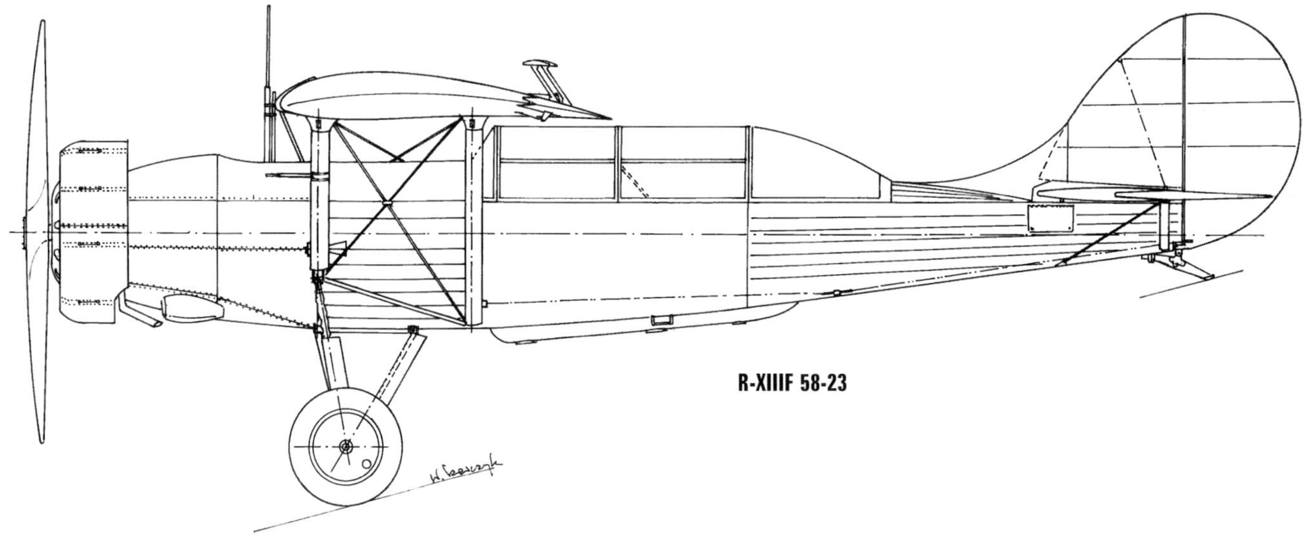

R-XIIIF 58-23

KAGERO

Drawings: Witold Szewczyk
Scale 1/48

Sheet 18

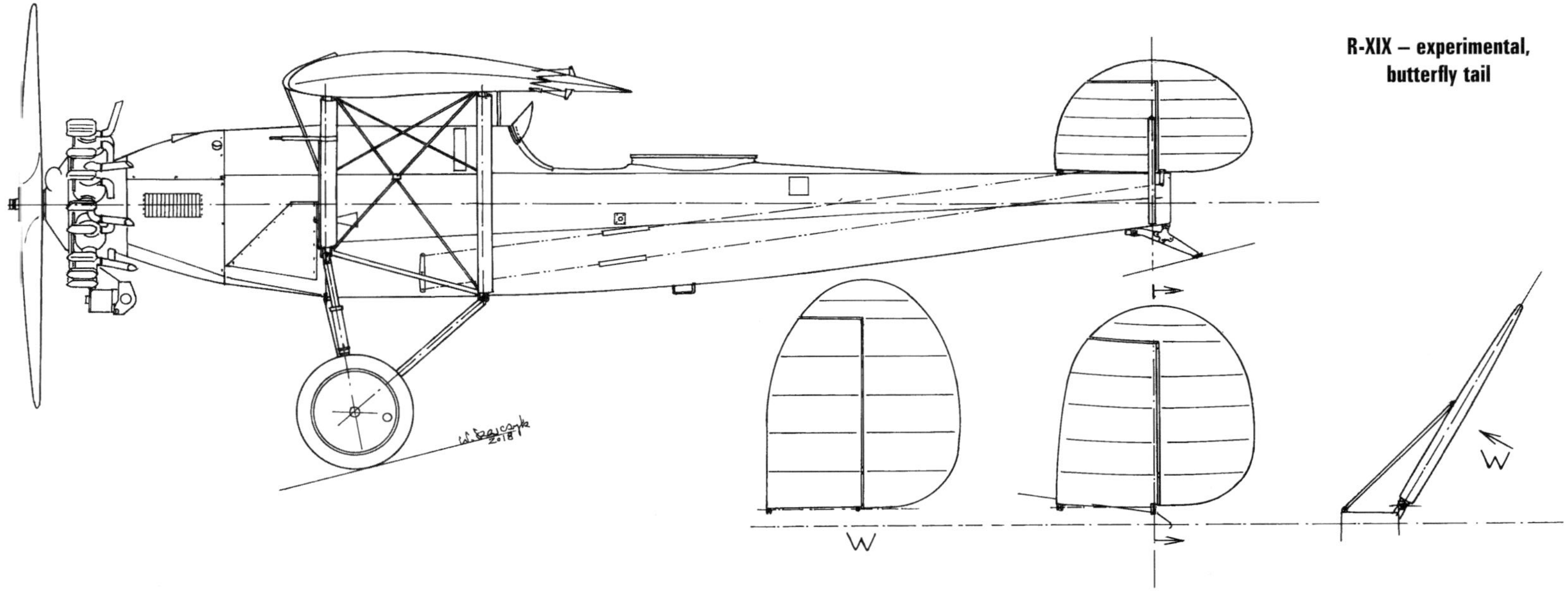

R-XIX – experimental, butterfly tail

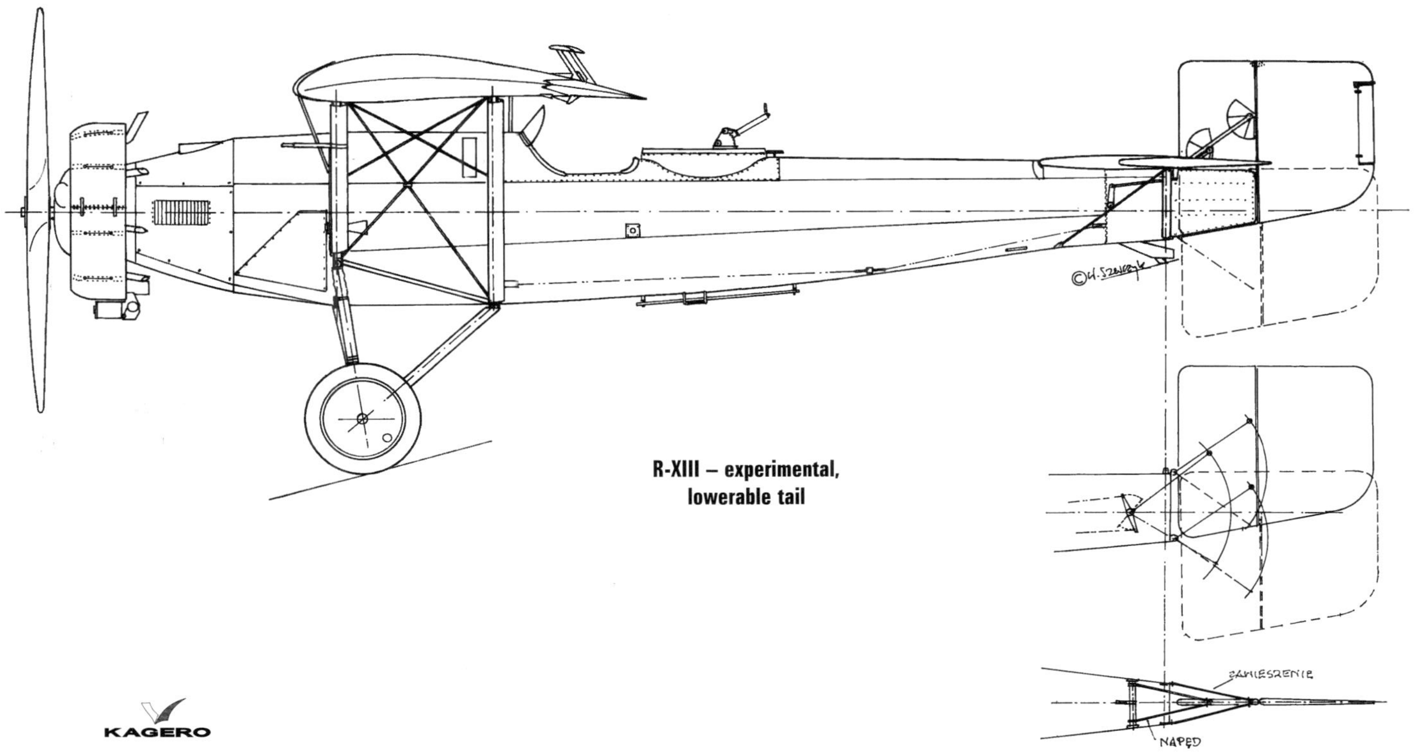

R-XIII – experimental, lowerable tail

Drawings: Witold Szewczyk

Scale 1/48

Sheet 19

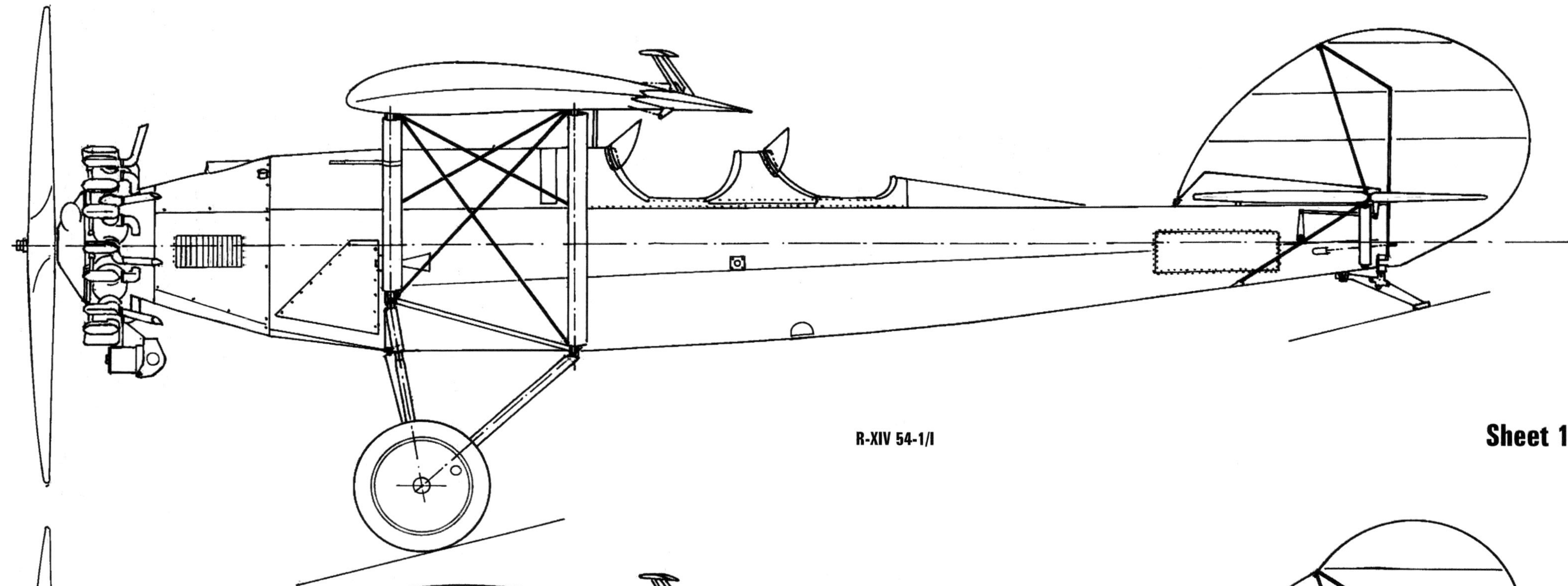

R-XIV 54-1/I

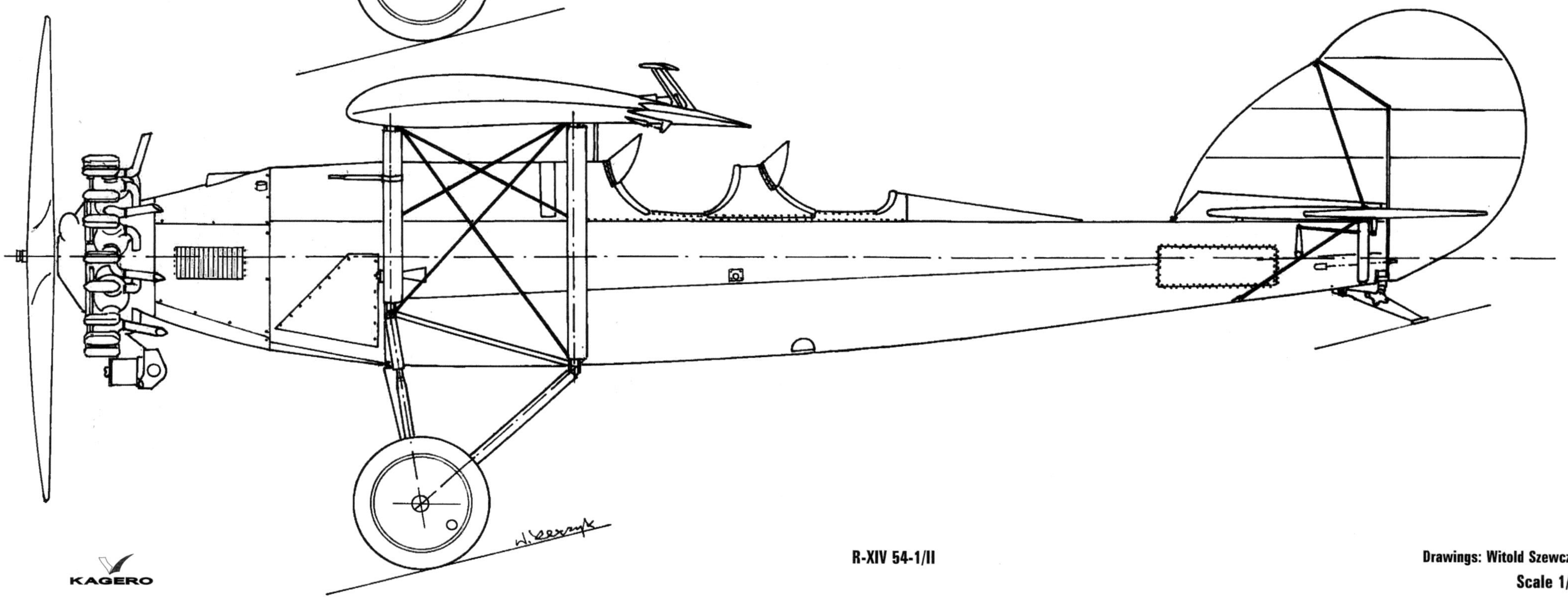

R-XIV 54-1/II

Drawings: Witold Szewczyk

Scale 1/32

Sheet 20

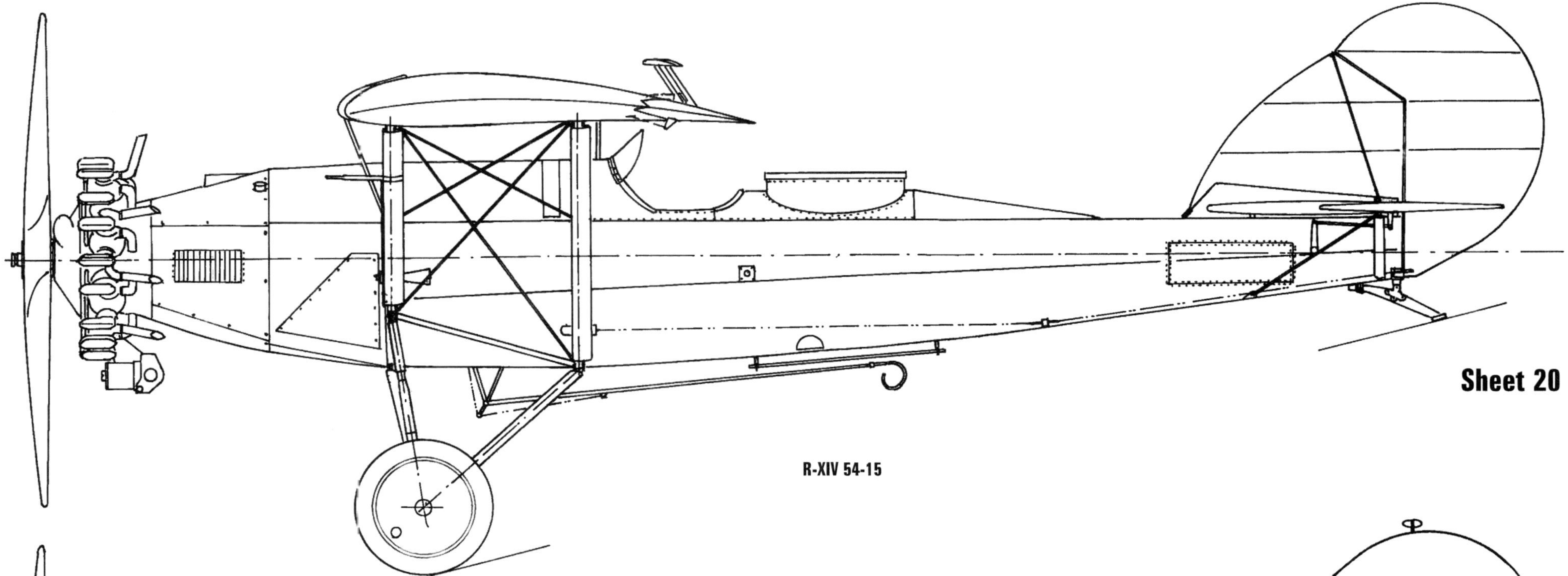

R-XIV 54-15

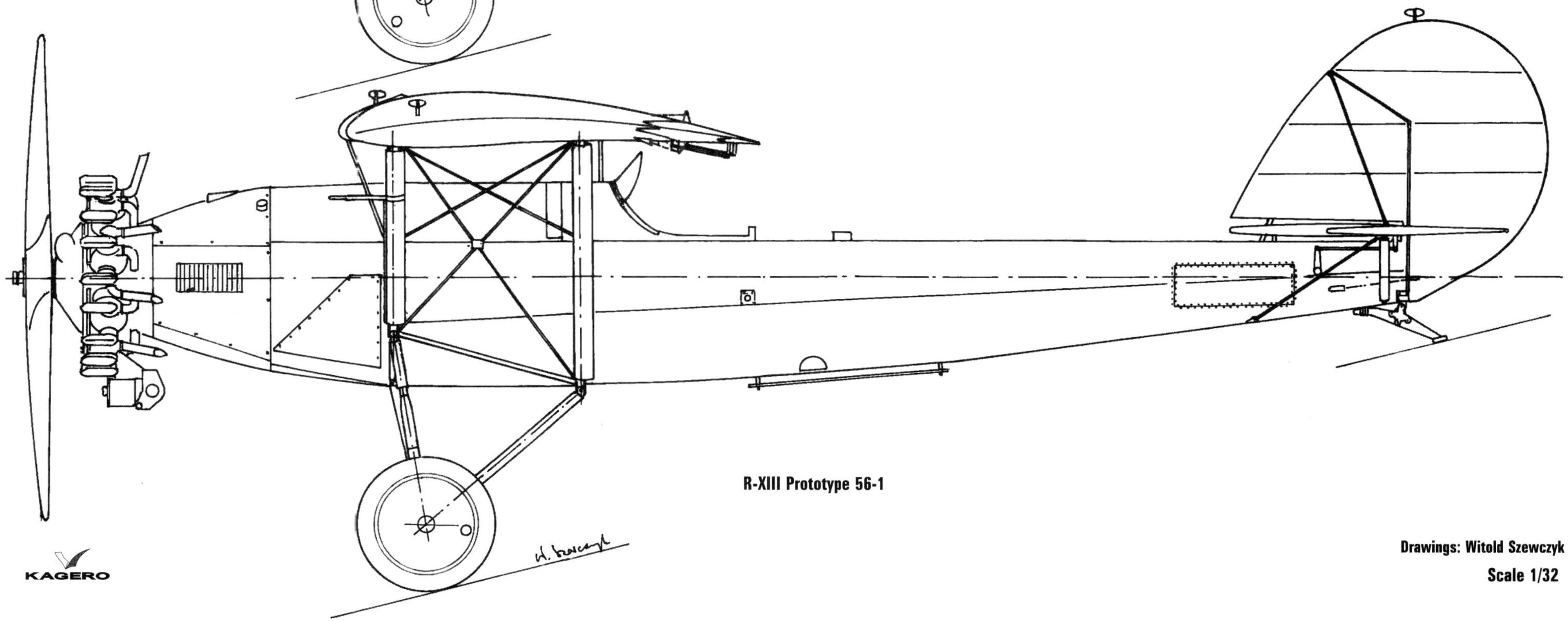

R-XIII Prototype 56-1

Drawings: Witold Szewczyk

Scale 1/32

KAGERO

Sheet 21

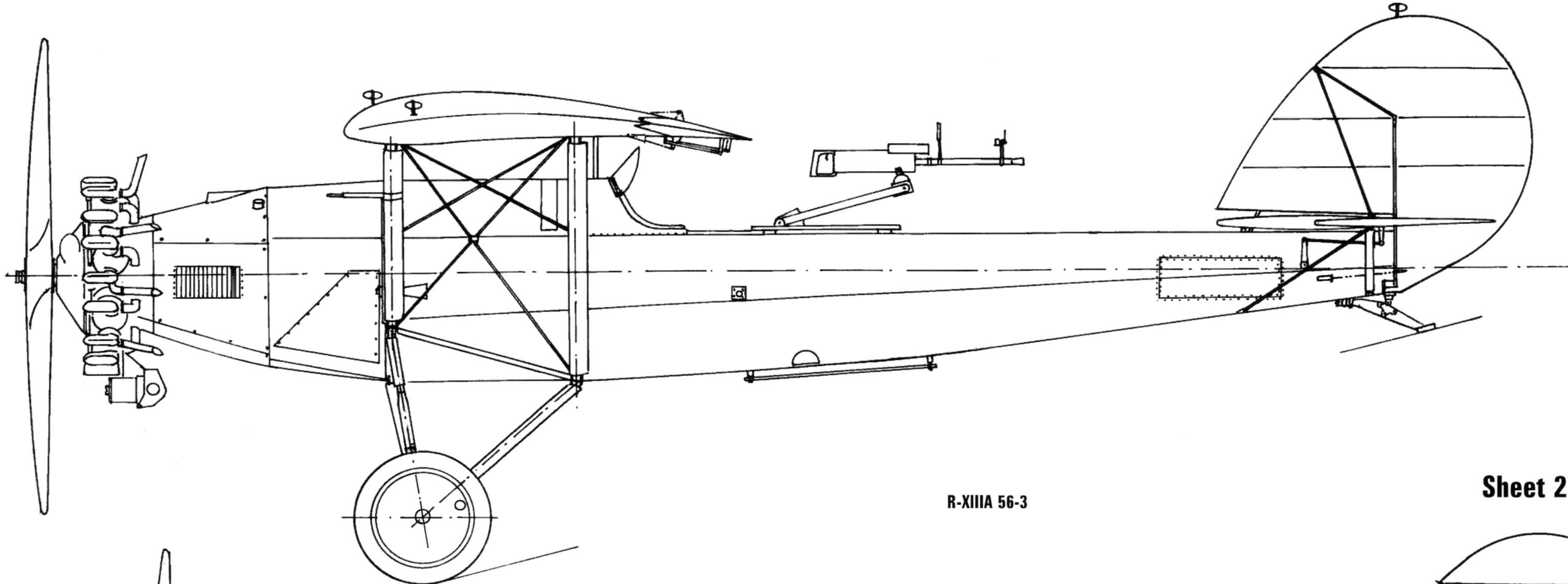

R-XIIIA 56-3

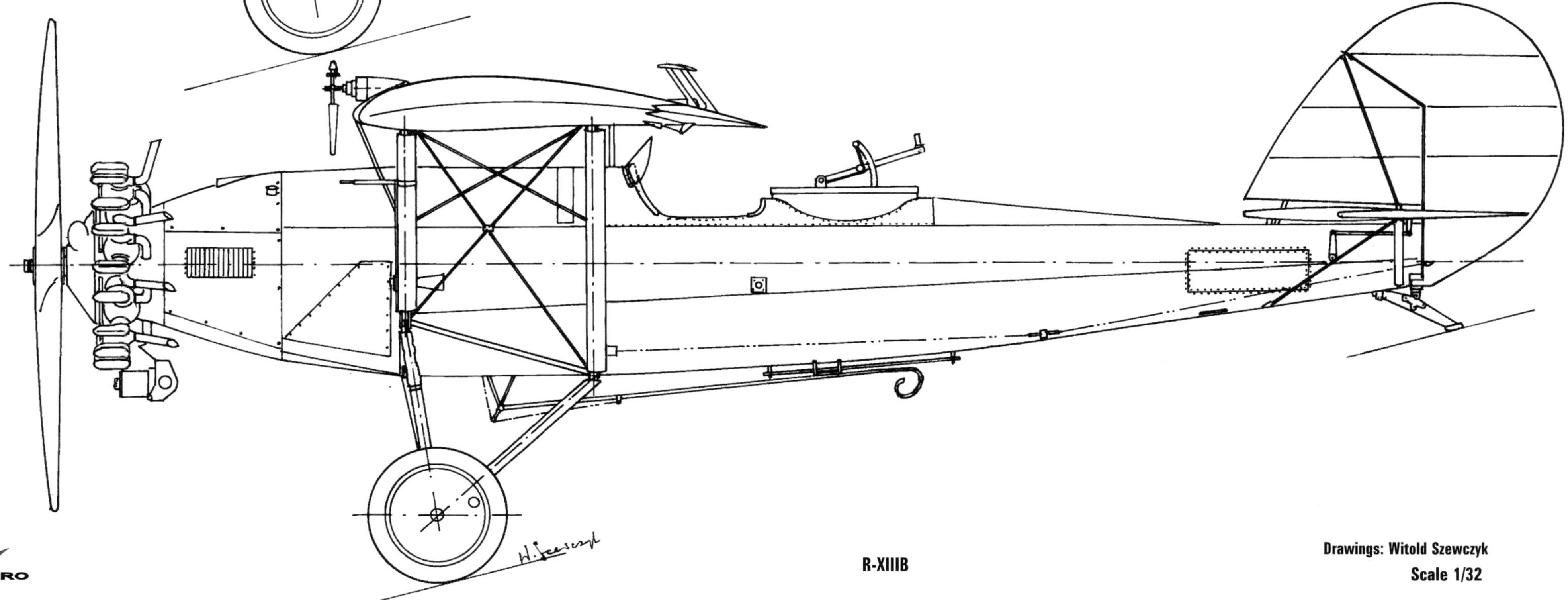

R-XIIIB

Drawings: Witold Szewczyk
Scale 1/32

Sheet 22

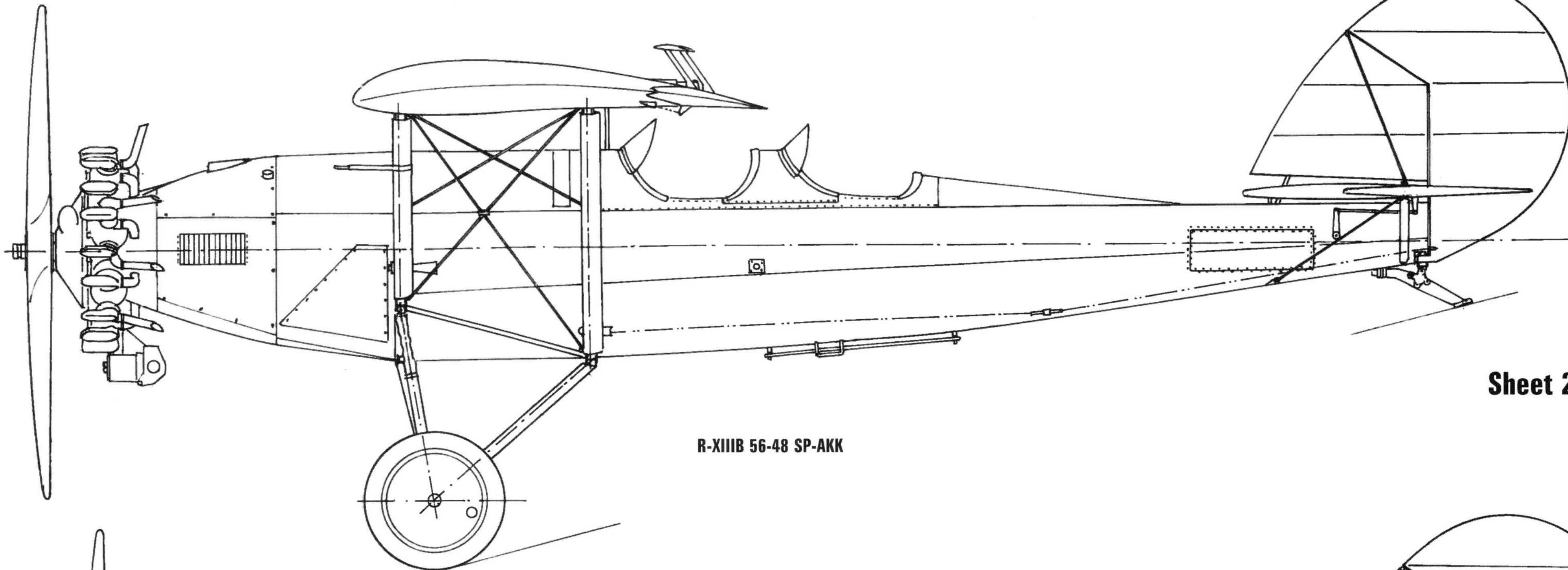

R-XIIIB 56-48 SP-AKK

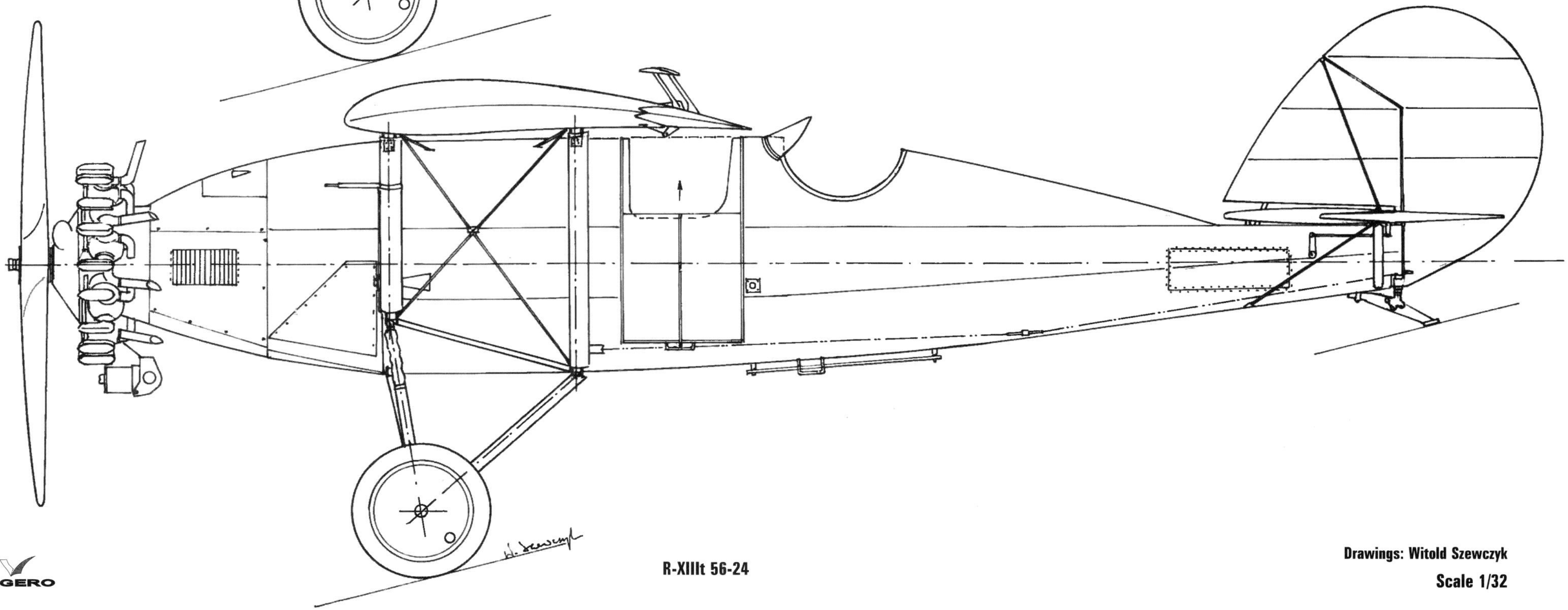

R-XIIIt 56-24

Drawings: Witold Szewczyk

Scale 1/32

KAGERO

Sheet 23

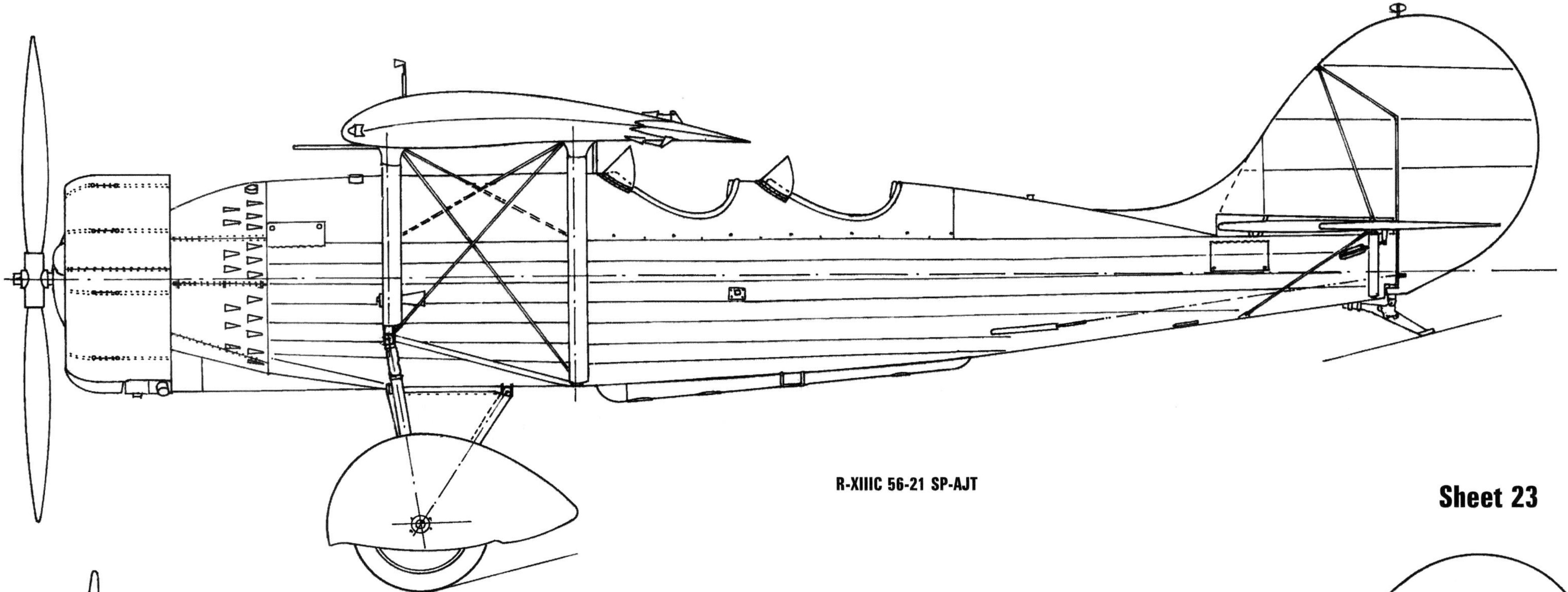

R-XIIIC 56-21 SP-AJT

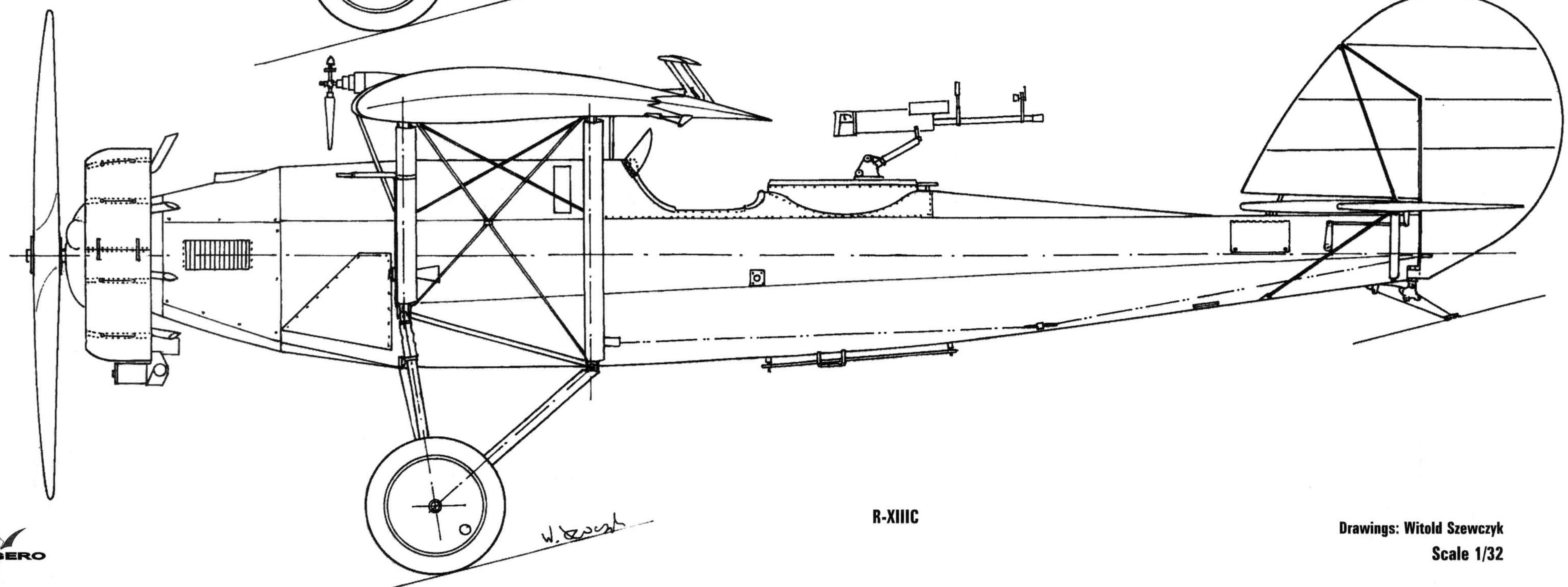

R-XIIIC

Drawings: Witold Szewczyk
Scale 1/32

KAGERO

Sheet 24

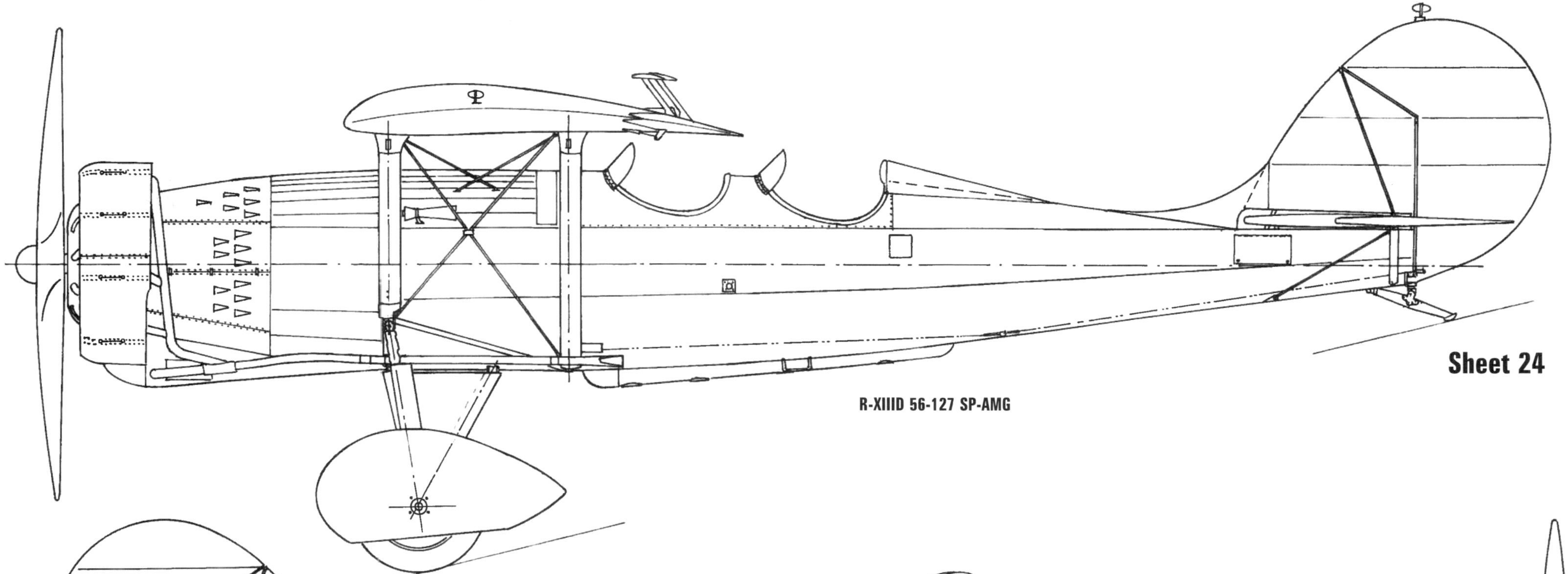

R-XIIID 56-127 SP-AMG

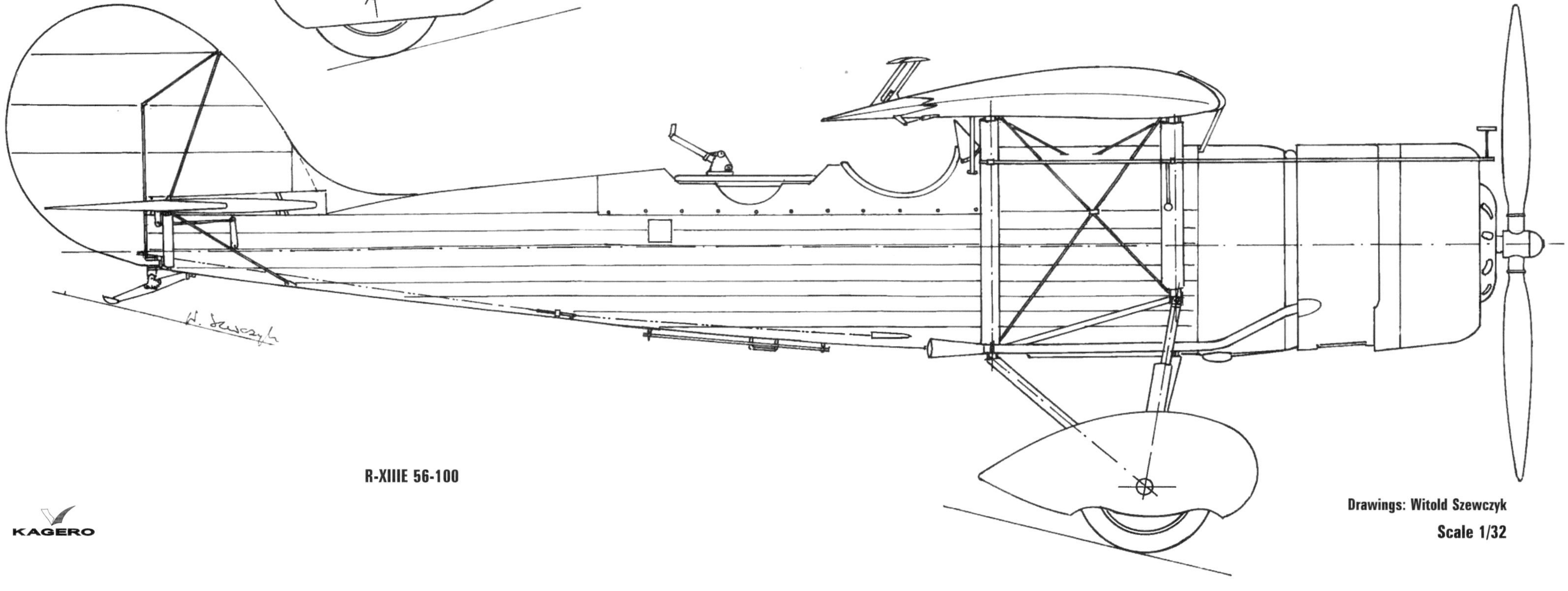

R-XIIIE 56-100

Drawings: Witold Szewczyk

Scale 1/32

KAGERO

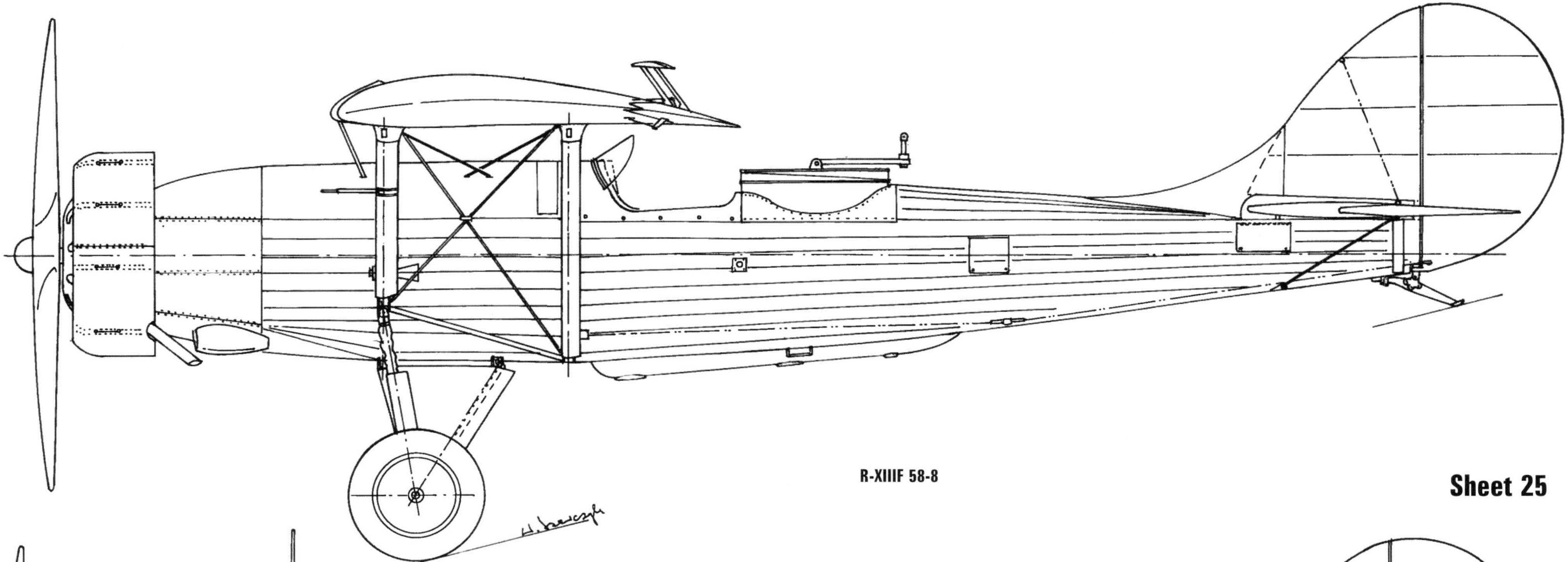

R-XIIIF 58-8

Sheet 25

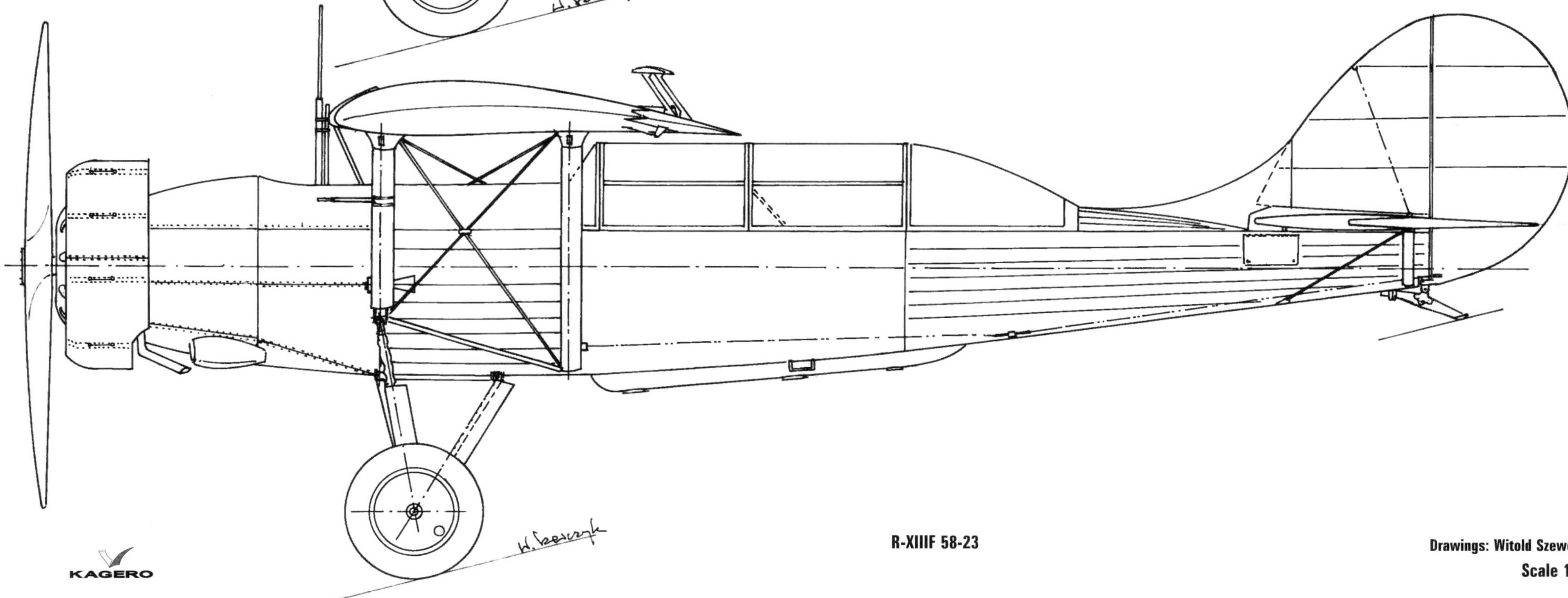

R-XIIIF 58-23

Drawings: Witold Szewczyk

Scale 1/32

KAGERO

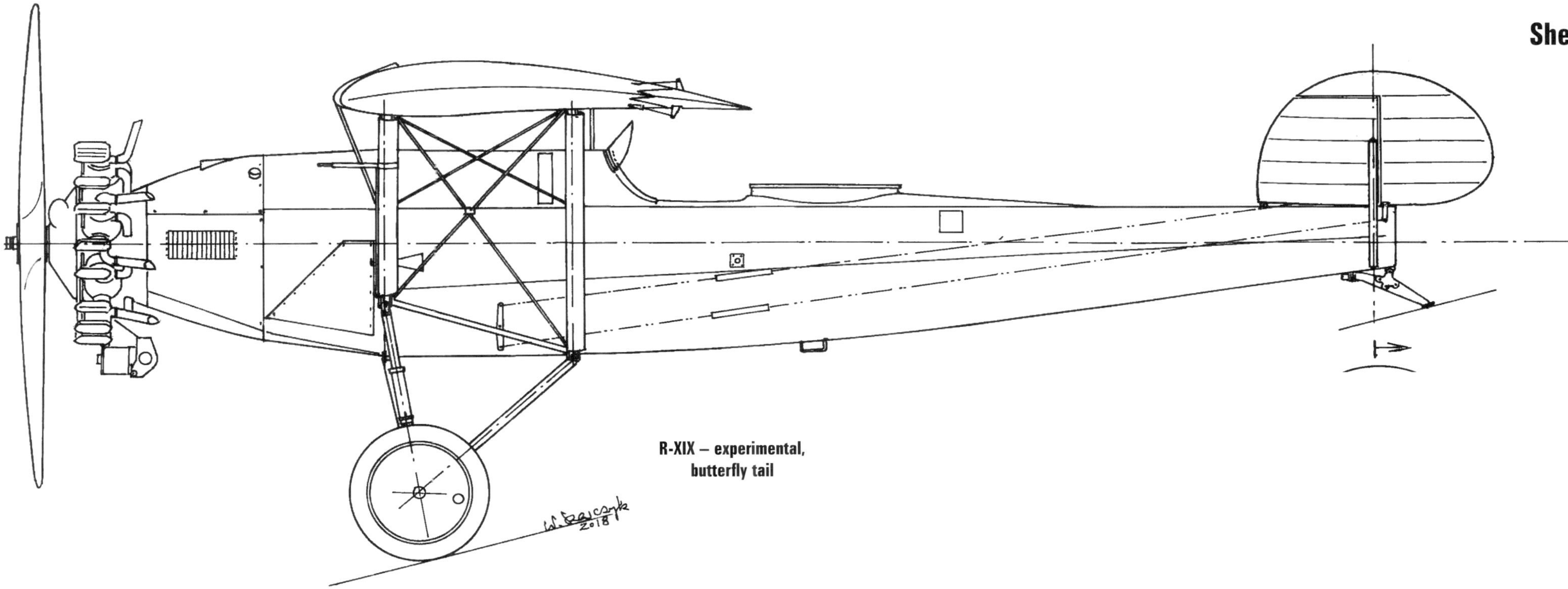

R-XIX – experimental, butterfly tail

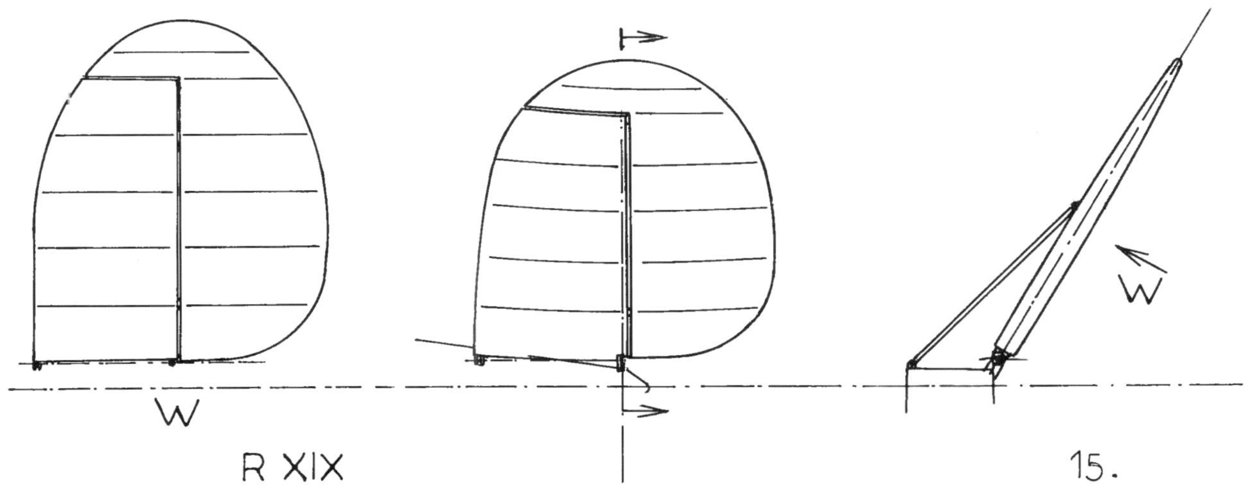

Drawings: Witold Szewczyk

Scale 1/32

Sheet 27

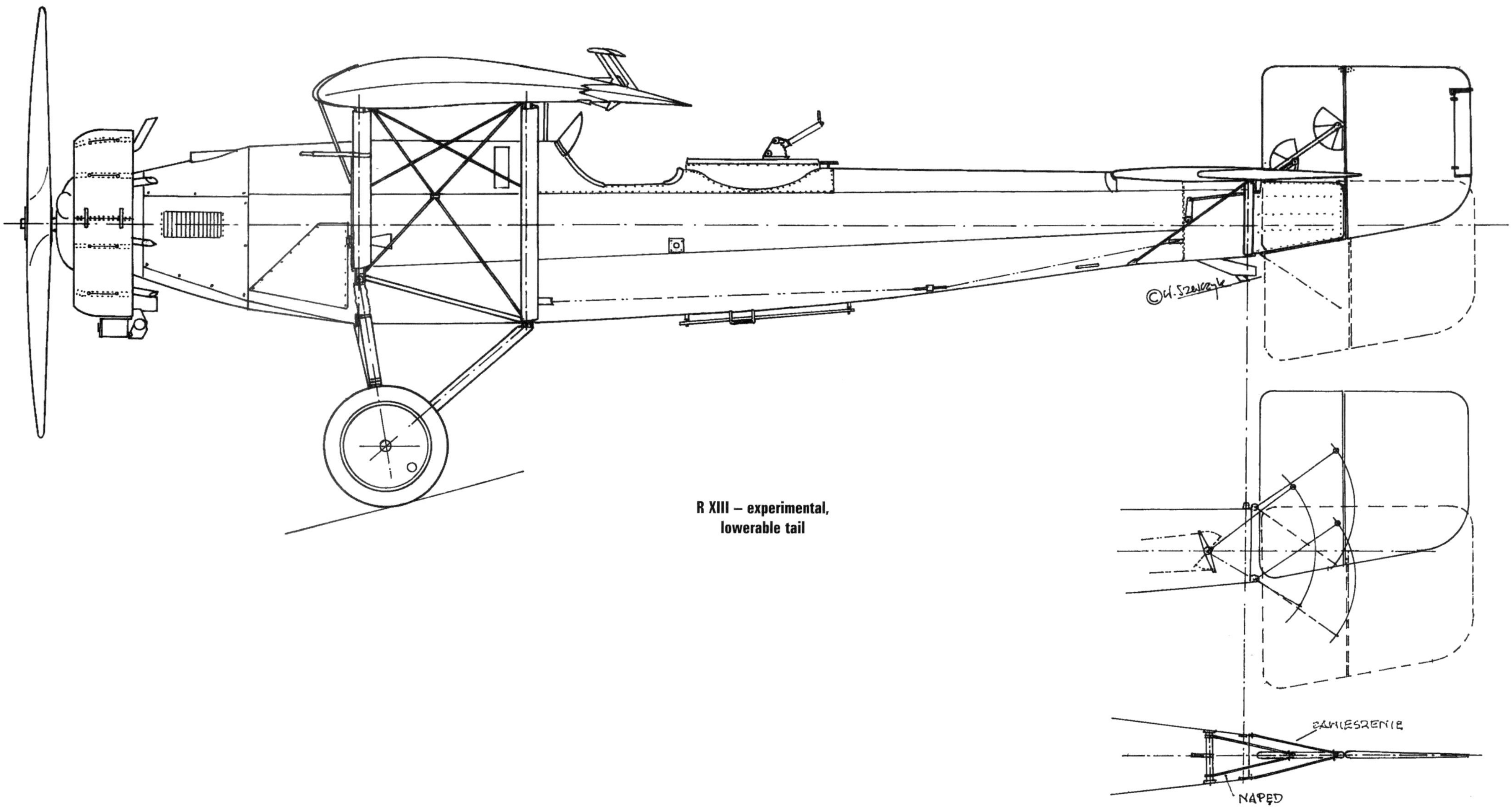

R XIII – experimental, lowerable tail

Drawings: Witold Szewczyk
Scale 1/32

KAGERO

Materials from Marek Trojanowicz (www.polskie-samoloty.pl)

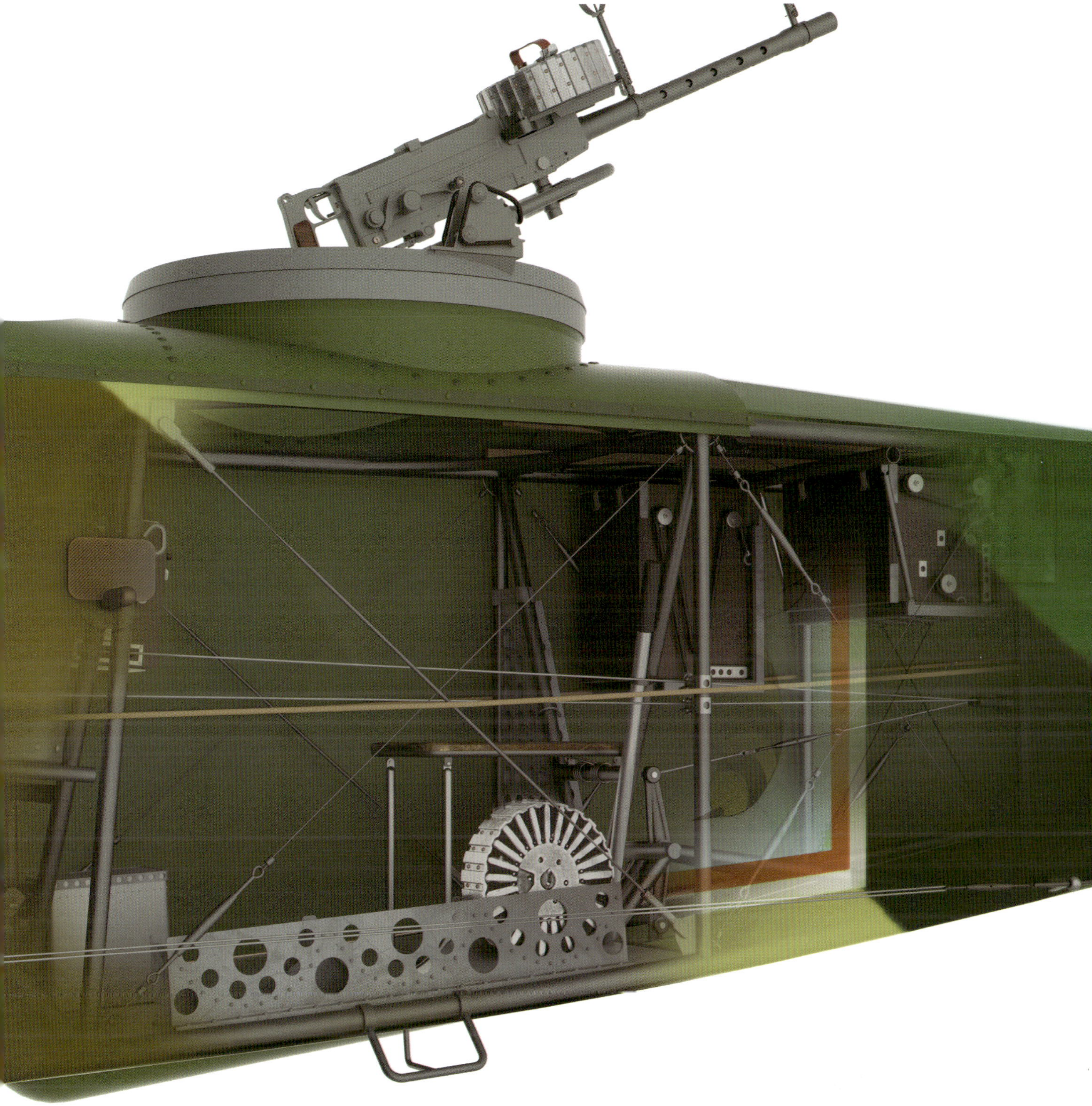

Fuselage's cross-section, observer's position.

Fuselage's cross-section, pilot's cockpit seen from the side.

Fuselage's cross-section, pilot's cockpit seen from the top.

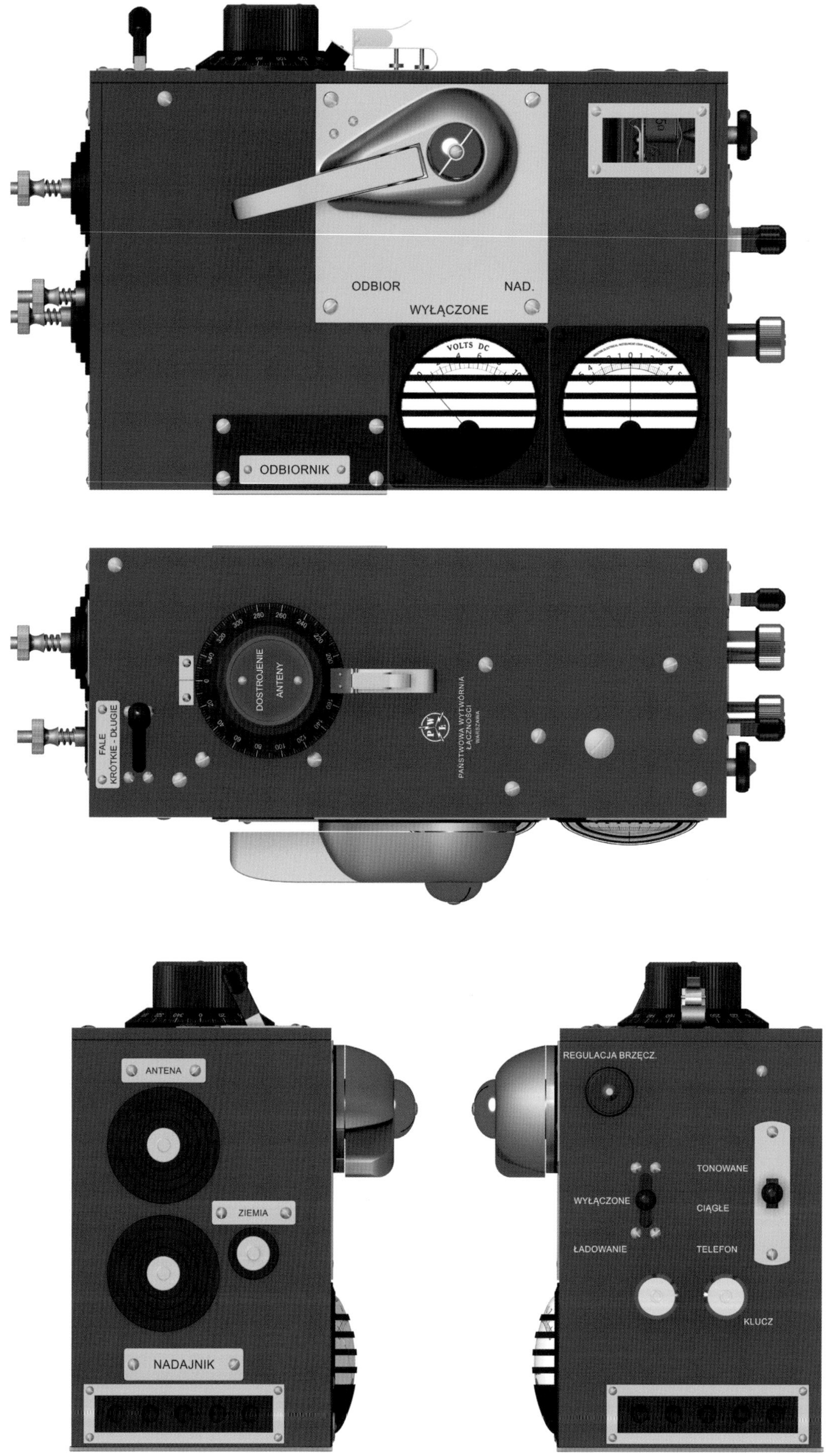

RKL/D radiostation, observer's box.

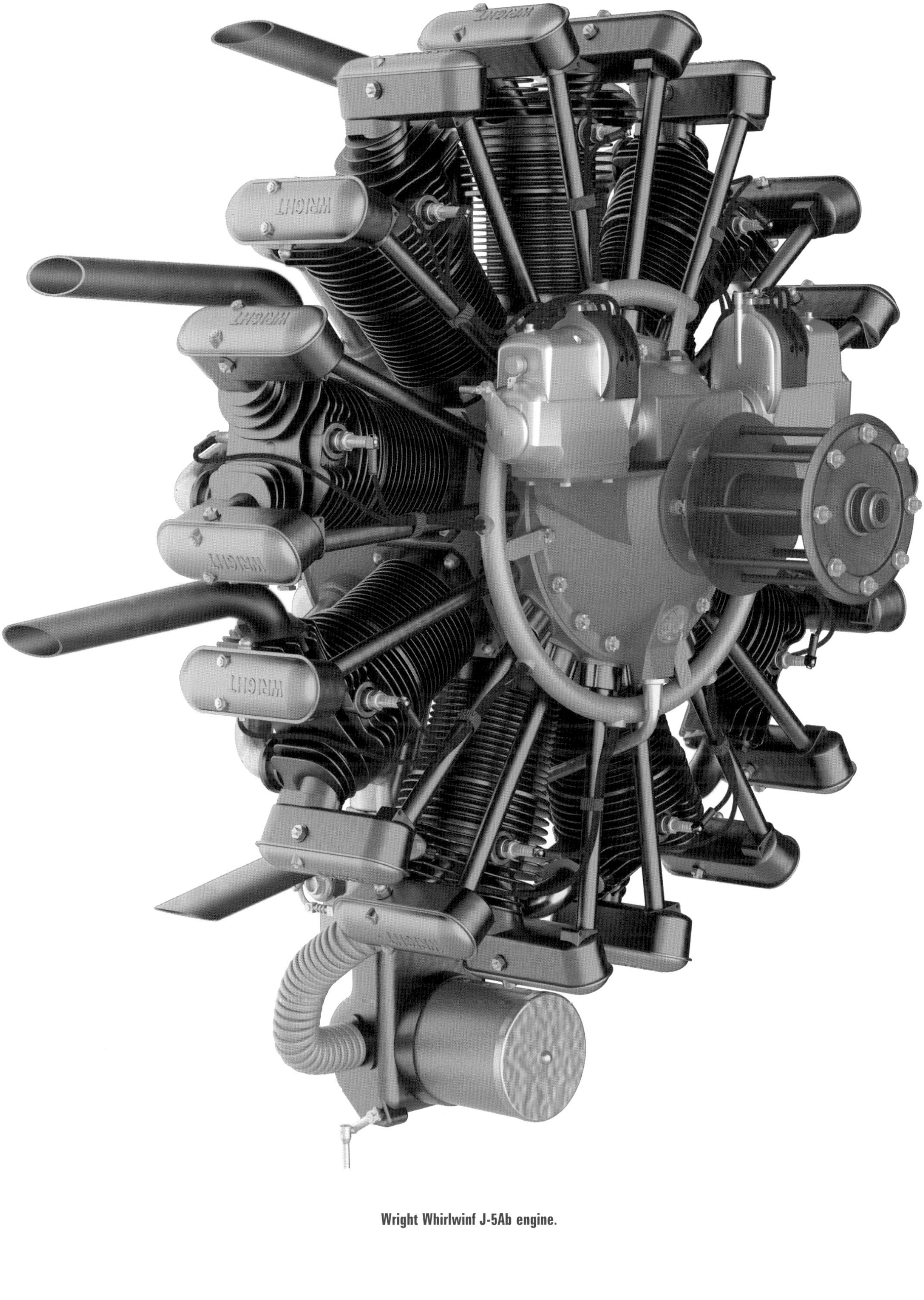

Wright Whirlwinf J-5Ab engine.

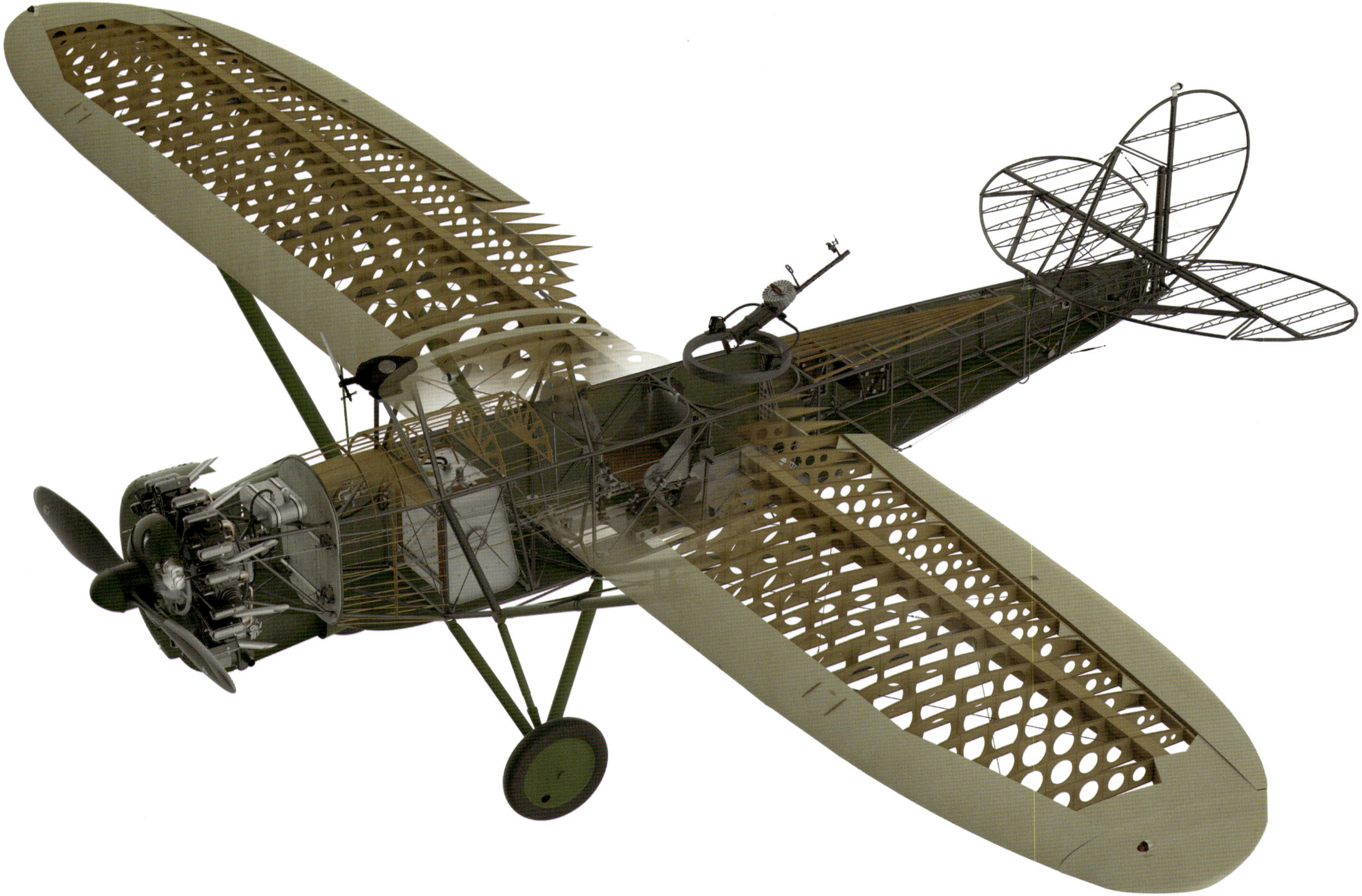

Cross-section of the whole aircraft.

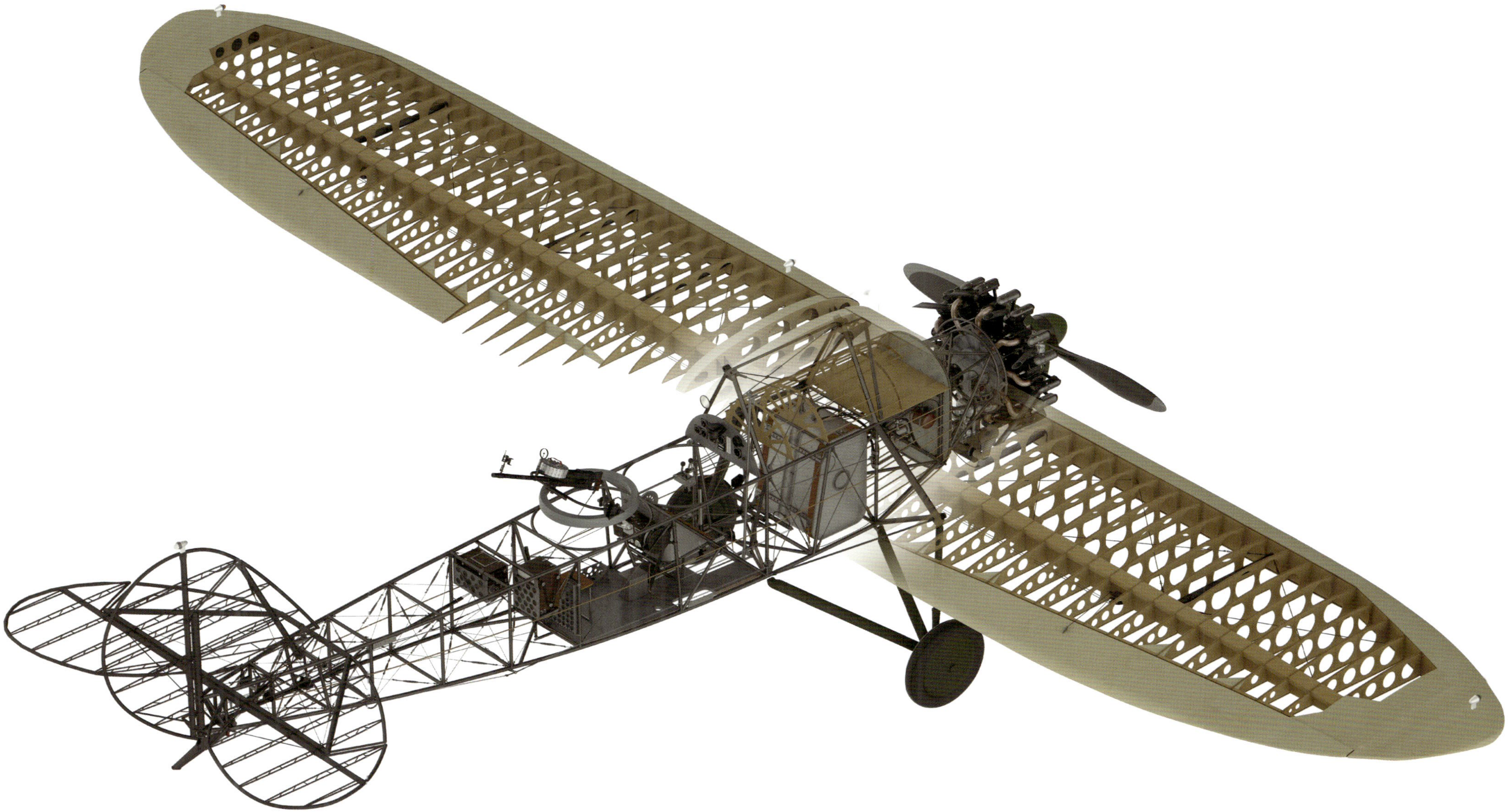

Cross-section of the whole aircraft.

Painted by Arkadiusz Wróbel

Rally Lublin R-XIIIDr with registration SP-AJT, named "Blue bird", on which Cpt. pilot S. Karpiński and mechanic W. Rogalski from 21st of October to 10th of November, 1935, flew a distance of 11.138 km visiting the following places: Warsaw–Bucharest–Istanbul–Adana–Aleppo–Baghdad–Bushehr–Jahrom–Karachi–Jaipur–Allahabad –Calcutta–Akyab-Rangoon–Bangkok–Preczubab (Kohiak). Raid was planned to Australia and back (42.000km) but on 10th of November, 1935, plane crashed during take-off from boggy airstrip of Kohiak airfield in Sinai. Damaged aircraft was shipped back to Poland and scrapped in 1936.

Rajdowy Lublin R-XIIIDr o rejestracji SP-AJT, „Niebieski ptak". Załoga w składzie kpt. pil. S. Karpiński i mech. W. Rogalski odbyła na nim w dniach 21 października – 10 listopada 1935 r. przelot o długości 11 138 km, pokonując trasę: Warszawa–Bukareszt–Stambuł–Adana–Aleppo–Bagdad–Buszehr–Dżahrom–Karaczi–Dziajpur–Ilahabad–Kalkuta–Akyab-Rangun–Bangkok–Preczubab (Kohiak). Planowano lot do Australii i z powrotem (trasa miała liczyć 42 000 km), ale 10 listopada 1935 r. maszyna rozbiła się przy starcie z grząskiego lotniska Kohiak w Syjamie. Uszkodzony samolot przywieziono statkiem do Polski i skasowano w 1936 r.

Lublin R-XIIID with registration SP-AMG. It was a personal aircraft of general L. Rayski. Besides white-red finish note the long exhaust pipes, which reached up to back strut.

Lublin R-XIIID o rejestracji SP-AMG. Był to samolot dyspozycyjny gen. L. Rayskiego. Prócz biało-czerwonego malowania uwagę zwracają długie rury wydechowe sięgające aż do tylnego zastrzału skrzydła.

Painted by Arkadiusz Wróbel

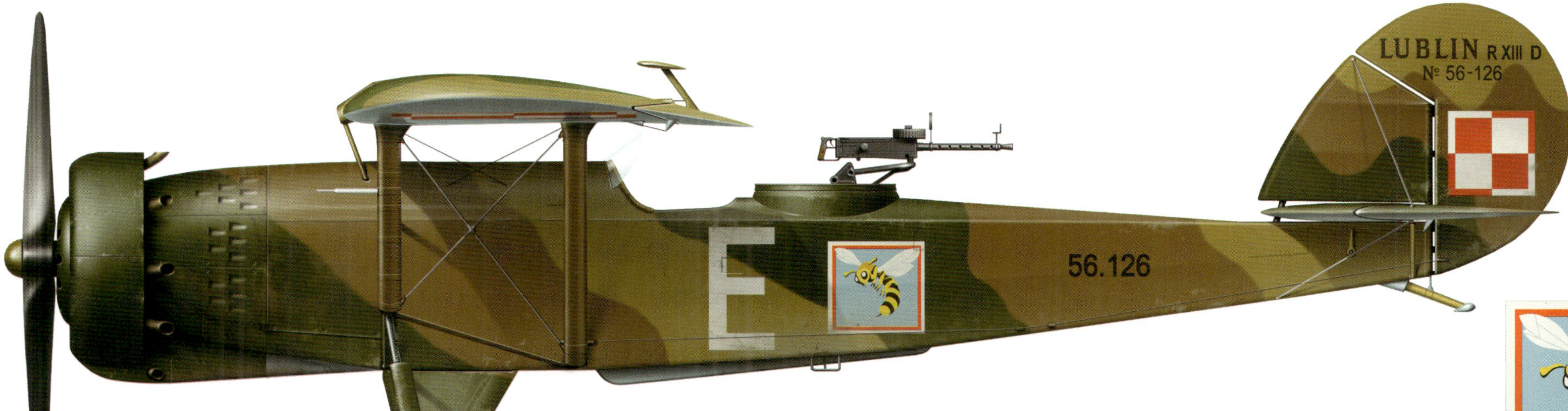

Lublin R-XIIID (serial no. 56-126) of 26th Observation Escadrille of 2nd Air Regiment. Kraków-Rakowice airfield, 1938. Note the individual marking as a letter, not number. Also note the unit's emblem – wasp on the blue square.

Lublin R-XIIID (nr fabr. 56-126) z 26. Eskadry Towarzyszącej 2. Pułku Lotniczego. Lotnisko Kraków-Rakowice, 1938 r. Zwraca uwagę oznaczenie indywidualne maszyny literą, a nie numerem, oraz godło eskadry – osa na tle niebieskiego kwadratu.

Lublin R-XIIID (serial no. 56-159) of 33rd Observation Escadrille of 3nd Air Regiment. Poznań-Ławica airfield, 1936. Unit's emblem was the dragonfly with binoculars on the white diamond.

Lublin R-XIIID (nr fabr. 56-159) z 33. Eskadry Towarzyszącej 3. Pułku Lotniczego. Lotnisko Poznań-Ławica, 1936 r. Godłem jednostki była ważka z lornetką na tle białego rombu.

Painted by Arkadiusz Wróbel

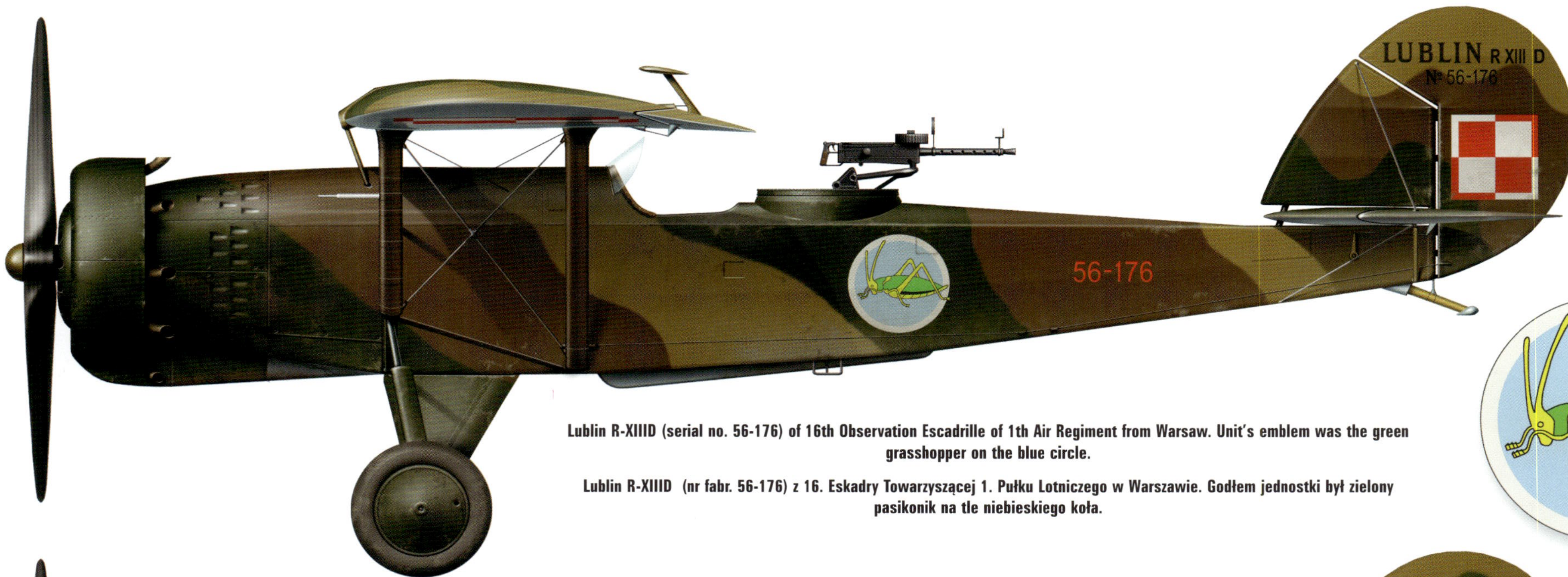

Lublin R-XIIID (serial no. 56-176) of 16th Observation Escadrille of 1th Air Regiment from Warsaw. Unit's emblem was the green grasshopper on the blue circle.

Lublin R-XIIID (nr fabr. 56-176) z 16. Eskadry Towarzyszącej 1. Pułku Lotniczego w Warszawie. Godłem jednostki był zielony pasikonik na tle niebieskiego koła.

Lublin R-XIIID (serial no. 56-27) of 66th Observation Escadrille of 6th Air Regiment from Lwów. Plane was originally built as variant "C", but during the overhaul it was upgraded to version "D". Unit's emblem was the green chameleon on the white circle.

Lublin R-XIIID (nr fabr. 56-27) z 66. Eskadry Obserwacyjnej 6. Pułku Lotniczego ze Lwowa. Samolot fabrycznie powstał jako wersja C, ale w czasie remontu przebudowano go do wersji D, pozostawiając stary numer seryjny. Godło jednostki to zielony kameleon na tle białego koła.

Painted by Arkadiusz Wróbel

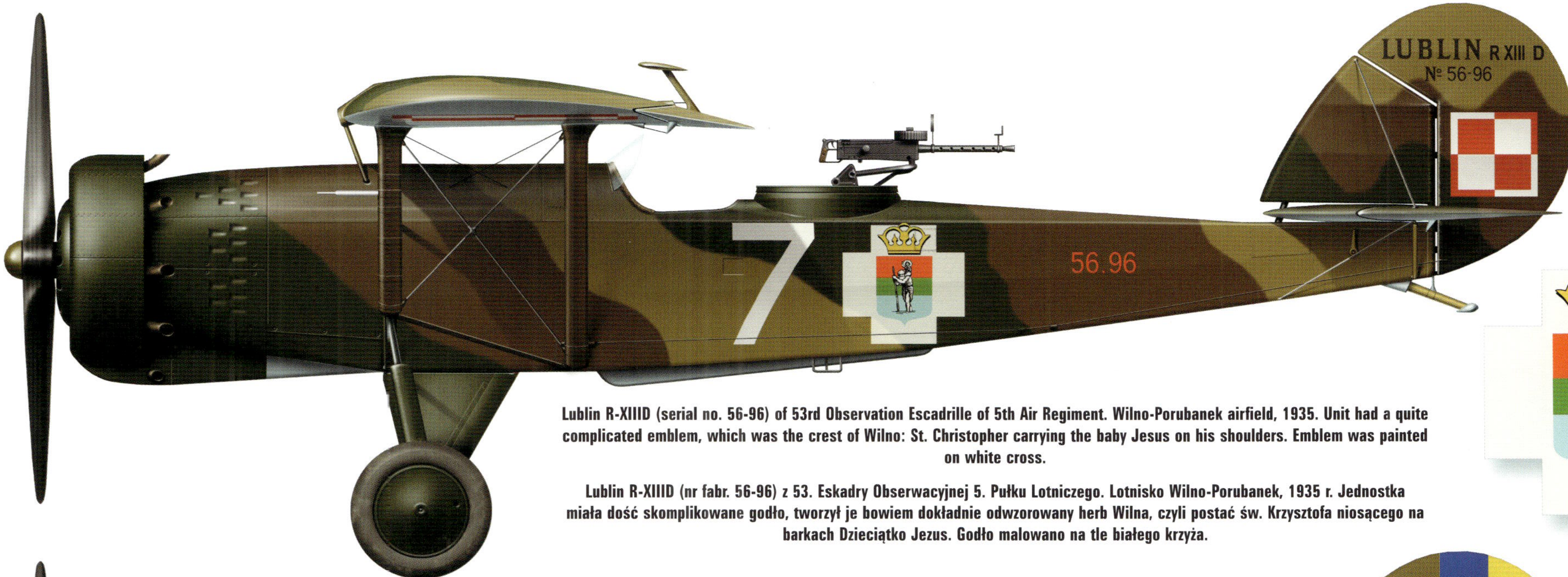

Lublin R-XIIID (serial no. 56-96) of 53rd Observation Escadrille of 5th Air Regiment. Wilno-Porubanek airfield, 1935. Unit had a quite complicated emblem, which was the crest of Wilno: St. Christopher carrying the baby Jesus on his shoulders. Emblem was painted on white cross.

Lublin R-XIIID (nr fabr. 56-96) z 53. Eskadry Obserwacyjnej 5. Pułku Lotniczego. Lotnisko Wilno-Porubanek, 1935 r. Jednostka miała dość skomplikowane godło, tworzył je bowiem dokładnie odwzorowany herb Wilna, czyli postać św. Krzysztofa niosącego na barkach Dzieciątko Jezus. Godło malowano na tle białego krzyża.

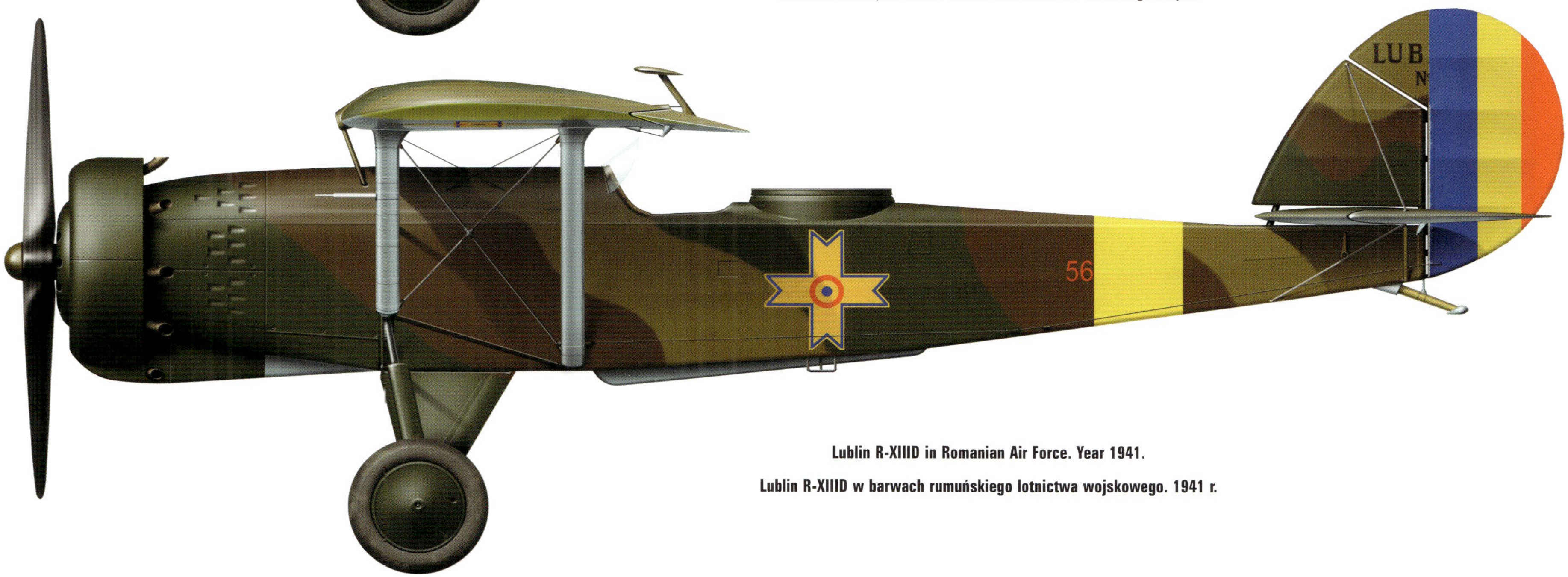

Lublin R-XIIID in Romanian Air Force. Year 1941.

Lublin R-XIIID w barwach rumuńskiego lotnictwa wojskowego. 1941 r.